Mongkut, the King of Siam

Somdetch Phra Paramendr Maha Mongkut, King of Siam from 1851 to 1868, as represented in a woodcut drawn from a photograph of the King in full royal regalia. This woodcut appeared during the King's lifetime in *Le Royaume de Siam* by Amédée Gréhan (2d ed.; Paris, 1868). The present reproduction is from the third edition (Paris, 1869). (Photograph from the Library of Congress.)

MONGKUT, the King of Siam

ABBOT LOW MOFFAT

CORNELL UNIVERSITY PRESS

ITHACA, NEW YORK

TO MY FRIENDS

Mom Rajawongse Seni Pramoj

AND

Mom Rajawongse Kukrit Pramoj

IN GRATITUDE

FOR PRESENTING ME TO

THEIR GREAT-UNCLE

King Mongkut

Preface

THERE are several millions of Americans and Europeans who feel almost personally acquainted with one of Asia's great statesmen, yet they do not know that he was a great statesman, and indeed few even know his name.

They know him as the King of Siam so whimsically presented in *The King and I* by Yul Brynner. They know him as the King of Siam so handsomely portrayed in *Anna and the King of Siam* by Rex Harrison. They know him as the King of Siam, the cruel and capricious despot of Margaret Landon's *Anna and the King of Siam*. They know him as the King of Siam in Anna Leonowens' books *The English Governess at the Siamese Court* and *The Romance of the Harem* (recently reprinted under the title *Siamese Harem Life*), from which the others are derived.

Each new presentation has naturally moved farther

away from a likeness of the real king as it was designed to appeal to a new and more distant audience. Even Anna Leonowens' books are the beneficiaries of a gifted imagination especially as they related to the King and his personal life. But then, it was by her lecturing and her books that she supported herself and her family after she left Bangkok. It obviously proved lucrative to thrill her Victorian audiences with gruesome tales of eastern harem life.

Anna's books shocked the Siamese Court, and it is said that the government tried to buy up all copies. When three-quarters of a century later Margaret Landon rewrote Anna's two books and *Anna and the King of Siam* became a best seller, many Siamese were highly indignant. Old tales told by Anna, which they knew to be fictional, were being repeated to a new generation of admiring readers as apparently true stories. The subsequent versions, in their opinion, offered even greater distortions in portraying King Mongkut. But deeper than any specific complaint was the feeling that these books and plays have presented to the world a caricature of one of their country's great men, and no country, big or little, likes the world to laugh—no matter how gentle and friendly the laughter—at one of its great men.

King Mongkut, King of Siam from 1851 to 1868, was in fact one of the great Asians of the nineteenth century. For seventeen years he steered his country through the conflicting pressures and territorial ambitions of France and England and set the course that preserved the independence of his country—the only country in Southeast Asia never to have fallen under European domination. Always there were evident in his life a deeply religious spirit that comprehended and believed in tolerance, an intellectual curiosity that caused a never-ceasing search for knowledge, and an unshakable determination to serve the Siamese people. In him surged the turmoil arising from the sudden impact of western civilization on an eastern civilization. It was this turmoil within him which caused those inconsistencies and incongruities that made him so striking and fascinating a personality. Yet through all his actions there is clearly visible the guiding purpose of his reign: the independence of Siam must be preserved. He realized that this required not only careful diplomatic action abroad but also a modernizing of the country at home. Even as one smiles at his foibles and his little weaknesses—especially at his English, of which he was so proud—the objectives underlying apparent trivia can be understood, whether in asking Queen Victoria for a decoration (as part of his campaign to emphasize the sovereignty of Siam) or in admonishing his people on the "inelegance" of throwing dead animals in the canals of Bangkok (as part of his campaign to adjust his people to the new and strange western ideas). Judged against his background and his times, he towers intellectually and morally over his contemporaries, not only in Siam but throughout Southeast Asia.

This little book is not intended as a refutation of any of Anna's stories.* As the Baltimore *Evening Sun* recently philosophized about them, "When truth gives fiction as much as one day's start, oftentimes, it is never able to catch up." [1] Moreover, most people do not consider whether those tales are literal history; nor, for that matter, do they care. They have enjoyed the books or the pictures or the play as light and charming anecdotes or delightful theater. That pleasure, however, need not preclude one from enjoying the remarkable true story of King Mongkut and knowing what the King of Siam was like in real life.

I have not tried to prepare a conventional biography of

* For comments on Anna as historian, see Appendix IV.

King Mongkut or a history of his reign. I have, rather, tried to sketch the man in his many facets, furnishing a factual outline but applying the color from his own writings, through which his personality and character shine so clearly, and from other contemporary sources. Some of his letters written in English have been published in the *Journal of the Siam Society* or have been quoted in books. In 1948 two of his gifted great-nephews, who felt that the western world should know something of the real King Mongkut, gathered together a substantial number of his letters, decrees, judgments, and state papers in the original English or in charming translations which they made from the original Siamese. M. R. Seni Pramoj was the Free Thai ambassador in Washington during the war and first post-war prime minister of Siam. He is today a leading lawyer in Bangkok. His brother, M. R. Kukrit Pramoj, a former member of Parliament, is a well-known newspaper editor and author. With these writings they included a brief sketch of King Mongkut's life in a manuscript entitled "The King of Siam Speaks." Most of the translations I have used are taken, with their permission, for which I am very grateful, from that manuscript. They appear here for the first time in English, except for a few of the decrees which were reproduced in an article by M. R. Seni Pramoj, "King Mongkut as a Legislator," in the *Journal of the Siam Society* in January, 1950.

I have inserted additional paragraphing and punctuation marks where these will make reading the translations from the Siamese easier, and I have corrected obvious misprints or errors, whether in manuscript or in print. I have not, however, made changes—especially not in King Mongkut's spelling or grammar—in letters written originally in English; nor have I changed the spelling of names as they appear in different places. The transliteration of Siamese words and names has always presented difficulties. As a result, the same names appear in the quotations in this book with varying spellings, but I am sure that readers will realize that those that look alike are in fact the same, as, Chau, Chao; Phya, Phraya; Suriwongse, Suriyawongse; Luang, Hluang. Etiquette requires that a man's title or rank always precede his name in Siamese. As this book is designed for western readers, I trust that any Thai who may read it will recognize that no disrespect is intended by my following western custom and referring to the Siamese King by his western name as Mongkut (he is scarcely known by that name in Thailand), just as I make reference to the British Queen as Victoria and to the American President as Lincoln.

I make no apology for quoting so copiously from King Mongkut's writings. Like the Pramojs, I have become convinced that no one could depict King Mongkut so well— and I think the right word is "endearingly"—as King Mongkut himself.

The King was photographed a number of times, and he often sent pictures of himself as presents to other heads of state. The daguerreotype he sent President Pierce was at one time in the Smithsonian Institution but cannot now be found. The Smithsonian has, however, a photograph, made many years ago in Philadelphia, which it believes to be of that daguerreotype. It is reproduced in this book. The daguerreotype which King Mongkut had taken with his beloved daughter and forwarded to Washington for President Buchanan arrived when Lincoln was president. Lincoln had it placed in the National Archives, where it now reposes. Unfortunately, over the years the picture has deteriorated and is not now suitable for reproduction.

Efforts to locate the daguerreotype sent to Queen Victoria by the first Siamese embassy have been unsuccessful. But Mr. Robin Mackworth-Young, Deputy Librarian, to whom my thanks are due, did find in the Royal Archives at Windsor Castle a letter from Earl Russell, the Foreign Secretary, dated September 22, 1861, which mentions that a letter from the King of Siam is to be submitted to the Queen "in a black bag of somewhat strange appearance." This was the letter in which King Mongkut made his "private proposal" to the Queen and in which he described the photographs of himself and of the Queen Consort that he was sending her.

The photograph which King Mongkut sent to Pope Pius IX just one hundred years ago is in the Vatican Library. Although it is somewhat stained across the bottom and the legs are a little out of focus, it is obviously a good likeness and also gives an authentic glimpse of the period.

The photograph of the King in western uniform is believed to be the best likeness that exists. It was taken in the latter years of his reign, but the date is not known. I am indebted to His Excellency, M. L. Peekdhip Malakul, the Royal Thai ambassador in London, for the use of this picture.

The other two pictures in the book are of woodcuts drawn from contemporary daguerreotypes or photographs of King Mongkut and appearing in books published during his life.

Probably the most interesting photographs of that period would be those taken by John Thomson, F.R.G.S., who traveled in the Far East during the sixties with camera, tripod, and the black cloth under which he could duck his head while focusing. He was in Bangkok in 1865 and not only took photographs of King Mongkut, for which the King sat, but also was given special facilities to photograph the tonsure ceremony of Prince Chulalongkorn. Ten years later he wrote:

Among other photographs which I took on the spot, one represents his majesty as he receives his son and places him on his right hand, amid the simultaneous adoration of the prostrate host. Mrs. Leonowens, who ought to have known better, has made use of this photograph in a work on Siam which appeared under her name, and described it wrongly as "Receiving a Princess." [2]

A woodcut was made from this picture, but unfortunately is not well drawn, and neither King nor Prince is recognizable. It is to be hoped that some day the plates of Thomson's pictures can be found and made available to the modern world.

In addition to thanking M. R. Seni Pramoj, M. R. Kukrit Pramoj, and M. L. Peekdhip Malakul, I want to express my appreciation to the Bobbs-Merrill Company for permission to quote from Cyril Pearl's *The Girl with the Swansdown Seat* about the first Siamese embassy to London; to Mr. Dan T. Bradley and Oberlin College Library for permission to quote from *Abstract of the Journal of Rev. Dan Beach Bradley, M.D., Medical Missionary in Siam, 1835–1873*, the diary of a minister who knew King Mongkut for twenty years; to Professor Mario Emilio Cosenza for permission to quote from *The Complete Journal of Townsend Harris, First American Consul General and Minister to Japan* about Harris' experiences when negotiating the treaty of 1856 with Siam; to Mr. Alexander B. Griswold for permission to quote from his article "King Mongkut in Perspective" about King Mongkut's religious reforms and also about Anna Leonowens as a historian; to John Murray

Ltd. for permission to quote from G. E. Mitton's *Scott of the Shan Hills* about the interest aroused when King Thibaw went two miles from his palace in Mandalay; and to Dr. Malcolm Smith and to Country Life Ltd. for permission to quote from his *A Physician at the Court of Siam* about, among other matters, the roasting of women after childbirth.

A. L. M.

Washington, D.C.
January 1961

Contents

Illustrations

THE designs on the cover and title page have been taken from two sides of a gold coin issued by King Mongkut. On the cover is the reverse of the coin, showing an elephant, symbolical of the Kingdom of Siam, within a sharp-edged discus. On the title page is the obverse of the coin, described by King Mongkut as "a picture of the Royal Crown," with "Royal Umbrellas supporting it on both sides" and "branches of trees, looking like flames, added to the background."

1

"High Prince of the Crown"

MONGKUT, the future King of Siam, was born on Thursday, October 18, 1804, eldest son of King Rama II and his Queen, Sri Suriyendra.

At that time the only European possessions east of India on the Asiatic continent proper, aside from the little Portuguese island of Macao near Canton, were Malacca, which for centuries had been held by various European powers, the island of Penang, which had been ceded to the East India Company in 1786, and Province Wellesley, a strip on the mainland opposite Penang acquired by the Honourable Company in 1800 to improve and protect the Penang anchorage.

There were three principal powers in Southeast Asia: Burma, Siam, and Annam.

Siam had been overwhelmingly defeated by the Burmese less than forty years before and Ayuthia, its capital for more than four centuries, so completely destroyed that it was never rebuilt. Yet Siam had already risen stronger than before and was now expanding eastward as opportunity arose at the expense of hapless Cambodia and of the Laos states. General Chakri, founder of the present dynasty, had been chosen king—Rama I—in 1782 and had built his palace at the little village or *bang* of Kok forty miles below Ayuthia, on a projection of land around which the river curves like a horseshoe, and erected a double row of fortifications within which the new capital city was growing.

In that same year Bodawpaya became King of Burma signaling his accession with two such hideous blood baths (in one district all living things including standing grain and fruit trees were destroyed) that, fearing an evil spell, he abandoned the historic capital of Ava and built a new capital at Amarapura. Two years later Bodawpaya conquered Arakan bordering the Bay of Bengal and so brought the frontiers of Burma into contact with India. In the following year he attempted a new conquest of Siam but was disastrously defeated. This defeat seemed to bring on a religious mania characterized by cruelties and the extravagant building of pagodas. All his people suffered, but especially the Arakanese, and at last, a decade before Mongkut's birth, a general revolt broke out in Arakan. Crushed, the refugees fled across the border into British territory hotly pursued by Burmese troops. This first border incident was settled peaceably, but it was evident that the new frontier was a source of potential danger. The British made numerous efforts to establish a satisfactory relationship with Burma; but in its willful isolation the Burmese Court failed to understand world realities. Such border incidents and a growing Bur-

mese ambition to conquer Bengal led in 1824, when Mongkut was nineteen, to the first Anglo-Burman war.

Until late in the sixteenth century, the Annamite kingdom had embraced most if not all the Vietnamese people,
but in the last years of the century the country became divided between two brothers-in-law—the northern area
(Tonking) falling to the control of the Trinh family, the
southern (Annam) to the Nguyen. Despite years of intrigue
and murder and a half century of warfare, neither family
could dislodge the other. There followed one hundred years
of peace. Then, about twenty-five years before Mongkut's
birth, power in Annam was seized by three brothers from
the district of Tay-son. The sole survivor of the Nguyens,
Nguyen Anh, was only fifteen years of age and forced to
flee. Civil war raged. The French bishop, Pigneau, gave
such aid as he could to the Nguyen cause. In 1787 he
finally appeared at Versailles with the eight-year-old son of
Nguyen Anh, was received by Louis XVI, and pleaded for
a military expedition to place Nguyen Anh on the throne.
An alliance was signed, but Louis could give no aid in those
late days of his own reign. The Bishop and his young companion returned to India. There he raised money for supplies, enlisted volunteers, and despatched several ships to
Saigon. Although the civil war continued for another thirteen years, this French help was possibly the decisive factor
that finally permitted Nguyen Anh to be crowned as King
of Annam in 1801. The following year his forces overran Tonking, and on June 1, 1802—two years before Mongkut was born—he proclaimed himself Emperor Gialong.
After two and a quarter centuries the Vietnamese people
were reunited. Gialong was the first of his dynasty. Bao Dai
the last.*

* Annam or the Annamite Empire were the Chinese names

Mongkut was five years old when his father succeeded to the throne. "The name my father . . . gave me and caused to be engraved in a plate of gold is 'Chau Fa Mongkut Sammatt Wongs,' " he wrote an American friend before he came to the throne. "Only the first three of these words, however, are commonly used in Public Documents at the present time." " 'Chau,' " he explained, "corresponds to the English word Lord, or the Latin Dominus: 'Fa' is sky: but when used in a person's name, it is merely an adjective of exaltation, and is equivalent to the phrase 'as high as the sky.' " " 'Mongkut' means Crown. The name 'Chau Fa Mongkut' means 'The High Prince of the Crown' or 'His Royal Highness the Crown Prince.' "[1] When he became king, he was generally referred to in Siam as Phra Chom Klao; but always with foreigners he retained the name Mongkut. In formal documents sent abroad his royal titles were written out: Somdetch Phra Paramendr Maha Mongkut. In letters he enjoyed using initials: S. P. P. M. Mong-

---

applied by foreigners to the country established by Gialong; but the term Annam was also applied specifically to the central section only, which had been an independent kingdom before being joined with Tonking and Cochin China. Late in the nineteenth century these three areas became administrative divisions of French Indochina and were called respectively Tonking or North Vietnam; Annam or Central Vietnam; and Cochin China or South Vietnam. Eighty per cent of the people in the empire were of the same race. To them the terms Annam and Annamite were alien and at the first opportunity they adopted the indigenous terms Vietnam and Vietnamese. Today both the democratic and communist governments in the territory once comprising Annam call their countries Vietnam. To add to the confusion, there was also a short period at the beginning of the last century when the term Cochin China was sometimes applied by Europeans to the whole country; but this term presently became restricted to the six southern provinces which later became the French colony of that name.

kut. A grandson, Rama VI, changed the names of his predecessors to Rama, and Mongkut is also known as Rama IV.

Mongkut's mother was the chief Queen, and he grew up
with all the honors accorded the heir apparent. He received the education of a prince prescribed in bygone centuries for those born to rule. His studies included literature
and poetry in Siamese and Pali—the ancient language of
the Buddhist religion. He was taught Siamese history—but
only the heroic deeds of former kings—and also the ancient
art of war, which included the use of unwieldy weapons and
the riding and control of elephants and horses. He learned
the rudimentary precepts of Buddhism together with numerous maxims from the Code of Morality of Kings. He also
studied the geography of legend which taught that Mount
Kailasa was the center of the universe, that the Gods dwelt
on its summit, and that on its slopes miraculous animals
were to be found in snowbound forests called the Him-
avanta. He was required to have a thorough knowledge of
royal ceremonies and customs down to the most minute detail. But of the great contemporary world outside the palace
he learned little. "Europe and England were to him then
hearsay, and America was mere gossip." His world was the
world of the Grand Palace.[2]

In nearly all religions there are rites connected with the
various stages of a person's life, especially childhood. In Indian Hinduism a series of propitiatory rites and ceremonies
marks each important phase of a child's life. In Siamese
Brahmanical books "ten auspicious ceremonies" are described, but most of them have become obsolete. At the
beginning of the present century only four rites were still
observed. The first involved the complete shaving of an infant's head when he or she was one month old, after which
a topknot was grown. This procedure was not followed,

however, by Siamese royalty. Siamese royalty continued to adhere to strict Brahmanical ritual and always left unshaven a topknot on the infant. Immediately following the shaving came a second ceremony, the "ceremony of giving the first name to the child," albeit a temporary name. At a later period came a third ancient rite, but from about the middle of the nineteenth century this, by custom, was reserved for princes and princesses of the very highest rank only. This was the "auspicious rite of taking the child out to bathe at a river (or sea) landing and teaching him to swim," and it was usually performed during the child's ninth, eleventh, or thirteenth years. As in many religions, the odd number was considered propitious.[3]

But the ceremony which developed into the principal one for all ranks was the formal tonsure ceremony. In Siam this rite was performed—equally for boys and girls—in the eleventh or thirteenth year. In origin the tonsure rites were probably purification acts, akin to ancient circumcision, but they have become a symbol of regeneration and an initiation into a new order of life. Indeed many of the rites are so similar to Christian baptismal rites that it has been argued they both stem from a common origin.

In his ninth year Mongkut, as a prince of the highest rank, was ceremonially bathed.[4] During his thirteenth year the celebration of his tonsure took place. Even for the lowliest commoner the tonsure of his child was an important occasion. The ceremonies for children of superior rank were splendid affairs. For the heir apparent the seven-day ceremonial was second only in grandeur and importance to his coronation. The royal tonsure ceremony, called a *sokan,* was intended to reproduce in all its pomp the scene at which the God, Siva, had performed the tonsure of his son, Ganesa, at his palace atop Mount Kailasa, and for this purpose an artificial mountain, 46 feet high, was built to represent Mount Kailasa, Lake Anotatta, and all the marvels in that region.

The ceremonies began on February 25, 1817, and for the first three days Mongkut attended in state the reading of appropriate Buddhist texts. The actual tonsure took place on Friday morning, the twenty-eighth, when one of his maternal uncles severed with golden shears three of the five tufts in which the topknot had been parted, each lock tied with a triple thread of gold, red gold, and silver. Two senior princes each cut one of the remaining tufts. Lustral waters were then poured over Mongkut according to both Buddhist and Brahman ritual, and finally he was received by his uncle—acting the role of Siva—on the top of Mount Kailasa, presented to the crowd which lay prostrate below, and led to the central pavilion on top of the mountain and there given a jeweled coronet and other insignia.

But this did not finish the day's activities. In the afternoon began the *somphot,* the consecration of the neophyte. Mongkut had to sit enthroned on a dais while lighted tapers were passed round and round him, the smoke being wafted toward him by hand (the same principle as incense from a censer). Then vestments, insignia of rank and other gifts were presented to him, and every relative and officeholder was expected to make a gift suitable to his rank and station. The *somphot* ceremonies continued on the two succeeding days. Only on the seventh day did the *sokan* come to an end when the severed hair, kept in a golden vase, was carried in state to a royal barge, rowed down river, and consigned to the water in front of Wat Arun, one of the two oldest temples in Bangkok. Formerly the hair was "floated"—the term still used—but in the case of royal hair it was feared that profane hands might touch it; an inner casket was therefore weighted and the hair sunk beneath the waves.

Mongkut's *sokan* was noteworthy as he was the first prince of the dynasty to be tonsured in full style. This clearly established his rank, but as an added mark of the importance which his father attached to the ceremony the King had a bronze stand, modeled on those anciently used at Ayuthia, especially made to hold the Buddhist relics in the central pavilion on Mount Kailasa.

Mongkut's younger full brother also received a royal *sokan* at the appropriate time four years later, but because of the cholera then prevailing the ceremonies were not so magnificent. Unfortunately, also, these ceremonies were marred when fire broke out in one of the palaces and interrupted the services while the King and court rushed to aid in extinguishing the flames. And then on the actual day of tonsure, after the *somphot* had begun, the smoke, the heat, and the fatigue proved too much for the twelve-year-old lad. He fainted, fell from the dais, and was unconscious for several hours. When the rites were resumed the next day, he simply—and successfully—refused to be dressed again in the state robes and wear the heavy *kieu* coronet, which bore the device of the reigning king.

Years later when Mongkut held a *sokan* for his son and heir, Prince Chulalongkorn, he made two important innovations. He substituted a gift of his own for the gifts which custom had required all relatives and officeholders to bestow; and he participated in the ceremonies. It was Mongkut himself who severed with golden shears the first three tufts on Chulalongkorn's head. It was Mongkut himself who acted the role of Siva, received his son on the mountain top, and presented him to the prostrate throng.

His *sokan* marked the end of Mongkut's childhood. Thereafter his father himself took charge of his education. Rama II was one of the great Siamese poets and to his influence Mongkut owed that purity of language and richness in style that made his Siamese writings so beautiful and effective.[5] It was at this time that in conformity with royal custom Mongkut was given a palace of his own and there established with his retinue and—presently—his harem.

It was formerly the practice in Siam for boys of good family, especially those of the royal family, to serve twice in the Buddhist church, first as a lad and then as a young man. In accordance with that custom Mongkut at fourteen years of age spent seven months in a monastery as a novice. Then when he was twenty he again donned the yellow robe. At that time he was already the father of children, and in the usual course of events he would have rejoined his family within a few months and reverted to the opulent life he had been leading. But he had scarcely entered the monastery when the King, his father, died.

The King had made no formal provision for the succession, and in those circumstances the selection of a successor devolved upon the Council of Princes and Ministers. It was generally assumed that Mongkut would be chosen. But whether, as some have said, as the result of political manipulation carefully organized by the mother; or whether, as others have surmised, because of the feeling that in those critical times (the Anglo-Burman war had just begun) an experienced hand was needed at the kingdom's helm, the choice fell not on the twenty-year-old Mongkut but on an elder half brother, born in 1787 of a mother not of royal blood. This brother had held important posts during his grandfather's reign and had been in charge of foreign affairs throughout his father's reign. In 1824 he became King Phra Nang Klao, subsequently better known abroad as Rama III.

Prince Mongkut decided to remain in the Buddhist church.

2

In the Buddhist Priesthood

IT is hard to conceive a greater change for any man. From a royal prince and heir apparent, living at the height of luxury and riches, he elected to become a simple monk sworn to poverty. From a life in the harem, he chose a life of celibacy. From the strict observance of court etiquette, he transferred to the wholly different, but even more rigorous, discipline of the priesthood, the Vinaya. Instead of being taught how to conquer and rule others, he was taught the art of subduing self. More important yet was the contrast in ideas to which he was subjected. Theretofore he had seen only a royal court and its autocratic principles. Now he entered one of the world's most democratic institutions, the Buddhist priesthood. Inside the monastery all were members of one brotherhood, all shared the common poverty, all were equal in the eyes of the Vinaya. Titles, ranks, privileges, all had to be forsaken on entering the priesthood. Only years of good conduct and superior knowledge brought seniority and precedence in the religious order.

Prince Mongkut, now known in the priesthood as Makuto Bikkhu, Mongkut the Beggar,[1] went first to Wat Samorai, where his father and grandfather had received their religious instruction. This was a temple given primarily to individual meditation, and the priests there professed disdain for the study of ancient texts and could not explain to the young priest how their practices conformed to those of the Buddha. He transferred to another monastery where for three years he studied the original texts and then did so brilliantly in the examination that he was presently given high rank and placed in charge of examinations. During these studies, however, he began to realize how far from the ancient disciplines his coreligionists had drifted, how much of the practices followed were done mechanically and without understanding of their inner meaning and purpose, and how many local customs drawn from other beliefs had become accepted through ignorance. It seemed to him a sacrilege to wear the yellow robe and to accept the privileges and the homage due the church as the only true continuation of the Buddha if one did not follow literally all that the Buddha had said. He went through an agony of doubt and thought of leaving the priesthood, but through the influence of a priest from Pegu in Burma whom he met at that moment his doubts were resolved; he returned to Wat Samorai and began the teachings which brought about a great reform in the Buddhist church and a renaissance of religion in Siam.

Just as among Christians there have been lengthy debates

on obscure and to the modern mind seemingly unimportant points of doctrine, so too among the Buddhists there have at times been arguments and indeed quarrels over such points as whether a monk should cover both shoulders with his yellow robe or only one. Mongkut's insistence on a literal observance of the Buddha's sayings tended at first to have a similar quality; but the essence of what he was seeking was that there be a knowledge of the meaning of the texts, not mechanical repetitions. He wanted to understand and he wanted others to understand the usefulness of the practices which the Buddha had initiated and the moral that they carried. His teachings aimed not only at eliminating patent abuses in the church but also at focusing Buddhist thinking on morality, purging it of superstitions and other accretions to the pure doctrine, and indeed minimizing speculation on the ego, on matter, even on the destiny of the being.

For seven years he made Wat Samorai his headquarters, preaching and expounding his ideas. It is a rule of the Buddhist priesthood that every monk go abroad at early dawn each day to beg for his daily food. This daily act, in all its simplicity and humility, brought Mongkut into contact with his own people and opened his eyes to a new world. Moreover, during the dry seasons he made many pilgrimages throughout the country. He was always accessible to all people, and on these pilgrimages he mingled intimately in the life of the people. He came to know their needs, their sorrows, their longings; and he came to understand the degree of progress which could be accomplished at a given time. Many of the reforms that he later effected were the direct result of these long pilgrimages, when he walked on bare feet from village to village and went each morning from door to door to receive his monk's alms. That these reforms were generally successful and formed a solid foundation for the more dramatic reforms carried out by King Chulalongkorn, his successor, was owing to the fact that they were not too ambitious to be realized and that they were appropriate to the actual social conditions of the country, which he had come to know at first hand.

Intellectual curiosity and development were keeping pace with Mongkut's spiritual development. He spent much of his leisure time in study. In addition to studying Sanscrit and Pali, he learned the languages of nearby countries: Laotian, Cambodian, Vietnamese, Peguan, Burmese, Malay, and Hindustani.[2] He delved in Siamese and Peguan astronomy, which was derived from ancient Hindu books.[3] He read deeply in history. It has been pointed out that the numerous little edicts on archaeological matters, on grammatical questions, and the like which were issued during his reign, although signed by others, were due to his initiative and that to him was due the publication which gives a concise history of Siam from 1350 to the destruction of Ayuthia. Furthermore, there came later from his own hand an English grammar and "Brief Notices of the History of Siam"[4] written in English, also numerous notices on obscure points of ancient history, archaeology, and tradition, which are of substantial value to the serious student.[5] It was while on one of his pilgrimages that in 1833 he discovered among the ruins of the ancient capital, Sukhothai, a stone pillar bearing the earliest known writing in Thai characters, the work, in 1293 A.D., of the first king of the first independent Thai kingdom in what is now Thailand. He also identified the ancient "Seat of Justice" used by that king and had it brought to Bangkok. It is now the Siamese Coronation Stone.[6]

An even more important event, which influenced his

entire life, occurred while Mongkut was at Wat Samorai. He came to know Bishop Pallegoix, the French prelate whose parish was close by. They became close friends and exchanged many an idea in long discussions. The Bishop was engaged on his monumental dictionary of the Thai language. Mongkut helped him with it and also gave him lessons in Pali. The Bishop in return gave Mongkut lessons in Latin.[7] In later years, Mongkut, when signing letters to foreign friends, would frequently add after his name "Rex Siamensium" or just the initials "R.S." Bishop Pallegoix was Mongkut's first important contact with western thought and knowledge.

In January, 1837, the King made Mongkut Abbot of Wat Pawaraniwesa. Although Rama III was a religious man, he probably had political as well as religious motives for this appointment. "Prince Mongkut, seated in a princely barge under a canopy hung with red cloth, escorted by a number of boats in pairs carrying his retinue, was conveyed to his monastery, in the precincts of which the King had just built for him a two-storied building in the so-called European style." The Second King had died and Rama III never appointed a successor. The title given the wat was "very similar to that by which the Palace of the Second King was designated. Thus," according to one historian, "everything contributed to represent Prince Mongkut as the Second King of Siam who had voluntarily retired from the world." [8]

This temple had been founded only ten years before, parts were still unfinished, and its religious community totaled only five priests. Mongkut remained there fourteen years. Under his leadership it became—and so continued for eighty years after he left—the most active center of the Siamese church. From it radiated an influence that had a profound effect in purifying and revitalizing religion in Siam.

Mongkut was already an object of veneration for his Pali scholarship; he made this wat the oustanding Pali school in Siam. He organized, with the approval of the King, a religious embassy to Kandy, Ceylon, which brought back many books that were lacking in Siam; after these were copied, they were returned to Kandy and other books, and also a Singhalese religious embassy, brought to Bangkok.[9]

Mongkut was particularly aware that four centuries had elasped after the death of Gautama before his sayings were first recorded in writing and that during this period, although the monks had endeavored faithfully to preserve his teachings and to pass them on from generation to generation by word of mouth, numerous errors and interpolations had inevitably crept into the original body of teachings; in addition copyists' errors in the two thousand years since then had caused further confusion. Mongkut and his followers felt that the true Doctrine or Law could be sifted from the accretions and distortions of twenty-four centuries only by studying the scriptures critically, not in the spirit of faith but in the light of reason.

Alexander B. Griswold has summarized clearly the two very different veins of thought which run through the Buddhist scriptures:

One of these veins of thought is rational and humanistic. The Buddha is a human being, a wise and gentle teacher. The Doctrine, lucidly exposed, is both a philosophy and a system of ethics. It maintains that no individual—whether animal, man, or god (if gods exist)—is permanent. Each is a compound, a putting together, of elements such as form, matter, and mental qualities; in each individual, without any exception, the relation of the component parts, constantly changing, is never the same for any two consecutive moments. No sooner has separateness, individuality, begun, than dissolution, disintegration, begins too. The single aim of mankind should be to abolish suffering. Belief in God is of no importance, while prayers for divine intervention are both useless and distracting. For the only way to abolish suffering is to do good and refrain from evil. Men must do good, not in order to reach heaven or to please God, but in order to be happy themselves and make others happy; they must refrain from evil deeds not because evil deeds are sinful but because they cause suffering to both victim and doer. Since this philosophy was not easy for simple minds to grasp, the Buddha tirelessly repeated the great ethical principle: "Take joy in the joys of others, take sorrow at the sorrows of others, be indifferent to your own joys and sorrows" —this program alone would abolish suffering. By rooting out all evil from their thoughts and deeds, men can become spiritually invulnerable and need no longer dread the otherwise eternal cycle of rebirths.

The other vein of thought in the scriptures is pietistic and transcendental. The Buddha has become a kind of super-god who performs miracles with ease, flies about from heaven to heaven, converts myriads of gods to his Doctrine, teaches his disciples charms to tame demons. The righteous worship him with an emotional extravagance in which blind faith crowds out reason. Forgetting that virtue alone can free them from sorrow and the cycle of rebirths, they have invented an easy technique to get to heaven by means of mechanical "acts of merit," such as adoring the towers that enshrine holy relics, or practising the trances.

In passages where the first type of thinking predominates, Buddha's own words seemed to be faithfully recorded. They had the ring of truth; they were the words of a supremely rational man. How could the same man have given his assent to the pompous follies of the other passages? . . .

In a touching passage, which was surely genuine, the Buddha had authorized a certain skepticism. He had begged his disciples not to accept any belief merely because it was handed down by tradition or preached by some respected teacher— even himself; they must test every belief with their own powers of reason. This was the criterion Prince Mongkut and his followers used, and the reconstruction of the true Doctrine followed naturally. The miracles were exaggerations, the accounts of gods and demons simply parables that had become confused with historical record, the absurd cosmography a spurious insertion.[10]

Mongkut felt that thus clarified no conflict existed between the Doctrine or Law and modern science. He did not reject the belief in transmigration, but he

gave it a more philosophic interpretation. He could point to the laws of physics to show that given causes produce given effects. If these laws govern the material universe, was it not reasonable to assume that similar ones govern the moral domain, so that every deed, whether good or evil, is inevitably followed by its appropriate consequence, either in this life or the future? Though there was no "soul" to be reborn, the "energy of action" was everlasting. Such conceptions were hard for simple people to grasp; and to them, if they had any doubts about transmigration, he gave the simple answer that Buddha himself had given: "If you are not sure, you had better be on the safe side. If you believe in it, you will lead a good life, gain the respect of all, and lose nothing even if it turns out you have guessed wrong. But if you reject it, you will very likely follow your own evil desires; and in this case if it turns out you have guessed wrong you will be like a traveller without provisions." [11]

Mongkut by his judicious selections and rejections of Buddhist scripture had, as he thought, revived the original Buddhist Law or had, as Griswold suggests, in fact created a new Buddhism. But he did not stop with this purely intellectual approach. He wanted the Buddhism and the moral principles in which he believed to be understood by the people as well as by the monks; he began to preach and he taught his followers to preach. Prior to this it was customary for a priest to paraphrase some Pali text and recite this as a rite; Mongkut, instead, undertook to deliver sermons in Siamese, seeking always to convince his hearers rather than merely to announce the truth. He did not read his sermons but spoke extempore with an eloquence that soon caused monks and lay persons to throng to hear him.[12] During the later years of his rule the number of priests regularly attached to the wat ran from one hundred thirty to one hundred fifty. Many years later his followers, the *dhammayutiakka,* "Those adhering to the Law," were recognized by King Chulalongkorn as a separate sect. By then, so great had been their influence on the Buddhist church as a whole and so effective had been the example they had set that there were no important differences between the old sect and the new.

It was about this time that Mongkut began to meet other foreigners. At first these were mostly traders and shipmasters, but "after them," to quote one history, "came the American missionaries, accompanied by their more than zealous wives, who must have been quite an innovation to the prince-priest, firmly fixed as he was in the idea that celibacy was one of the necessary conditions of priesthood. They staunchly pushed in before them Presbyterianism, and in their energetically religious trail they brought along pictures, books, newspapers, printing-presses, schools, hospitals and the inevitable harmonium."[13] Mongkut observed their medical work—indeed he was several times attended by the Reverend Dan Beach Bradley, M.D.[14]—and the scientific and other apparatus that the missionaries brought with them. He decided to learn English, and three years after he became abbot he arranged to take lessons from Dr. Bradley.[15] For some reason the arrangement did not prove satisfactory. Six years later, in 1845, Mongkut began his studies with the Reverend Jesse Caswell and for eighteen months received an hour's instruction four times a week. Caswell died in 1848. In later years Mongkut always referred to him as his "revered teacher" who had taught him English. He erected a monument over his grave and on two occasions sent funds to his widow in the United States.[16]

A glimpse of Mongkut at this period is found in the diary of Dr. House, another medical missionary, who recorded the details of his first call on the prince-priest at Wat Pawaraniwesa: "I looked around the room," he wrote, "Bible from A. B. Society, and Webster dictionary stood side by side in a shelf of his secretary, also a Nautical Tables and Navigation. On the table a diagram of the forthcoming eclipse in pencil with calculation, and a copy of the printed chart of Mr. Chandler. . . . His manners were rather awkward at introduction, and his appearance not prepossessing at first, though we became more interested in him as we saw him more. . . . He understands English when he reads it, but cannot speak it well yet." [17]

There was at least one reason for this and why his English always took a highly original turn. There was at that time no Siamese-English dictionary, and Mongkut found it necessary when essaying English to translate a word from Siamese into ancient Pali and then search for an English equivalent of the Pali word in a voluminous Pali-English dictionary that he possessed.[18] As he never could be certain which of the English equivalents listed in the dictionary gave the precise meaning he wanted, he was apt to insert at least two alternatives in his composition. Informed, some years later, that a visitor had been born in Edinburgh, he exclaimed "Ah! you are a Scotchman, and speak English I can understand; there are Englishmen here who have not understanding of their own language when I speak." [19] For all its idiomatic quaintness, Mongkut was—rather naturally—proud of his ability to speak English, particularly as he felt that it was this more than any other single attribute that had won for him the respect of the western powers.[20]

Mongkut also studied geography, physics, chemistry, mathematics, and especially astronomy.[21] He became increasingly interested in the scientific knowledge of the west and in its mechanical application. From the American missionaries he also learned much about the major western countries, their histories, what was taking place there currently, and the methods by which they were governed. He began to read English books and newspapers and to acquire western devices and machines. He even installed a printing press in the monastery, the first press outside the Catholic and Protestant missions and the first to be operated by Siamese.

In the latter years of King Phra Nang Klao's reign, the court became nationalist and isolationist. There was some murmuring against Mongkut that he had criticized the Siamese form of Buddhism and adopted a form derived from Burma, traditional enemy of Siam; nor was his friendship with foreign missionaries approved. But none of Mongkut's activities smacked of politics; he had never interfered in the affairs of government; the most powerful of the aristocracy recognized his worth as well as the need for a better understanding of the outside world; he was popular with all the people; and finally there was still the feeling that Mongkut was in fact the rightful heir. As a result, when King Phra Nang Klao lay dying and tried to name his own son as successor, the Council of the Crown refused. A few days later Mongkut was asked to become king.

3

His Majesty's Gracious Advices

IN a letter dated April 21, 1851, which he signed as "newly elect President or Acting King of Siam," Mongkut announced his succession to Governor Butterworth at Penang: "Whereas His Majesty the late King was expired and demised on the 2nd instant, on next day of which day I was elected and entered to this place where I am living happily with great business or affair of presiding of whole kingdom, but my enthronement or exaltation will be on 15th May for waiting of the greatest preparation the ceremony of my crowning as more pleasant than those of my predecessors, as they thought that I and my brother . . . are purer by birth both sides, paternal and maternal. Our people, both of capital and dependent districts and tributary countries around Siam, with their principal heads of

Governors, were seemed to be unanimously glad to us for our being successors to the throne." [1]

The move from monastery to palace was even more dramatic than the earlier move from palace to monastery, for now Mongkut was King of Siam and at least in theory an absolute monarch. In addition to the total change in his personal life, his new role at long last gave him the opportunity to do those things which he felt were necessary for the welfare of Siam and for which the preceding twenty-six years had given him such unique training and knowledge.

Traditional political thought in Siam, as elsewhere in Asia, wished to isolate the country from foreign contacts, but Mongkut had seen what was happening to his neighbors and what had already happened to mighty China. He had discovered for himself the technical superiority of the west and he knew the power of the west. Events forced him to be conscious of the aggressiveness of the west. Years later he expressed the problem of Siam in these words: "Being, as we are now, surrounded on two or three sides by powerful nations, what can a small nation like us do? Supposing we were to discover a gold mine in our country, from which we could obtain many million catties weight of gold, enough to pay for the cost of a hundred warships; even with this we would still be unable to fight against them, because we would have to buy those very same warships and all the armaments from their countries. We are as yet unable to manufacture these things, and even if we have enough money to buy them, they can always stop the sale of them whenever they feel that we are arming ourselves beyond our station. The only weapons that will be of real use to us in the future will be our mouths and our hearts, constituted so as to be full of sense and wisdom for the better protection of ourselves." [2]

He walked warily between England and France, the two countries he had most reason to fear, and he did all that he could to make his country known and understood abroad and to ensure respect for its sovereignty. He developed and carried on throughout his reign a voluminous correspondence with heads of state and influential men in other countries. He even initiated an exchange of letters and gifts with Pope Pius IX. He saw to it that Siam played a conspicuous part in the Paris Exhibition of 1867.

In addition, however, he realized that both by legislation and example he must effect such reforms in the laws, customs and institutions of the country as would bring them in line with western thinking and so minimize excuses for external interference. During his seventeen-year reign, assisted by a small band of able men, especially Chao Phraya Sri Suriyawongse, the *Kralahom* or Prime Minister, he effected a bloodless revolution in Siam that laid the solid base on which the even better-known reforms of King Chulalongkorn were constructed.

Almost his first acts were, in accordance with the desires of the European community, to reduce import duties, to permit the export of rice, and to establish an opium monopoly to ensure its control.[3] Within a few years he voluntarily "opened" the country for foreign trade. He completely did over the financial organization of the kingdom. He established a Royal Mint—in the palace—for the issue of flat coinage "equal in every respect to the coinage of that State of Europe which is called France"[4] to replace the bullet-shaped ticals and cowrie shells then in use.* He

* This was in 1860. At first only flat silver coins were minted.

promoted the construction of waterways and roads, substituting paid labor for the former feudal *corvée,* and he
encouraged shipbuilding. He employed westerners as advisers both to spread western ideas and knowledge and,
where necessary, to act as administrators while the new
ideas were making headway. He sought equal justice for
all before the law and curbed some, at least, of the privileges of the nobility which had set them above the law.
He established an official Gazette. He took the first steps

In 1862 Mongkut added flat coins of smaller value composed of
an alloy of tin, copper, and unsmelted powdered tin ore. In 1863
he introduced three gold coins for general use pointing out in a
long decree that all important countries issued gold coins. These
gold coins were modeled basically after the English sovereign and
half-sovereign, but there were two major differences. Mongkut
never placed the sovereign's head on any coins. Instead, on one
side of the gold coins appeared a likeness of the royal crown with
a royal umbrella on each side. On the reverse was a representation
of the chakra—a sharp edged discus—in the center of which was
an elephant symbolical of the Kingdom of Siam. The chakra, used
as a mark of the Chakri dynasty, was a symbol of Vishnu. The
other major difference arose from his fear that the Siamese people would look askance at any gold coins that were not of pure
gold. For purposes of hardening the coin the English sovereign
was made of an alloy of gold and copper (22 carat). Mongkut required that his new coins be of absolutely pure gold with no alloy.

The flat tin and copper coins displaced the cowrie shells which
had been in use for barter purposes in Siam from time immemorial.
Thereafter cowrie shells were used solely in the public gambling
houses as counters in playing fan tan and other games. The bullet-
shaped ticals, which the flat silver coins were intended to replace,
were not actually demonetized until 1904. At that time some fourteen million of these ticals were withdrawn from circulation and
recoined in the modern style.

Mongkut also issued, in 1853, the first paper currency in Siam,
but paper currency did not come into general use until the next
reign.[5]

to eliminate slavery. He enacted laws to improve the status of women and children. He authorized the common people to look at the King!

It is hard in the twentieth century to conceive of a monarch unwilling to travel and hiding from the people's gaze; yet that was the tradition, derived from India and based on the king's divinity, among conservative royalty in Southeast Asia. Even as late as 1880, J. G. Scott (who as Shway Yoe wrote the classic *The Burman: His Life and Notions*) in a letter from Rangoon, exclaimed: "King Theebaw has at last left the Palace and visited Mandalay Hill [less than two miles distant]. This may seem to you a very simple matter and hardly worth the trouble of recording. But when a King of Burmah leaves his palace and deigns to show himself to the world, there is a tremendous to-do. King Mindōn [Thibaw's father] only came from behind his stockade two or three times, during the last ten years of his reign. King Theebaw till this present pilgrimage, had never been out at all. If Golden Foot goes by water, all bridges have to be destroyed, for never can descendant of Aloungpayah pass beneath where mortal has trod above. All houses he may pass must have a wooden grating put up in front of them." [6]

In Siam, King Mongkut's predecessor had left the palace only once a year, to visit the temples of the city. Mongkut set the tone of his revolution by traveling frequently, extensively, and on occasion, unconventionally. The first steam vessel to arrive at Bangkok had been the English steamer "Express" which on January 11, 1844 "came walking up the Menam about 10 o'clock a.m. producing a great swell and stirred a great excitement." [7] Early in his reign Mongkut ordered a steam vessel of his own. One day late in 1855 "an extraordinary event happened," exclaimed Dr. Bradley. "It is that the King of Siam ventured his own person on board his new steamer and rode up the river two or three miles above his palace, to the grave astonishment of his court and people. The ride was wholly unpremeditated alike to himself and all others. But seeing his Prime Minister on board and two of the missionaries and observing with great admiration the working of the boat he could not resist the temptation to go aboard himself. He had just returned in state from visiting temples and stepped directly out of his State barge into the steamboat." [8] Few contrasts could have been more dramatic, for the King's state barge was a great dragon-headed, gilded affair, with curtains of regal crimson, propelled by a host of paddlers who at each stroke raised a shout to testify to the importance of the royal personage they were transporting. It was attended by a large number of other barges, all in a line, and all being paddled with great rapidity. "In the King's own boat were several men with long staffs, from which were streamers of white horse-tails; these they threw into the air and brought down, striking violently on the bottom of the boat, in time with each shout of the crew. All other boats on the river stopped and their crews crouched down on the seats." [9]

In Siam the law and custom dating back to the Old Capital had been very similar to that in Burma. During a royal journey on the water, "any boat which crosses the line of the royal barge or speeds abreast the procession renders the owner thereof liable to the punishment prescribed by law; and any person who shows disrespect by walking, standing or looking out of the window at the moment when the royal procession passes his way is . . . liable to be shot at by the sergeants-at-cross-bow." [10] This last, it is true, had been modified by Mongkut's father because a woman had, in fact, been hit in the eye by a crossbolt, and the crossbowmen were thereafter limited to "threatening persons showing disrespect." Mongkut found, however, that whenever he went abroad, whether on land or on the water, the police and all the accompanying guards were accustomed "to chase His Majesty's subjects out of His way and, further, to order them to close all the doors and windows in their houses, boathouses and shops." Not only did Mongkut put a stop to all this; he expressly encouraged the people to view the royal processions and to be available for him to speak to as he wanted. At the same time, although the practice of prostration before royalty was not abolished until the next reign, he provided an entering wedge against the system by authorizing tolerance of foreign ways.

"A Chinese," he decreed, "may, at the passing of the royal procession, choose either to prostrate himself in accordance with the Thai custom or to stand and kowtow in such manner as a Chinese would stand and bow to his Emperor. The same act of prostration is permitted to a Farang [Siamese term for member of the white race] who prefers the Thai custom. Should he prefer to stand up, take off his hat and bow or salute in the custom of his country or in the manner of a foreign Asiatic, let him be. No officer proceeding in the royal procession, no City authorities or Nai Amphur [district officer] or any of the officers responsible for maintaining order among the crowd, nor any among the Thai people in attendance on His Majesty shall forbid him his choice or force him to do homage against his own custom and inclination."

Mongkut issued many decrees in the course of his reign. Normally, statutes do not make light reading, but Mongkut's laws possess great charm in their combination of simple rule and lucid explanation for its enactment. For instance, in 1856 he issued a "Notification" setting forth "His Majesty's Advice on the Inelegance of Throwing Dead Animals into Waterways, the Construction of Fireplaces, and the Manipulation of Window Wedges."

By Royal Command, Reverberating like the Roar of a Lion,
    Be it declared to all servants of the Crown of higher and lower rank and to the people of the Realm as follows:

Whereas it has been brought to the attention of His Majesty that in the words of foreigners and provincials who are Laos, Cambodians and dwellers in the upland who draw their supply of water from wells, as well as other peoples, the inhabitants of the City Divine are great polluters of water. For it is said that the Divine City dwellers do dishonour to their own city by throwing carcasses of dead animals into the river and canals where they float up and down in great abomination, and having thus contaminated the water, the City dwellers themselves do make an inelegant habit of constantly using the same water for purposes of drinking and ablution.

Wherefore, His Majesty is graciously pleased to advise that under no circumstances whatsoever should any person allow himself to throw a dead dog, a dead cat or the carcass of any other dead animal into the river or canal, whether big or small. The people are requested . . . to bury the offensive carcasses on the spot and to bury them deep enough so as to prevent their escape on to the waterway where they will float up and down in great abomination.

By the exercise of a little imagination it should not be too difficult to perceive that other people using the water along the waterway do object to such an exhibition. Were provincial priests and novices . . . or other country gentry to pay a visit to the Divine City and find the same objectionable custom still in practice, they would undoubtedly carry away the impression that conditions inside the City are not as healthy as outside it, the water supply in the City being so unclean as to breed in the dwellers thereof a number of unhappy ailments. The same or similar impression would be given to Englishmen, Chinese and other foreign Asiatics who come to do business in the Divine City.

Appeal is, therefore, made to the better instincts and humanity of City dwellers who are requested not to throw carcasses of dead animals into the waterways to the revulsion of their fellow dwellers. Henceforth, should any person disregard His Majesty's gracious advice . . . he shall, after due testimony being given against him by his neighbours, be conducted in ignominy around the City by the Nai Amphur [district officer] so that the spectacle may serve as a sorry object of warning to others against committing such an inhumane and irresponsible act of water pollution.[11]

Then the same law proceeds to advise householders how to build fireplaces so as to avoid

conflagration from occurring, whereby property is destroyed by fire, lost during graceless removal or stolen in the confusion, as well as putting the people to a great expense of building new houses. . . .

From now on house-holders are required to build their fireplace not too near the inflammable partition and to build it with bricks, lime or earth after the model fireplace which is placed on exhibition at the Royal Field by the Twin Buildings bordering the main avenue. Should the poorer people find it too costly to copy the model for use in their house-hold, they are requested to give the partition near the fireplace a coating of a mixture of earth, clay and paddy husks, and also to remove the pile of faggots to a safe distance. . . . The police will be instructed to examine every house in the City and to order the vacation by the owner of any house found to be a source of danger from failure to follow His Majesty's advice. . . .

Finally, in the same act, Mongkut advised his people to be a little more original in protecting their homes against burglary:

It transpires that cases of burglary and house-breaking regularly conform to a strange and identical pattern, that is to say, the burglar would ascend the window by a ladder, cut a hole in the partition, lift the window wedge and enter the somnolent household to make leisurely appropriation of gold and silver articles to be found for the unlawful taking.

The advice given was "to keep moving the window wedge beyond the reach of the burglar's guessing, that is to say, by the tactic of inserting it at the top or bottom of the window and placing it at other times sideways."

In connection with this decree, it is interesting to observe that Sir John Bowring, who was in Bangkok the preceding year, noted "If, even *by accident,* a house should catch fire, the owner of it is seized, and led through the town, three days on shore and three days on the river. He is obliged to repeat, every few minutes, 'My house caught fire; take care, and be warned by me.' He is then, if rich, put into prison, and only released by paying a heavy fine. This severity is not unnecessary in Bangkok." [12] Bowring also reports that on one occasion Mongkut pointed out his kitchen with pride, saying, "That is my cook-house; I built the first chimneys in Siam." [13]

In another decree the King observed that during celebrations of the New Year, the great majority of men "see fit to get themselves drunk all over the place." [14] These celebrations, he noted, involved eleven days altogether—five in honor of the lunar year and six in honor of the solar year—including a day of preparation for each, the three or four days of actual celebration, and another for sobering up. The police could not cope with all the brawls that resulted. He requested his people therefore to do their celebrating in their own homes. "Any urgent business," he concluded, "which they may wish to perform abroad before they get over the reaction of their overindulgence, must wait until they are sober."

In an even more optimistic spirit he once tried philological reform by decree.[15] Both in the common language and in the court language certain condiments were miscalled. He furnished the correct words and directed everyone to use them thereafter. A few months later he had to concede defeat. Notwithstanding his new law, he lamented, "the majority of the people in the Capital still use the words kapi and nampla as of old. Worse still, advantage is being taken by some rogues who, by impersonating the Nai Amphur, have, on many and increasing occasions, extorted money from the people. Be it, therefore, declared that from now on the people may continue to use the words kapi and nampla as they have been used to do so from the time immemorial," although at court the correct words must be employed.[16]

On one occasion, when two judges had died and their places were to be filled, Mongkut decided on a noble experiment. By royal command it was announced by the Minister of the Royal Household * that it had been reported to His Majesty

that in accordance with the practice in other countries persons to be appointed by the Ruler as judges are first elected by the people, whereby only the choices of the people are assigned to the task of sitting in their judgment. Being graciously desirous

---

* It was customary for decrees to be issued "By royal command" over the name and titles of the appropriate minister. The official "bearer" of this decree was "Chao Phraya Dharma Dhigoranadhibodi Srisuvira Mahamatwongse Rajabhongse Nigoranuraks Mahaswamibhak Boromrajopakarabhiromya Sarabodomkichvicharn Mahamonthirabal Bodinrajanives Nintramatya Antepurikanath Senabodi Aphaibiryakrombahu."

of promoting the peace, prosperity and happiness of the people of the Realm, His Majesty deems it fit to modify existing custom in favour of such an election.

Wherefore, be it declared to all princes of the Royal House, whether ennobled or as yet un-ennobled and to servants of the Crown . . . that they are invited to make their choice in the coming election. . . . The elector is requested to put down in writing his own name and the names of the persons he elects to the two posts just mentioned. No one is obliged to make his choice among the servants of the Crown attached to the Palaces of the First and Second King. On the contrary, any person, even though he be a slave, who is believed to be so sufficiently possessed of wisdom and restraint as to be able to give clear and satisfactory judgment in accordance with truth, justice and the law may be elected as judge.

Election slips will be distributed to all the princes and servants of the Crown by the officers of the Department of His Majesty's Secretary, with the request that each prince and servant of the Crown may please to fill in one slip only and return the same to His Majesty. The princes and servants of the Crown are further requested not to treat this election as a joke. Nor should they dilly-dally, thinking that perhaps their choice would not meet with His Majesty's approval, or that perchance they would lose face if whomsoever they elected were rejected by other electors. Such a habit of thought should be entirely discarded. For human hearts vary one from the other, and well may the choices in the election differ because it is His Majesty's wishes that they be freely made.[17]

Naturally, not all of Mongkut's decrees were of this nature. Part of the inscription on the stone pillar which, while he was still a priest, he had recovered at Sukhothai read:

In the entering in of the gate is a bell hung up there. If folk aggrieved within town or city have controversies or matters that distress them within and cramp their hearts, which they would declare unto their lord and prince,—there is no difficulty. Go ring the bell which he has hung up there. Prince Khŭn Ram Khămhaeng, lord of the realm, can hear the call. When he has made investigation, he sifts the case for them according to right.[18]

One of Mongkut's major acts was to reinstitute this ancient Thai right of direct petition to the king to redress injustice. He considered this right so fundamental to the welfare of his people that on his deathbed he enjoined on those around him that this practice must not again be allowed to lapse. Prajadhipok who was king from 1925 to 1935 estimated that during his reign he personally examined nearly a thousand petitions a year.[19]

As in all of Mongkut's decrees, a disarming simplicity pervades the statute which establishes the right of petition. "Should the petitioner," he wrote, "be a commoner without any person to assist him in submitting the petition he shall go and wait before the Sudhai Swariya Palace on any day preceding the Buddhist Sabbath, that is to say, on the 7th of the Waxing or Waning Moon in the full month or the 13th in the incomplete month. There, in the afternoon and eventide when not otherwise occupied in other affairs of the Realm, and provided that it will not be raining at the time, His Majesty the King, . . . will appear on the throne in the said Palace or on the Penja throne in front thereof to sit in judgment, whereupon the Judgment drum shall be beaten calling all the petitioners before His gracious presence where they may personally present Dikas [petitions] to their King by holding the same up over their heads." [20] He insisted, however: "The language used in the petition is required to be concise, and care shall be taken to avoid subtlety, prevarication and circumlocution. Under no circumstances must a malicious slander of any noble be included in the

petition and the use of obscene language is strictly forbidden."

At the time that Mongkut became king one of the principal sources of royal revenue was the sale by the king of
exclusive rights to farm commodities. At first, the only monopoly had related to spirituous liquors; but as the years
had passed one after another every species of industry was
handed over to be farmed until practically everything required by the people was affected. The list included tobacco,
oils, torches, leaves for covering roofs, combustibles, timber,
condiments, markets, fisheries, mining, hunting, and gaming.
Even the right to import opium, which had been declared
contraband in the 1826 treaty with England, had been
farmed to a wealthy Chinese. The export of teak was prohibited and of rice unless there was on hand in the kingdom
a three years' supply. One of Mongkut's first acts was to
authorize the export of rice and teak. He wiped out the entire monopoly system which had proved so thoroughly pernicious for the people, substituting in its place revenue
derived from a reasonable tax on imports and exports, and
he encouraged foreign commerce generally.

These were very bold strokes because they brought him
into direct conflict with most of the nobility, who had a
deeply vested interest in the old system, since monopolies
were secured through their influence and they derived
much of their wealth therefrom. In a matter as vital to his
country and its people as this, however, Mongkut would
not hesitate. On the other hand, the nobles constituted the
ruling class; he had to work with them and through them,
and he had to have their support. Moreover, Mongkut was
conservative when it came to matters of rank on which the
whole structure of the monarchy rested. While he did not

want abuses, he had no intention of curtailing privileges which did not bear heavily on the people.

As a result even some of his major reforms furnish re-remarkable reading, as in the judgment he rendered in response to a *dika* submitted by a girl who had been abducted by the man her parents wanted her to marry, whereas she wanted to marry her lover:

Whereas by existing custom a man is pleased to consider any woman his wife whom he is able secretly to compromise. So is the general belief of litigants and so has the Court passed judgments handing women over to the men by whom they have been compromised. These women are not animals. Even so, the old law concerning the freedom of divorce was once re-pealed. However, such a measure cannot be deemed to be just. For the choice of separation should be freely exercisable by either the husband or the wife. Therefore, the old law is hereby confirmed, and all judgments on the status of a wife under the custom above referred to shall be revised to conform to the rule of free will in the woman.[21]

He denied that this decision was inconsistent with certain other judgments that he had rendered: "For the judgment in the other cases was based on the dignity of the nobles concerned." He summarized one of these cases and then continued:

One would criticise this last judgment as drawing a distinction between the nobility and the common people. But far better it is to draw the distinction than to displease the nobility in these cases. Were the rule of free will to be followed with regard to their women these nobles would be stricken with surprise and mortification, whereby to see a judgment allowing any of their womanfolk to be brought to dust by the effrontery of a com-moner would provoke in them a painful suspicion that the Ruler

no longer upholds their honour and tradition. No amount of
damages paid to them in compensation would assuage such a
pain of such a suspicion. Even were the compensation amounted
to one hundred catties, having spoken their word of disapproval
these nobles would never take it back. The judge in such a case,
therefore, would be a fool to follow the rule of free will in the
woman. . . .

Wherefore, in deciding cases arising in the City as well as outside it the judges are hereby directed to consider the degree of
nobility involved. Among the people of lower birth they are to
follow the rule laid down as in the foregoing, whereby the doctrine of marriage by mere touch and compromise is overruled,
and the wishes of the woman are to be followed, whilst those of
the parents and kinsmen are to be consulted among the nobles.

The fact is undeniable that people of lower birth are more
interested in acquiring wealth than in furthering the welfare of
their children. As the result, children, who should receive nothing but kindness and mercy from their parents, are oft consigned
by the latter to miserable slavery in mere exchange for gold and
silver. Therefore, the rule of free will must be made applicable
so as to prevent havoc being brought upon the persons of
women oft sold into bondage by their parents.

The rule, however, must be otherwise in application to the
nobles. For in such a case even a small liberty taken of the
woman through a marriage contracted below her rank grows
big and intolerable in the eye of her sensitive kinsmen. If liber-
ties must be taken of the woman, her nobility of kinfolk prefer
that they be taken by a nobility of equal rank, so that through
fear of their power and influence the general public, who perceive something insinuating, would find wisdom in keeping their
mouth shut, whereby dignity would be saved and the scandal
relegated in the course of time to happy oblivion.

The consideration for the nobility's sensitivity shown in
the foregoing judgment did not, however, prevent Mong-

kut from taking startlingly direct action when he thought it necessary:

Notice is hereby given to all servants of the Crown attached to the Ministry of the Royal Household that the Prince Davorayos and the Prince Alongkot Pricha are in the habit of getting drunk whilst resident within the confines of their respective palaces. Wherefore, with the exception of the Officers of the Oars and Lawn Sweepers under the command of the Prince Davorayos and the Officers of the Rifles and Arsenal under the command of the Prince Alongkot Pricha, no person is permitted to enter into their palaces for any purpose whatsoever. . . . The purpose of this injunction is to prevent the caller at the said palace from becoming an object of the carousing Prince's unjustifiable outburst. . . . as by law the presumption in cases of brawl committed within the household lies against the caller. . . . Be it clearly brought to the attention of all likely callers at the palaces aforesaid that the Princes hardly ever get sober. Wherefore, no one is guaranteed a safe and uneventful visit thereto. Even those who come under the exemption . . . are advised to exercise due care and prudence. . . . While the Princes are on the rampage, they had better stay outside.[22]

This concern about possible trouble must be read with the realization that it was against the law—a relic of ancient taboos—for a person to touch any part of the body of those of high rank. For touching the king or queen the punishment was death. In 1883, Queen Sunanta was drowned within sight of many people when her boat overturned and an official forbade those nearby to rescue her. Of course in actual practice the law was not applied to those in daily attendance who helped with dressing or acted as masseurs; but even these had always formally to request permission to touch the individual concerned.[23]

Mongkut firmly rejected any idea that members of the royal family were exempt from trial for criminal offenses. Certain judges had declined to accept jurisdiction in a criminal case involving several members of the royal family. Mongkut wrote the Council of Ministers: "The phrase, 'members of the Royal Family cannot be brought to trial,' if used, is a direct disparagement to the honour and dignity of the Royal House." [24] Elsewhere he made it clear that he also, the absolute ruler of Siam, was not above the law. "If any of the officials or one of the people should complain against the King let such complaint be accepted. Let orders under the seal of the Rajawongse Pavara Sthan be issued to all ministers and the lady officials inside the Palace. Let them take evidence on the case and let judgment be given. If such evidence is not sufficient or not clear, let a letter be addressed to us as King and we will reply according to truth." [25]

4

Agreement with England

IT was in his relations with foreign countries that Mongkut achieved the most striking reversal of traditional ways.

The Siamese had never forgotten or forgiven that extraordinary period in their history when the Greek adventurer, Constant Phaulkon, became what today would be called Foreign Minister and conspired with the French Court of Louis XIV and the Jesuits to bring about the conversion of Siam to Christianity. In execution of the plan, not only were commercial concessions and extraterritorial rights acquired by the subjects of Louis XIV, but also a number of Jesuits came with the French negotiators, and French troops occupied the *bang* of Kok forty miles below the capital and also Mergui on the Tenasserim coast facing the Bay of Bengal. The fears of foreign domination which were aroused

led to a revolt and the public execution of Phaulkon. The
French garrison at Kok was besieged but, after negotiation,
was permitted to evacuate to Pondicherry in India. The
smaller garrison at Mergui fought its way out, although
with heavy losses, and also reached Pondicherry. French
traders and missionaries were persecuted, and many were
killed. The antiforeign feelings aroused by this experience
became a part of Siamese tradition and reinforced the con-
servatism and isolationism which characterized Siamese
thinking and indeed the thinking of all eastern Asia in the
mid-nineteenth century.

A treaty had been signed between England and Siam in
1826, but its primary purpose was to settle certain political
issues. In 1833 a treaty was signed between the United
States and Siam, but this was little more than a polite exchange of good will. Neither treaty permitted the posting of
a diplomatic or consular officer in Siam, and there was no
"opening up" of the country to trade.

By 1850 the British had felt the need for revision of the
1826 treaty in order to encourage commerce, and the
United States was also dissatisfied with conditions under
the 1833 treaty. Sir James Brooke (who had become Rajah
Brooke of Sarawak four years before) came to Bangkok on
behalf of England to negotiate a new treaty. He failed. As
he departed, an American commissioner, Ballestier, arrived.
Ballestier had been a merchant in Singapore, apparently
not too successful in his commercial operations, and, as Sir
John Bowring wrote, "it may be doubted whether the nom-
ination of a commercial gentleman whose history was well
known to the king and nobles at Bangkok was judicious:
it was certainly not deemed complimentary to the proud
Siamese authorities." [1] His failure was more ignominious
than Brooke's. He was not even permitted an audience with

the King, and he left without presenting the letter he had brought from the President. Both Brooke and Ballestier were convinced and so recommended to their governments that the only way to secure new agreements with Siam would be by a warlike demonstration.

But the following year Mongkut became king. Brooke was again selected to proceed to Siam, but even before he could have learned of this Mongkut wrote to Governor Butterworth and asked that any negotiations be postponed until after the cremation of the late king. "The ceremony of the burning of the Royal King's corpse ought to be done with the greatest pomp, which cannot be finished quickly. If therefore in this interval before conclusion of the King's funeral ceremony, the Mission of British Government may come to our country, it might be great troublesome to us." [2] Actually, Mongkut did not wait until the cremation—royal cremations sometimes do not take place for a year or even longer—but after a few months, by proclamation, he effected the major reforms relating to import duties and the export of rice that had been the primary objects of the Brooke mission. As a result, pressure for new negotiations dropped. After much discussion, however, between the Indian Board and the Foreign Office and in consequence of petitions submitted by merchants seeking to have trade with Siam placed on a sounder basis, it was decided that a new treaty should again be sought.[3]

In 1855 a British Mission headed by Sir John Bowring arrived in Bangkok and concluded within the space of one month the treaty which completely altered the relations of Siam with the western world. Not only did the new treaty limit the duties on goods imported by British merchants and permit British subjects to buy or rent property near the capital, but it also regulated the taxes which might be im-

posed on them, and it granted extraterritorial rights authorizing the residence in Bangkok of a British consul who was
given civil and criminal jurisdiction over all British subjects in Siam. In the fascinating account of his mission given
by Bowring in his *The Kingdom and People of Siam,* he
describes the Siamese protocol and pageantry for receiving
the mission which, for lack of other precedent, followed
exactly the procedure adopted on the occasion of receiving
the embassy from Louis XIV in 1685. He makes clear the
conflict between the old school, who were opposed to dealings with foreigners, and the new thought, of which the leading proponents were Mongkut and his prime minister, the
Phra Kralahom. He recounts the various stages of the negotiations. But he makes no mention of the correspondence
which he and the King of Siam had before his arrival.

On July 18, 1854, the King had written to Bowring:

Your Excellency's former correspondence with me were considered as private, and the contents were not made known to our
Council, as it is not customary. I am desirous therefore that
Your Excellency should write and announce your intention of
visiting Siam, and determine a time for your arrival here, say at
least two or three months after the date of Your Excellency's
letter, and also express the manner of, and the number of
vessels and people that will accompany your visit. Please let our
officers of State be aware of the time of Your Excellency's arrival here, in order that they will know without doubt, and make
proper preparations to receive Your Excellency and retinue with
all suitable honors and respect, and also our officers of State
knowing of Your Excellency's intention will be enabled to quell
the fears of the people, who are of various races, and prevent
exaggerated reports, because it is very seldom foreign vessels of
war or steamers visit Siam.

His Excellency, Sir James Brooke, K.C.B. announced his
visit three months previous to his arrival, so it has become a

custom which I would be desirous of Your Excellency's following.

At the same time I would be glad if Your Excellency would
write also to me privately, and inform me of the nature of your
visit, and give the substance of the Treaty you would be desirous
of entering into, so that I might consult with my Council, and
know what clauses in the proposed Treaty they would be willing
to agree to, and what they would not. I would therefore inform
you of the same for your consideration, and thereby will save a
good deal of time and discussions after Your Excellency's arrival here.[4]

Six months later he wrote another personal letter to Bowring telling him that everything was satisfactory and that the
government was now ready to receive him.[5] He suggested
that Bowring try to come in April or May so as to see a white
elephant which had recently been captured and which would
be in Bangkok by then.

Bowring arrived in Siam on March 27, 1855, and the
treaty was signed on April 18. It was taken to England for
ratification by Harry S. Parkes, who had served as Bowring's
private secretary during the negotiations. Parkes (afterwards Sir Harry Parkes, K.C.B., K.C.M.G., and one of the
most distinguished of British diplomats in China and Japan)
reached England on July 1. Although only twenty-seven
years old, he was already an expert in Chinese matters—he
was as competent as he was good looking—and he was held
in London on consultation for many months by the Foreign
Office. Late in November he met a charming girl, wooed
her, and on New Year's Day, 1856, they were married. Ten
days later he and his bride set out for Canton, where he was
to take temporary charge of Her Majesty's Consulate, but
he was directed to go to Bangkok on the way and present
Queen Victoria's reply to the letter from King Mongkut

which had accompanied the treaty to London, to exchange ratifications of the treaty, and to deliver the royal gifts that the Queen was sending.* Parkes reached Bangkok in mid-March.

The royal letter was received by the King with all traditional splendor; a few days later ratifications of the treaty were exchanged with more ceremony; and on the following evening "the ratified copy of the treaty which was brought from England was . . . placed in the table before the throne in which Her Britannic Majesty's letter was placed, the Congregation of many Englishmen who accompanied H. S. Parkes Esquire . . . came in our Palace and took their seats at the frontier spot. . . . A pleasant theatrical entertainment was performed in honor to Her Britannic Majesty's royal letter and ratification until the midnight at near of which" the King made a little speech in English.[6]

Immediately thereafter, however, what Mongkut called a "commentary document" had to be negotiated because the British wanted an "explanation of certain articles and clauses of the new treaty which seemed to be gloomy or obscure." One "gloomy" clause, for example, set the distance within which British subjects might buy or rent a house, lands or plantation at "anywhere within a distance of twenty-four hours' journey from the city of Bangkok, to be computed by the rate at which boats of the country can travel." [7] It appeared the British felt this was not precise enough to indicate the exact distance involved. The new understanding was written in English in the first instance, but the Siamese interpreter had trouble preparing a written translation. The Siamese commissioners naturally did not want to sing the English version without a Siamese version

* A description of these royal gifts and what befell them will be found in Appendix I.

they could follow; Parkes was anxious to be on his way. So the King—he recorded all this with natural pride—orally translated the English document into Siamese while the commissioners checked off the points that had been agreed upon. When from this oral presentation it was found that the English version conformed to what had been stipulated, the commissioners signed it.

Then came the question of a Siamese embassy to London. Here again Mongkut overturned Siamese tradition. For generations it had been against the law for any high-ranking Siamese to go out of the country. While he was still abbot, Mongkut had written friends in upstate New York of his regret at not being able to visit America: "On hearing of your desire that I may pay visit to New York &c. I was most sorry for I know the opportunity would not be to me during my life for arrival the same with my body. The exact description of New York I have read in some books & heard frequently from mouth of my teacher and friend so that I was desirious long ere to visit, my whealth or property is as much as enough or sufficient for let me meet all the countries of the Europe & America." [8] But it was out of the question "owing to bad custom of our ignorant ancient & modern Government who prohabit alway the getting abroad of all royal persons as I am except the expedition for war." [9]

Even at the time of Bowring's arrival to negotiate the treaty there had been no change. When he had suggested in the course of conversation with the welcoming officials that presently some high Siamese functionary might go on a return mission to England, he was promptly informed, as he recorded in his diary, that it was against the laws of Siam for any exalted person to leave the country.[10]

Nevertheless Mongkut quietly pursued his revolutionary determination and when the time came had his way. In 1857

the first Siamese ambassadors left Siam.* The British government had made available the steam frigate "Encounter"
for their transportation to Suez and the steam despatch
yacht "Caradoc" from Alexandria to Portsmouth. The King
wrote Lord Clarendon to express his appreciation and also
to request Clarendon's care of the embassy "during their
being in boards Her B. Majesty's men of war in their ways
of going & coming & their stay in England." [11] At the same
time he gave the embassy a short personal letter of greeting
to be delivered to Queen Victoria. This letter concluded
with the paragraph and signature: "Above lines are genuine
our manuscript, from Your Majesty's distinguished Friend,
by race of the royalty affectionate Brother, and by humble
respect most obedient Servant. S. P. P. M. Mongkut, Major
King of Siam and its dependencies." [12]

The reference, Major King, recalls a Siamese custom
which dated back nearly four centuries.† This was the elevation and crowning of two kings. The Second King was the
most important person in the country after the First King;
he had royal privileges and responsibilities, he maintained
his own court and army, and he had almost unlimited access
to the Treasury. If the First King died, he succeeded to the
principal throne. The system clearly stemmed from an effort
to ensure stability and orderly succession, avoiding a minority reign, because it was usual for an adult son to be
named Second King, or if there were no son of suitable age
or one whose mother was of royal birth, then a brother
would be named. During the Chakri dynasty no Second

* A description of the ambassadors' reception in England will
be found in Appendix I.

† This custom was not confined to Siam; practically all the kingdoms of Southeast Asia had the same custom, and, indeed, some
in India.

King succeeded to the principal throne because each, in fact, predeceased his First King.

When Mongkut, who then had no royal children, was asked to become king he insisted that his only full brother should be chosen as Second King. This was a logical choice and fully acceptable to the Council of Princes and Ministers. Unlike Mongkut, his brother had decided to accept service under their half-brother when the latter became king, and he had held various civil and military posts, including active service as head of the navy during a war with Vietnam. Like his brother, he was full of intellectual curiosity. Among his earliest studies were navigation and the art of shipbuilding. "Captain Coffin, who took away those twins that have been the wonder of the world," to quote the *Siam Repository,* "was one of his first teachers." [13]

In later years, he constructed a model steamer "not twenty feet long, with smoke-pipe, paddle wheel, all complete," [14] which he personally ran on the river a few years after the "Express" visited Bangkok.* With the advent of the Amer-

* This accomplishment was actually reported in the New York *Tribune* (April 7, 1849, p. 2) in an article captioned "A Royal Siamese Machinist":

"The *Singapore Free Press* of Oct. 19, 1848, published the following communication from Bangkok, Siam, describing the proficiency attained by a native prince in mechanical art.

" 'Some time since, it was intimated that his Royal Highness . . . [the future Second King] had commenced the construction of a small steam-engine. This, under the most indefatigable and persevering exertions, on his part, has at length been completed, and the Siamese can now boast of having running on the river Menam, a steamboat, every portion of which has been made and manufactured here, and entirely by native artificers. She is $26\frac{1}{2}$ feet long, 3 feet $10\frac{1}{2}$ inches broad; the engine being 2 horse power. This little phenomenon has made several trips up and down the river, his Royal Highness the Prince generally acting

ican missionaries he studied English and ultimately secured an excellent command of the language. He developed a beautiful "copper-plate" handwriting. Unlike the bolder Mongkut, however, he never would dispense with a secretary even in his simplest correspondence, not trusting his ability at composition and wanting to be sure to avoid errors. He was more westernized than Mongkut and was accordingly more popular with the foreign colony in Bangkok. He was deeply interested in scientific progress—he was far more expert in astronomy than his brother [15]—and he maintained an excellent library in the English-style residence that he built. He was fond of martial exercises, hunting, and all forms of sport, which Mongkut did not care for. He seems, however, to have been more cautious or politic than his brother. For several years before the death of King Phra Nang Klao, the future Second King, conscious of the current antiforeign feeling, stopped seeing his European friends, although as soon as Mongkut and he became kings he again saw much of the foreign residents and had many foreigners in his employ. In later years also there were occasions when he was conveniently out of town when it seemed as if there might be trouble with foreign countries, or at least so thought Mongkut.[16] He is said to have had very democratic political views. Among the names he gave his eldest son was George Washington, after his favorite hero. When Chulalongkorn

---

steersman himself, in full view of thousands of astonished and admiring spectators, who crowded the banks of the river on each occasion. . . .

" 'The workmanship of even the most minute part of the engine itself is truly admirable, and reflects the greatest credit on its royal constructor, who had every portion of it made under his immediate superintendence and constant inspection, and by workmen all self-instructed, being his Highness' body servants and retinue.' "

became First King in 1868, Prince George Washington was chosen by the Royal Council to be Second King. When the latter died in 1885, the ancient office was abolished. Chulalongkorn then made his eldest son the heir with a new title equivalent to Crown Prince.

The Second King was usually consulted on all important state affairs, but Bowring, when negotiating the treaty which was signed by both kings, could not ascertain what responsibility and authority the Second King really had. "He is supposed to take a more active part in the wars of the country than does the First King," he wrote, but he "appeared to me more occupied with philosophical pursuits than with state affairs; and probably such a course of abstention is both wise and prudent." [17] Early in 1855 an American missionary commented to the Prime Minister on the fact that Siam had a First and Second King. He noted in his diary the Prime Minister's reply: " 'Second King,' he said, 'is no King'; by which I understood him to mean that the Second King was not allowed to have any part in the government, but that one will alone ruled." [18]

Mongkut was about five feet eight inches tall and had an erect and commanding figure, but he was far from handsome. "He had a very homely as well as old face," according to the wife of one missionary.[19] "Of middle height, thin, with a somewhat austere countenance," is Bowring's description.[20] "An expression of severe gravity was settled on his somewhat haggard face," we are told by a Fellow of the Royal Geographical Society who visited Bangkok in 1865.[21] A Frenchman who was received by Mongkut two years later wrote: "Sa Majesté Siamoise, agée de soixante-trois ans, est parfaitment laide, et tient beaucoup du singe," but then, he was a critic who made mock of many things and persons Siamese, except the King's children whom he found entrancing—especially one thirteen-year-old girl clad only in jewels.[22]

When Mongkut was in his late twenties or very early thirties, he had suffered a partial paralysis of the facial muscles—quite possibly Bell's palsy, the result of a virus infection—from which he never fully recovered, so that his large mouth had a droop on one side.[23] Furthermore, even before he became king, he had lost all his teeth, a common enough affliction in those days, and had those in the lower jaw replaced by a set made of sapanwood, a hard wood of deep-red color.[24] In 1854, Dr. Bradley presented the king with "a valuable casket of artificial teeth with a daguerre-otype of President Pierce, a present from Dr. D. K. Hitch-cock of Boston, to the King through me," but the teeth apparently were not a success.[25] It was only a year before Mongkut died that an adventurous dentist, Dr. Collins, traveling from China, came with his wife to Bangkok from Singapore because he had heard the King would give $1,000 for a good set of teeth. Poor Collins encountered much trouble and perplexity because the King would not let him touch his mouth in getting the needed wax impressions, but would always take these himself. The impressions were not perfect, the plates which Dr. Collins made did not fit smoothly, and the King lost his temper (for which he apologized the next day) when Dr. Collins wanted to look in his mouth to see what needed to be done to make them fit. A few days later Dr. Bradley was authorized to put his finger in the royal mouth and it was found that the plates could not be corrected. Finally, the King allowed Dr. Collins to take a new wax impression, "and the teeth that were made by it pleased his Majesty." Dr. Collins collected $560 from the King; and $108 for a set of teeth for one of the older princes. Then he and his wife started cheerfully overland for Burma, going upriver six days from Kanburi and hoping after that to go by elephant to some "navigable stream in Burma on which they expect to glide to Maulmein." [26]

By contrast, the younger brother was good looking and had a rather dashing personality, or at least so it seemed to Mongkut, who never ceased to poke envious fun at those qualities in the Second King. The younger brother, in turn, loved to tease Mongkut by calling him old-fashioned and senile. He usually referred to him as "Pi Thit" or "Pi Then," terms corresponding roughly to the English words "padre" or "prelate." [27] For some years the two brothers worked together in reasonable harmony. Then the Second King went to reside in the north, coming to the capital only when necessary on affairs of state. The Second King, who died in 1865, was much more urbane and westernized than King Mongkut, was generally, at least among foreigners, considered the cleverer of the two, and was more popular personally with the westerners residing in Bangkok. There can be little doubt but that Mongkut was jealous of his brother's popularity.

He was always very conscious of western opinion. "The King is eager to procure everything that is published regarding Siam," wrote Harris, the American envoy, in a confidential dispatch to the Secretary of State, "and quite as thin skinned on the subject as we are said to be in analogous ones." [28] A critical or inaccurate remark by a foreigner was often given undue importance in his mind, apt to be remembered, and presently thought of as representing foreign opinion. In 1852 Frederick Arthur Neale, "formerly in the service of His Siamese Majesty," had published his *Narrative of a Residence at the Capital of the Kingdom of Siam*. In this book he stated that there were seventy thousand floating houses in Bangkok and that the whole city, except for

a few named houses, was built on rafts.[29] Harris, to whom
this work had been recommended by the American Consul
at Singapore, commenting on this "Munchausen history of
Siam," solemnly recorded in his diary: "From all I see and
from all I can learn, I think there are seven thousand, not
seventy thousand floating houses in Bangkok, and I *know*
that more than nine tenths of the whole city is built on terra
firma." [30] But Mongkut continued sure that the world, or at
least Englishmen, thought otherwise.

At about the same time, Dr. Bradley had a disturbing
experience. "The Prime Minister sent for me to-day [Feb.
7, 1852] to give some explanation of a matter which has
just come to the knowledge of the King and with which he
was troubled. It was that he finds that I did not translate the
account of his inauguration [which the King had written]
correctly. But that I had made a grave mistake by making it
appear that his younger brother was endowed with more
wisdom and ability than himself. My reply was that I did my
best to give a true translation of the paper which was put
into my hands. The Minister said that the King was very
angry and that himself and his brother, the assistant Phra
Klang, were in circumstances to suffer much from the royal
displeasure. I requested that he would obtain the original
manuscript which I translated and examine the paragraph
which was so greatly exceptionable. He did so. Having read
along a few minutes he came to a place and struck his hand
on the book, and said 'Ah, here it is. Here is the mistake in
the Siamese.' He found that the mistake had arisen from a
loose and ambiguous mode of speaking of the First King,
so that even a Siamese would think that it meant the Second
King. . . . The Prime Minister seemed to acquit me entirely of any blame in the matter. I was very thankful to
God that he thus delivered me. It is quite a serious matter
to lie under a suspicion that I had a thought of conspiracy

against the Senior King and was publishing to the world that his brother was the more able man of the two." [31]

In 1857 Bowring published his account of his embassy and included the indiscreet statement: "Captain K[nox],* an Irish gentleman, has been opening his mind respecting the position of the Second King, whose agent he is. He says that the Second King is thrown too much into the shade, but that he is the cleverest man in the Kingdom, and has two thousand troops at his disposal; and intimated that . . . he would probably take a more active part in public affairs." [32]

Mongkut always selected Siamese as his ambassadors to represent him on important missions, never foreigners. They were chosen from the ablest of his entourage, but naturally they had had little or no diplomatic experience. Accordingly Mongkut was accustomed to write them long chatty letters giving rambling explanations of current situations, revealing his anxieties for their conduct and the impression they were making, furnishing encouragement or admonition, and adding gossipy news of their families and his own.

Mongkut's humor often ran to sarcasm, but in a letter he wrote the following year to his ambassadors in London, the inner feelings roused by these books and similar views appearing occasionally in the press are not too well concealed. He wrote:

I am very pleased indeed with this lot of letters and despatches. Mom Rajothai has certainly improved them by adding English characters wherever English words or names appear, which

---

* Thomas George Knox was an Irish adventurer who had been in Siam for many years. Formerly in the British Army, he had shortly after his arrival secured the post of drill master to the troops of the Second King. He learned to speak, read, and write Siamese fluently and became interpreter at the British Consulate. He succeeded Sir Robert Schomburgk as consul in 1864.

make them more easy to understand. The letters themselves are very entertaining, and I have read them over and over again to the ladies and gentlemen of my court. I have read them to the priests in their monasteries and to the laity in their homes. There are, of course, some philistines who have shown by their sceptical smiles that they doubt your report of having been invited to tea with Queen Victoria, the truth of which I and the senior members of the nobility have never entertained the least doubt, for we have some knowledge of English manners and customs.

We feel assured that the news concerning the activities of your Embassy cannot be embroidered with lies as had been done in the case of the Embassy to Peking, for the simple reason that all matters of interest are now reported in the newspapers, with more details than are usually described in letters. Moreover, there are always some Englishmen, newly arrived in this country, who are able to give accounts of the activities of the Embassy before we read of them from your letters.

For instance, I have already read in the newspapers, some time in the first half of the fourth month, that Sarapeth had ordered a sword to be made for me. I have learned about the Embassy's tour of British towns and boroughs since the second half of the third month. As regards the wedding of the Princess Royal to Prince Frederick William of Prussia, the papers were so full of it that I could not be bothered to read all of them. The postponement of the Embassy's return from England was largely talked of here, since the end of the fifth month. I have also learned of the Embassy's request for a loan of 4000 pounds from the Treasury of Queen Victoria, of the Embassy's three drawings of money on Phra Bidespanich [Siamese Consul in Singapore] amounting to 14,000 dollars at the London Exchange, and many other things besides, no matter whether they have been mentioned by you in your letters to me or not. To all these things I gave no objection whatsoever, but there is one small matter which worries me.

I hear that you have made the statement that the First King

had 1000 soldiers under his command while the Second King had only 500. As this statement is not quite in accordance with fact, would not people there accuse you of telling lies? As a matter of fact, I only have 800 soldiers under the command of Phra Bahol, another 400 in the "Bayonetted-Rifles" Royal Guards and only some 300 raw recruits. Have not the Second King got as much as 600 or 700 annamite mercenaries and over 2000 new recruits? Do you not know that it is the common talk of the town that the Second King has more military strength in the country than all other persons, who are nothing but names, and that only His Majesty the Second King, Prince Chao Fa Israphongse, and His Majesty's children are the hope of the people?

A great number of Englishmen have been and are now residing in this country. They seem to have an accurate knowledge of everything that is to be known here, but it is rather regrettable that they still retain a fixed idea regarding four phenomena characteristic to this country. The four unchanging phenomena, according to them, are that the river running through Bangkok has no other name but "Menam" [its name is the "Chao Phya"; "menam" means "river"]; that three-quarters of the houses in Bangkok are built in water, only one quarter being built on dry land; that nine parts out of ten of the local population are Chinese; and that the First King is a decrepit old man, so weak and thin and stupid as to be entirely incapable of conducting any official business. The only reason why he ever became King at all was that he happened to be elder brother to the Second King, who is actually at the head of affairs, and by whom both the present Treaty with Great Britain and the Embassy to that country have been originated. The First King is really so ancient that his power of speech is now restricted to only "ohs" and "ahs," punctuated by meaningless nods of the head. Whenever he is called upon to receive foreign guests, the Second King must always be behind his back, to tell him what to say.

The Second King, on the other hand, is a strong young man

who delights in riding either a great tusker elephant in must, or a stallion over five *sok* [seven and a half feet] high. His Majesty shoots every day, loves all things military, is so very learned and so full of culture as to become the central figure surrounded by worshiping pundits and the intelligentsia. The Second King is also a ladies' man. . . . I came to the throne when my age was four years less than the Second King's present age, but I was then already alleged to be old. The Second King is now more than three years older than I was when I came to the throne, but people still say that he is a young man. He cannot make even a chance visit to any provincial towns without being offered the daughters of governors or officials. He went to Saraburi and came back with a daughter of the Deputy Governor; he went to Nakorn Rajsima and came back with nine or ten Lao wives; he went to Panas Nikom and came back with a daughter of another Deputy Governor; and after his trip to Rajburi in the sixth month last, he returned with another wife. I have not been able to discover the identity of her father.

As for me, I am always looked upon as an old man wherever I go. No one has ever presented me with his daughter, and I always have to return home empty-handed, on account of my being an ancient relic. Although my hair is getting thin, I am not really bald, and whatever hair there is left to me is naturally black without the aid of hair-dyes, but people looking at me from a distance always insist that I am completely bald. I have even gone to the expense of buying myself a riding cap, and have taken pains to go out riding wearing it with the hope of creating an impression of youthfulness. I was a failure; people still maintain that I am old and still refuse to give me their daughters. . . .

These false impressions have been going on for a long time now, no one has ever been able to rectify them, not even in Bangkok itself. If you, who are abroad, tell truth, you will not be believed, since people have tried to make things sound otherwise by writing to the papers that the government of this country is carried on by the brains and influence of the Second King alone, the First King being aged to the point of imbecility. Have you not been a little careless in your speech, in making an understatment of the Second King's military strength, which is in reality much greater than that of the First King? I have an uneasy feeling that people abroad may say that the Siamese Ambassadors are nothing but liars. . . .

You seem to have spent a great deal of money in the purchase of goods. If it later transpires that these goods are for sale, I am afraid the English newspapers will say that the real motive of the Siamese Embassy to London is a commercial one. But since people will always find some scathing remarks to make about the Siamese and his character, you need not pay particular attention to this warning of mine, as long as you feel that your good services to the State remain unimpaired.* Moreover, if the English people should remark on your undue amazement at whatever you see there, there is no need to take it as an offense, since it is natural for you, who are barbarians visiting

---

* Just the same, Mongkut was somewhat disturbed and after the return of the embassy to Bangkok he wrote a letter to Lord Clarendon in which the King's English got rather out of control: "We fear a little however that on their some admiration, marvel and wonder in various articles which are very curious to them, when they have seen in various streets in London and other places in England, their desire to have purchase such various articles must be stronger than their usual desire here, it might produce some blaming consideration upon them even to ourselves, that the Siamese are very covetious or greedy, perhaps. They confessed themselves to us that upon this occasion they have entered to a most pleasant paradise or city of the Angels upon heaven, they could not help or suffer only in their mind the very interesting admiration &c., as the Siam is only a poor country and they never saw such the pleasant important city before, which city has not been seen by them even by their remote and foremote Ancestors. We would beg therefore your Lordship's and other's pardon upon them." [33]

paradise, to be amazed. My only regret is that, having had the good fortune to behold the beauty of angels, you have to return home empty-handed, for you cannot buy them and bring them back like Chinese women. Nevertheless, it might be a good idea to buy some of their costumes and bring them back home to dress up some of our earthly beauties here for the sake of variety.

There is no official business of any importance in Bangkok. . . . I and the members of my family are all in good health, with the exception of my son Kasemsant, younger brother of Yingyowalaks, who has been suffering from a long illness. I have not much hope for his recovery. His Honour Phya Sri Suriwongse has sprained his ankle in a riding accident; he has been unable to walk for over a month.

We are expecting your return daily. We keep on telling each other that the date of your return would be on the morrow or on the day after, so that we have become, in a manner of speaking, like Bua, the wife of H. E. the Minister of Harbour, who is in continual expectancy. Rumour had it long ago that she had been daily expecting a blessed event. Some said it would be on the morrow, some said it would be on the day after, but as far as I know, up till the first half of this month she was still expectant.

As regards the case of Phra Intradit who has committed adultery with your wife, Sarapeth, I have ordered the judges to hold a trial. They have decided on fines and compensations amounting to over 28 catties of money [the equivalent of about U.S. $1,300 at that time]. The fines are not to be paid to the Government, but are to be paid to you, since I have sent you far away from home. I should like to bring to your notice the fact that the amount of fines decided by the Law Court in the case of abduction of one of the King's women from a royal boat was a little more than one catty of money only [a little less than U.S. $50].[34]

The ambassadors finally returned to Siam, again on a British warship, late in May, 1858. They brought a royal letter from Queen Victoria which pleased Mongkut. "We are very much rejoiced and happy," he wrote in an official reply, "that our noble Embassy, when they were in London, and when they were travelling in post of England have right in their doing every where, without mistaken in proper conducts, pleased to your Majesty and your Government. There is nothing in them for any reproval or blame, so Your Majesty recommended our favour on them." [35] The Queen had doubtless read in *The Times* that the chief Siamese ambassador admitted "to the luxury of 58 wives" and within four hours of landing at Portsmouth had permitted his eye—so it was related of him—to light "on a young lady whom he would have liked to make the 59th, at the purchase-money of 3000 *l.*" [36] But had Victoria, one wonders, heard that in London, while staying at Claridges at Her Majesty's Government's expense, they "were conducted, with suitable escorts, to Kate Hamilton's where one of the senior envoys, Phya Mantry Suriywanse, glittering in golden robes, and displaying a belt encrusted with rubies, made a profound impression on the whores who had just swept in from Mott's and the Argyll. With an aid of the Royal Interpreter, Mom Rajoday, who was also picturesquely accoutred, the amiable diplomat ordered unlimited champagne for all. He continued to dip liberally into the treasures of the two Kingdoms until daybreak, when he was respectfully hauled into a waiting cab, and on to his hotel bed." [37]

5

The Americans

THE conclusion of the British-Siamese treaty had been the signal for other countries to negotiate similar treaties. In 1856 both the United States and France concluded treaties with Siam, and in the following years treaties were signed with most of the countries of Europe.

Pomp and ceremony were naturally important at the Court of the King of Siam, and Mongkut was always careful when dealing with foreigners to adhere to precedent lest he err and offend some western power. A letter from a foreign ruler was always received by the King and the full court with the same protocol and pageantry as if the ruler in person were being received. When the American treaty had been signed, he wrote in most formal style to President

Pierce describing minutely all the proceedings. His letter began:

"Somdetch Phra Paramendr Maha Mongkut by the blessing of highest Superagency of whole universe the King of Siamese Kingdom and the Sovereign of all interior tributary countries adjacent around in every direction, viz, Laos or Shiangs on North Western and Northern; Lao kaus on North and North Eastern; Cambodia from North Eastern to South Eastern; most of Malay peninsula in Southern and South Western, and Kariungs on Western to North Western point, and the professor of Magadhy language and Buddhistical literature &c &c &c

"To Franklin Pierce, President of United States of America &c &c &c

"Sendeth Greeting!

"Our distinguished and respect friend,

"Your appointed envoy plenipotentiary * Townsend Harris Esquire has conveyed your letter and presents to Siam by board United States Steam Frigate 'San Jacinto' which

---

* Harris had not, in fact, been appointed officially as envoy plenipotentiary. In a confidential report to the Secretary of State on his mission to Siam, he wrote: "You will observe that in the letter I wrote to the Minister of foreign Affairs, I took the title of Envoy Plenipotentiary. I did this after mature reflexion and advice. I believed, that if I presented myself as Consul-General to Japan, it would originate a series of difficulties that might defeat my Mission. I assure you I assumed the queer compound above quoted, solely for the purpose of aiding me in the execution of the duty which the President had entrusted to me, and not from any feelings of vanity. The salute I received on leaving the ship was carefully counted, and reported to the King; and I know that when it was asserted to the King, that I was simply a Consul, that assertion was fully met by the statement that I had received a salute of Seventeen guns on leaving the San Jacinto. I trust that this explanation will be satisfactory to the President and to yourself." [1]

was arrived the anchor place at mouth of Chau Phya river on the 12th day of the April, 1856." [2]

The "San Jacinto" lay off the bar for eight days. Then Harris was brought by royal steamer to Bangkok where he was suitably housed by the government. The king "had just gone through a grand ceremony of receiving an autograph letter from the Queen of Great Britain," Harris wrote Secretary of State Marcy. "At first he was decidedly disposed to making a palpable difference between the mission of the President of a republic and the regal head of a mighty empire. At last it was decided that I should come up to Bangkok 'with all the honors,' and my audience, the manner of presenting the President's letter, and the ceremonial to be observed thereon, was left for future decision. This accounts for the eight days delay between my arrival at the Bar and my arrival at Bangkok." [3]

At Bangkok further delay ensued. Someone had informed the king that the American president "had a title no higher than that of Excellency and consequently had not higher rank than an English admiral or a Governor or envoy." There was much discussion among the Siamese. "At last," reported Harris, "Prince Krom Hluang [Wongsa],* brother of the kings applied to me for the style of address used in writing to the President pretending it was wanted by the king and that he might write to the President. I was fully aware of his object, and informed him that we had no titles of rank in the United States, that such individuals, as were honored with an office, took the titles of that office; that we considered the office of 'President of the United States' as the most exalted on earth, and that to place any title before

* Prince Krom Luang Wongsa, a brother of King Mongkut by a different mother, was a physician and a member of the New York Academy of Medicine.

it would in our eyes degrade it, that the high officers of government in writing to him, addressed their letters 'To the President' or 'To the President of the United States.' I then showed him my full powers where it was headed 'Franklin Pierce, president of the United States.' This settled the whole matter."

The king's letter to the president naturally makes no allusion to these topics, but proceeds to a description of the audience:

On the first of May we have ordered the supreme court consist of principal high princes and noble councillors to be assembled in great meeting at the Pyramidical Royal residence named "Tusit Maha Prasad" with their full dresses and articles for their insignia for receipt of the letter addressed us from the President of the United States, which letter was on that day conveyed with escort and honoring procession as great as like manner of that in time of receipt of the letter from late President of the United States of America which was brought by Edmund Roberts Esquire, the American Envoy for negociation of the old Treaty of friendship and commercial intercourse between United States of America and our kingdom in the year 1833, and met with salute of 21 guns at the landing-place from the gilt boat and was thence brought to our court accompanied with Townsend Harris, Esquire, and Commodore Armstrong and other officers of the steamer San Jacinto, the former of whom has held the golden vase upon which the letter addressed us from United States of America was placed and which letter was so conveyed to the presence of our throne and stationed upon the table by the Envoy himself who has proclaimed immediately his being sent from the Supreme Government of United States of America for negociation and amendment of the Treaty of Friendship and Commerce with authority and people of Siam &c after which proclamation he had handed the letter with its outer fitting and Great Seal to our royal own hand. We have so acknowledged the receipt of your letter which we have opened immediately and read it in English style and let all American men at that assemble convinced that we understood its content throughout and translated orally its meaning to the great congregation of Supreme Court of Siam.

Two of the American participants have left detailed and colorful accounts of the ceremonies. The audience, which had originally been scheduled a day or two earlier, was postponed until May first because the current Siamese month was inauspicious, and the Siamese hoped that the change in the foreign month might offset the disadvantages inherent in their own. On the first, Harris appeared, resplendent in the uniform he had had made in Paris, on his way out, expressly to wear at the Siamese Court. It comprised a *chapeau bras* —a small three-cornered hat capable of being folded flat and carried under the arm—with black cockade and gold eagle, a single-breasted blue coat lined with white silk having a straight standing collar embroidered with gold, the cuffs similarly embroidered, and the button holes slightly embroidered, "white cassimere breeches, gold knee buckles, white silk stockings, and gold shoe buckles," and a sword.[4]

About eleven o'clock the boats sent by the King arrived to bring Harris and his suite in formal procession to the palace landing place. "First went boats containing the band; * then followed the boat with the President's letter, which was deposited upon an elevated and canopied throne. In this boat were four standard-bearers with triangular silk banners. The letter itself was laid in a portfolio of embossed purple velvet; heavy white silk cords attached the seal, which was shut in a silver box ornamented in relief with the

---

* This navy band was, by official direction, financed from a slush fund. A brief account of its origin and some of its musical adventures in Bangkok will be found in Appendix II.

arms of the United States. The cords passing through the seal and box were terminated by two heavy white silk cord-tassels; the whole was inclosed in a box in the form of a book bound in purple and gold; over this was thrown a cover of yellow satin. The marine guard, in two boats under command of Lieutenant Taylor, escorted that containing the letter.

"Next came a richly-canopied and curtained boat containing specimens of the presents from the United States to the king. This was followed by the barge containing the commissioner [Mr. Harris], his interpreter, Rev. Mr. Mattoon, and his secretary, Mr. Heuskin, with one of the ship's coxswains carrying the United States flag. The Commodore, his secretary and I [Surgeon to the Fleet Wood], occupied the next boat and then followed the remaining officers of the suite. . . . The whole procession must have extended along the river for at least half a mile. The river fronts, the floating houses, were covered with a dense mass of Siamese, through which we were pulled for two miles, our rowers shouting and whooping like wild Indians, as their paddles rapidly struck the water; this being one of the modes of indicating that they bore what they consider honorable burthens." [5]

A detailed program for the day's ceremony had been carefully worked out and distributed a few days before. After listing the order in which the boats and their occupants should proceed to the palace landing place (an order, incidentally, which was not observed), the program provided:

7 On arriving at the palace landing place, a salute will be fired which will be returned by the band playing "God Save the King";

8 After landing, the procession will be formed again in ex-

actly the same order as in the boats, with the exception that the American Flag borne by the Commodore's coxswain, and supported by two boys, will be placed between the band and the guard; all gentlemen will be carried in chairs.[6]

A few weeks earlier, at the reception of the letter from Queen Victoria borne by Harry Parkes, "the procession formed and walked under a triumphal arch which the King had caused to be erected with the words *Welcome Her Britanic Majesty* inscribed on it," [7] but it is to be remembered that this letter marked the ratification of the King's first treaty, and, besides, it was signed, as the King had delightedly ascertained in advance, by the Queen as his "affectionate Sister." [8] The program for the American audience continued:

9   On arriving at the Hall of Justice, the band, Flag and guard will halt, and the remainder of the procession will proceed on to the Audience Hall;

10   On arriving at the Audience Hall, the procession will be formed in four lines, as follows [fifteen names follow]. . . . By request of the King the three last mentioned gentlemen join the procession [These were Dr. Bradley and Mr. Chandler, American missionaries, and Mr. David O. King, "an enterprising American Merchant, who has just established himself in Bangkok" [9]].

11   The procession, having fairly entered the Hall, will halt, and make one bow, being uncovered; it will then proceed up the Hall in the same order to a place marked by a table, when the procession will halt, and, after bowing again, the gentlemen will be seated, Commodore Armstrong occupying a cushion on the left in front.

Mr. Harris will then place the President's letter (which he has borne from the entrance of the Hall) on the table and remain standing by it. On receiving a signal he will advance and

present the President's letter to the King, after which he will
return to his place and, still standing, will read his speech, on
the completion of which (which will be known by his bowing and
handing a paper to Mr. Mattoon) the gentlemen will please rise
again, bow and be reseated.

12 In marching up the Hall and in being seated, gentlemen
are requested not to crowd on the rank in front, and to cover
their file leader.

At the landing place, when the procession was formed,
it was found that "two chairs, carried on men's shoulders,
were provided for the Commodore and commissioner, and
for the remainder of us simply red cushions upon a seat
without back or sides, and supported on arms resting on
the men's shoulders. . . . Our seats were very uncertain.
We must have sat there very awkwardly, for the crowds of
Siamese through which we passed rent the air with shouts of
laughter." [10]

"All along the road," wrote Harris, "we passed through
a double file of soldiers, dressed in a most fantastic manner.
Some companies were armed with long poles, furnished at
the top with a round knife, others with battle axes, cross-
bows, old flint muskets. Some wore long gowns and looked
like women, others looked like the Swiss montagnards of a
Chatham theatre. Twenty elephants, each with a howitzer
on its back, of Spanish manufacture of two centuries ago.
A salute was fired of twenty-one guns." [11]

At the Legation Hall, still some little distance from the
Audience Hall, the gentlemen "dismounted." At this point
there was a fairly long pause; then the procession went forward on foot. "As we turned a corner we came suddenly
upon an appalling sight—files of a hundred men on each
side of our road, and each man had under his left arm an
oblong drum; in his right hand was a bone, looking like a

deer's antler. The moment we made an appearance, these two hundred drums received simultaneously a single blow —and the crash was awful; and then, after a short pause, another. Having passed through the drums, a band of wind instruments received us, and then we were at the door of the audience hall." [12]

"Arrived at the Hall of Justice," Harris recorded in his diary, "the nobles who had escorted me from the Hall of Legation, fell on their knees as soon as the door was opened, made three salaams and preceded us to the throne, crawling on hands and knees, among a crowd of nobles all prostrated in the same manner, and dressed in rich gowns, interwoven with gold. Everyone had the insignia of his rank,—*viz.*, a gold betelnut box, gold teapot, swords, etc., near him. The Hall of Justice is a large building of immense height, built in the form of a cross, the centrum supported by four slender and most graceful looking pillars, rather in the Egyptian style. Between the four pillars, the white state umbrella of nine stages; at the upper end of the hall, the throne richly carved and gilt. The throne has no steps, the King entering it outside the hall, and has no communication whatever with the hall but the opening of the throne where the King is seen sitting. . . . On each side of the throne two state umbrellas of seven stages and ten others of five stages. Immediately under the throne, four swordbearers and two guards armed with a rifle." [13]

Wood added some details: "Along each side of the long hall, in two rows, lay the nobles of the kingdom, resting upon their elbows and knees upon red velvet cushions. They were clothed in the richest golden tissues, some having golden muslin over under garments of rich silk, and some fine muslins over tunics of uniform gold. My old friend, Prince Wongsa, and the prime minister were among those most richly and tastefully costumed. . . . Before each noble was arranged his paraphernalia of golden vessels, some of them as large as a soup-tureen. There must have been from ten to twenty thousand dollars before each noble." Then turning his attention to the throne, he wrote, "The curtains of the front of this throne are drawn back, and in the open space is seated the king, also clad in golden fabrics, and upon his head a crown of purple velvet, glittering with jewels, and having a single bird-of-paradise plume falling over to one side. He is a small, thin, pleasant and intelligent-faced man, of a hue scarcely differing from that of his dress and surroundings." [14]

"Two cushions," wrote Harris, "were provided for the Commodore and myself, my suite had to sit or lie down on the floor, covered with rich Smyrna carpeting. Having gone through the ceremonial alluded to in the program and presented His Majesty with the President's letter (I could hardly hand it to him the throne being so high [a stool had to be provided for Parkes!]), on a signal I read my address [he had found 'it hard work,' he had written a few days earlier when composing this, 'to reconcile my republican ideas with the strong language of compliment I *must* use' [15]] as follows":

May it please Your Majesty,

I have the honor to present to Your Majesty a letter of the President of the United States containing a most friendly salutation to Your Majesty, and also accrediting me as his representative at your Court.

I am directed to express, on the President's behalf, the great respect and esteem that he feels for you, and his warm wishes for the health and welfare of Your Majesty, and for the prosperity of your dominions.

The fame of Your Majesty's great acquirements in many difficult languages and in the higher branches of science, has crossed

the great oceans that separate Siam from the United States, and
has caused high admiration in the breast of the President. The
United States possesses a fertile soil and is rich in all the products of the temperate zone. Its people are devoted to agriculture,
manufactures and commerce. The sails of its ships whiten every
sea; its flag is seen in every port; the gold mines of the country
are among the richest in the world.

Siam produces many things which cannot be grown in the
United States, and the Americans will be glad to exchange their
products, their gold and their silver for the surplus produce of
Siam.

A commerce so conducted will be beneficial to both nations,
and will increase the friendship happily existing between them.

I esteem it a high honor that I have been selected by the
President to represent my country at the court of the wisest and
most enlightened monarch of the East, and if I shall succeed in
my sincere wish, to strengthen the ties of amity that unite Siam
and the United States, I shall consider it as the happiest moment of my life.[16]

Harris dismissed the balance of the audience with a brief,
"The King opened a commonplace conversation; asked how
many treaties had been made between the United States
and Eastern nations; how long the actual President would
remain in office; the number of our States, etc. Gave to me
and each of the officers his visiting card." [17] But Wood,
once again, furnishes the details: When Harris had finished
his address, "we all rose, made the stipulated bows, and
resumed our seats. The king then commenced a conversation with the commissioner . . . through Mr. Mattoon,
who sat near Mr. Harris, and a Siamese official interpreter,
who lay next Mr. Mattoon with his head bowed to the floor,
and his hands pressed together before his face. At each
communication he raised his head slightly, and prefaced
his message by some of the magniloquent titles of the king.

During the first part of the conversation, the king was loosening the clasps of the President's letter, which he seemed impatient to get at. He asked how long Mr. Pierce had been President, and how many Presidents there had been. Having by this time got out the letter, he noticed the seal, and asked if we had a new seal with each President. He then opened the letter, and read it aloud in English, with a French accent, and then said to the commissioner, 'Did you understand me?' 'Perfectly.' 'I will now read it in Si-amese,' and he did so to his nobles.

"He then inquired how many treaties we had with the East, and with what nations. He remarked, that in any treaty we might make with Siam we could expect no ex-clusive privileges. The commissioner replied that we desired none.

"The king then went on with quite a long history of the various embassies which had visited Siam, and held up a gold-scabbered sword which had been presented through Mr. Roberts [when the American treaty of 1833 was ne-gotiated] to the then king, and had fallen to him. He seemed to prize it highly.

"He then inquired what were our usages in receiving presents, and was told by Mr. Harris that the Constitution of our country prohibited our receiving any. He inquired what was done with such presents as had been made to officers of our government, and was told they were deposited in the State Department. I suppose he made his inquiries, because he had heard that such were our arrange-ments. . . .

"During the audience I felt some one lightly pushing my elbow; and, looking around, found it was a young man, the nephew and private secretary of the king, on his hands and knees, pushing before him a silver cup of cigars and a box of lucifer matches, and also a small stand of wine in cut rose-tinted decanters, and with glasses to correspond.

"Notwithstanding the sacredness of 'the presence,' smoking was not against etiquette, and was therefore freely indulged by the commissioner and others of us smokers during the hour and a half that the audience continued." [18]

"At the end of the audience," concluded Harris, "a large curtain is drawn concealing the throne from our sight in three strokes, and at every stroke the crouching nobles make a salaam by raising their joined hands to their foreheads." [19]

But to return to the King's letter to President Pierce:

Also Townsend Harris, Esquire, has handed us upon the same time the list of valued Articles of useful and curious presents,* your portrait of living size &c. . . . We beg to offer our sincere thanks to you and beg to assure that these articles of presents will be kept in our possession for the token of your remembrance and mark of the good friendship existed between our kingdom and United States of America as well as the golden fitted sword which has been presented to our Royal half-brother and predecessor . . . when the old Treaty of U.S.A. has been done by Edmund Roberts, Esquire on the year 1833, and which royal sword we have shewn to all American visitors upon this time of ceremony. . . .

On the 2nd May the American envoy and his accompanied American persons Commodore Armstrong &c. has visited our younger royal full brother, the Second King at his palace where they met with cordial welcome good treatment as well as they have here before that day.

Protocol of the audience with the Second King followed closely that with the First King, including the delivery of a formal address. In this address Harris offered the interesting comment: "A new state of the American Union [California]

* A list of these presents will be found in Appendix I.

had lately sprung into existence, from which the voyage to Siam can be made in one month. This makes the United States the nearest neighbor that Siam has among the Caucasian races and is a strong reason for uniting the two nations." [20] During the conversation following the address, the Second King "said he knew all the names of the Presidents with the exception of the late President, and he wanted to know the actual Vice-President's name." Wood noted that he "seemed to have a particular affection for General Jackson respecting whom he made minute inquiries." [21]

Thereafter the Siamese plenipotentiaries were appointed. They were the most important men in the kingdom: Prince Wongsa, as representative of the royal family; the uncle of the Phra Klang, who held a position analogous to that of elder statesman in Japan; the Phra Kralahom (Prime Minister); the Phra Klang (Foreign Minister); and the Lord Mayor of Bangkok. These same officials also represented the King, however, in the discussions with Mr. Parkes and were still engaged in working out the "commentary document" on the British treaty. As a result, there was a fortnight's delay in starting the official conversations; then the American treaty was negotiated rapidly and signed on the twenty-ninth of May.

Once the treaty was signed Harris departed with a speed that irritated the King, who obviously thought it unseemly and scarcely courteous. "Your envoy," he continued in his letter to President Pierce, "was in a very hurrying haste for his departure and determined his being staying here but two days, after the conclusion of the Treaty, in which most narrow space of time we are very sorry to say indeed we could not have time to prepare our letter in answer to your letter . . . and pack suitable articles of presents that

would be designed to you from us . . . and your envoy
could not be detained longer little while than he has determined by a single word at once . . . and took leave [of]
us on the morning of the 31st instant." A little later the
King referred to "the hest or hurried departure of your envoy who did not delay and got down to sea in evening of
the said day and went by the steamer San Jacinto [which]
steamed away on the morning of the 1st June instant."

Townsend Harris was a distinguished merchant from
New York who had been president of the city's Board of
Education and the inspiration and driving force behind the
founding of the College of the City of New York [22] when
he succumbed to the lure of the East. For six years he had
made long trading voyages visiting many Pacific islands,
and he had traveled, lived, and carried on business in China,
Malaya, India, and Ceylon. Increasingly, however, his pas-
sionate desire was to go to that secret country—Japan. He
had applied in vain for permission to accompany Commodore Perry on his famous trip. He returned to the United
States just as the Perry treaty arrived and promptly sought
the post of consul which that treaty authorized. He secured
appropriate endorsements. He saw the President. He wrote
to him, "I have a perfect knowledge of the social banish-
ment I must endure while in Japan, and the mental isolation
in which I must live, and am prepared to meet it. I am a
single man, without any ties to cause me to look anxiously
to my old home, or to become impatient in my new one." [23]
On August 4, 1855, he was appointed first American Consul General to Japan. And just then word was received in
Washington of the British success in negotiating a new
treaty with Siam, and Harris, who would be passing near
that country en route to his new post, was entrusted with
the mission of negotiating a new treaty for the United States.

Just as today some people become impatient with the newly independent countries of the world because they do not make decisions or act with the speed or precision which those from older countries with their trained and established civil services have come to expect—so Harris, arriving in Siam, failed to make allowances for the revolutionary change in foreign policy that Mongkut was inaugurating and all the difficulties attendant upon that voluntary effort to open the country to foreign trade and influence. Indeed he seems never to have realized that it was the King himself who had inaugurated and was actively pressing forward the new policy. Harris ignored the facts that Mongkut and his supporters were of necessity feeling their way and balancing each proposed step; that the King had almost no officials who had had the experience or were qualified to understand the new relationships he was trying to establish; and that an inordinate load of work, which in other countries would be done by trained subordinates, had to be executed personally by the King. Harris failed to evaluate, for example, the significance of the entries in his own diary to the effect that the King "was much annoyed by the number of letters which Mr. Parkes had written to him, or rather the labor it had thrown on him." [24] On the other hand, Harris took it for granted that the Siamese authorities would know that a short courteous reply to President Pierce would meet the requirements of international protocol; he never dreamt that Mongkut might believe it necessary that he himself write a long letter to the President minutely describing Harris' visit, or that the King would personally have to check the translation and correct in his own handwriting the official copy that went to Washington.

Harris considered it "folly" that time should have been wasted while the King, before granting an audience and determining the ceremonies to be followed, tried to resolve his uncertainty as to the status of the American Republic and its President and the appropriate protocol for receiving Harris and the President's letter.[25] He lamented his inability to secure a private audience with the King in advance of the official reception of the President's letter. "The greatest difficulty exists," he noted in his diary, "in the fact that the King is totally ignorant of the power and greatness of the United States, and he will remain in that state unless I can have a private interview and convince him that we are to be both feared and respected."[26] He resented the delay in the issue of credentials to the Siamese commissioners. By the tenth of May Harris was complaining that "the King has now the strange fancy for executing public documents connected with Americans and English in the English language. This must cause more delay and I *think* is so intended."[27]

He became increasingly indignant when he finally came to realize that the Siamese were in no hurry and would not begin negotiations with him until they had concluded their discussions with Parkes. He wrote in his diary disdainfully that the Siamese did not feel competent to carry on two negotiations at once. He seems not to have considered that from the Siamese viewpoint there was no reason why they should: the negotiations with Parkes were taking all their time and were the more important negotiations since they involved substantive interpretations of what they had already agreed; it would naturally be better for them to know exactly what more had to be conceded the English before they took on another country; and a short delay in starting negotiations with Harris would do no one any harm.

In contrast to Harris, Surgeon Wood, who throughout his visit was trying to understand the Siamese and their

King Mongkut early in his reign, as shown in a woodcut drawn from a photograph given to Sir John Bowring and published by him in 1857 in *The Kingdom and People of Siam*. Below is a facsimile of Mongkut's signature with the Latin phrase he often added, "Rex Siamensium." (Photograph from the Library of Congress.)

King Mongkut with Queen Debserin. This illustration is taken from what is believed to be a photograph of the daguerreotype sent by the King to President Franklin Pierce in 1856. (Photograph from the Smithsonian Institution.)

viewpoints, had seen the situation clearly enough soon after their arrival in Siam: "Mr. Parkes, who brought out the English ratified treaty, is still here," he wrote, "and has been for some weeks endeavoring to launch it into successful operation, in which he has found some difficulty and many obstacles. Mr. Parkes is uncertain when he will get through. The presence of this gentleman is no doubt some obstacle to our negotiations being commenced. . . . I suspect they [the Siamese] do not want too much on their hands at once; and soon the French mission will be pressing them. . . . This treaty-making is a difficult and responsible business among such a people. It is contrary to the traditions, notions and habits of the masses to be in appearance surrendering rights to foreign powers, and especially western powers. It is contrary to the interest of the nobles to be opening for general competition a trade of which they now have the monopoly. The enlightenment and education of the two kings, being so far in advance of their nation, may prove their ruin." [28]

By the fourteenth of May, the day Parkes had a farewell audience with the King, Harris was fuming. Gone were the sentiments he had expressed in his address. He entered in his diary contemptuous references to the King; he had found the solution for all the delays. In his confidential report to the Secretary of State he elaborated his views. "The delay of fifteen days in appointing the Commissioners," he explained, "arose from the peculiar habits of the King. He is pedantic almost beyond belief, and squanders a great deal of time in the most trifling pursuits indeed. I fancied I could trace strong resemblance between him and James the first of England, whom the great Sully called 'the most learned fool in Christendom.' After some twenty years, spent in the rigid celibacy of the Priesthood, the King gives up a large portion of his time to voluptuous pleasures and his self-indulgence appears to be growing rapidly on him. It often occurs that his Nobles come to the morning audience at 8 o'clock and remain there until 5, 6, or 7 o'clock, in the evening, prostrate on the floor of the audience-hall, without ever seeing the King, but knowing he is indulging himself in a manner equally repugnant to decency, and the laws of his Religion, of which he was a stern supporter, while in the Priesthood." [29]

Parkes left Bangkok on Thursday, May 15. On the same day the tropical poisons which had gradually been making Harris' world gloomier and gloomier broke forth and Harris developed "many boils, etc. etc., indigestion, etc." [30] (eloquent "etceteras" for those acquainted with the tropics!). And on the very next afternoon Harris met with the Siamese plenipotentiaries to commence negotiations.

During his courtesy call on the Phra Klang a few weeks before, Harris remarked that he expected the British treaty to serve as the basis for the American treaty. The Phra Klang had said, "There would be no difficulty in regard to it." But in reply to Harris' remark he added, "No more than that yielded could be granted. The boat was already full, pressed to the water's edge, and would bear no more." [31] Now Harris handed the Siamese a Siamese version of the treaty he would like to have. It was essentially the British treaty, but with several variants. There was discussion, argument, dissent; there were affirmative changes that the Siamese wanted. The meeting adjourned until Tuesday, the twentieth.

Harris was no Job, and as each day he entered in his diary "still unwell," life became grimmer; each day became an eternity; people were actuated by the most despicable motives in everything they did. On Tuesday and Wednesday, the Siamese were impossible, especially, as he discovered and wrote in his diary on Wednesday, "the Commissioners *cannot* do any single thing without first consulting the King." [32] On Thursday, at the fourth meeting, "thinking quite time enough had been wasted, I gave them my ultimatum, *viz.,* the Treaty as I had given it to them in Siamese" with one minor change requested by the Siamese.[33] The commissioners promised to give him their answer on Saturday, and on Saturday they accepted Harris' proposal.

"I hope this is the end of my troubles with this false, base and cowardly people," he exploded in his diary. "To lie is here the rule from the Kings downward. Truth is never used when they can avoid it. A nation of slaves. . . . I never met a people like them, and hope I may never again be sent here. The proper way to negotiate with the Siamese is to send two or three men-of-war of not more than sixteen feet draft of water. Let them arrive in October [when the river is high] and at once proceed up to Bangkok and fire their salutes. In such a case the Treaty would not require more days than I have consumed weeks." That evening he gave notice that he would leave on the following Saturday.[34]

Parkes had had a far more difficult task than Harris. He had had to negotiate a new meeting of the minds; Harris had only to garner for the United States the benefits of the British negotiations. Each man contended with the same difficulties. Mrs. Parkes recorded in her Journal: "The Siamese are so very dilatory in all matters of business, and it is such hard work to uproot their old prejudices and customs and to introduce new ideas, that Harry says he has to go over the same ground over and over again before we can reconcile them to any change, even if it would prove beneficial to themselves; for they are so selfish and dishonourable themselves that they judge of others' conduct by their own, and consequently imagine that foreigners have some sinister design to their country in whatever they may propose; and none of the Commissioners appointed to arrange matters can take a single step without referring it to the King. They generally meet at Prince Kroma Luang [Wongsa]'s for discussion, and it is often two or three A.M. before Harry gets away." [35]

But however discouraged or irritated Parkes may have been, he never ceased to be diplomatic in his manner, and his final verdict has the ring of clear and sympathetic understanding. A few weeks after he left Siam he wrote to his brother-in-law: "I was fortunate in securing and maintaining throughout the friendship of the First King, who listened to several of my propositions even against the wishes of his Ministers. He is really an enlightened man. His knowledge of English is not profound, but he makes an excellent use of what he has acquired, and conducts his correspondence in it in a very creditable manner. It is scarcely a matter of surprise that he should be capricious and at times not easily guided; but he entered into the Treaty well aware of its force and meaning, and is determined, I believe, as far as in him lies, to execute faithfully all his engagements, which are certainly of the most liberal nature." [36]

But Parkes had not been ill whereas Harris had suffered from those etceteras which becloud the vision, warp the judgment, and are the particular nemesis of the diplomat. Even though by Sunday, the twenty-fifth, he was able to enter in his diary, "I am now quite recovered," [37] he never recovered a mellow outlook or escaped from the judgments he formed during this period.

Some days would have to pass while the treaty was being translated, copied, compared, and prepared for signature, but Harris' one desire now was to quit Siam as soon as possible. At Singapore, on his way out, he had seen the French ships waiting for the French envoy to carry him to Siam, and he had been anxious to complete his negotiations before that diplomat should arrive.[38] [Montigny, the French envoy, did not arrive in Bangkok until July 14.] [39] But that was no longer a pressing matter, and there is nothing in his diary to indicate that he needed to leave on May thirty-first, but having said he was going to do so he intended to depart that day, regardless.

On Tuesday afternoon, the twenty-seventh of May, Prince Wongsa "requested me to delay my departure until Monday, saying the King had not the letter to the President ready, nor could he give me an audience of leave, as he had engagements for all the time. These were mere childish pretence, as plenty of time exists between this and next Saturday morning to do all they require, and moreover I told the Prince *last* Saturday that I must leave next Saturday. I accordingly sent word that I should much regret not having an audience, but it was absolutely necessary I should leave on Saturday, as the bread was running short in the ship, and that if I did not go before Monday I should lose the June mail from China [to the United States]," [40] and, as he offered in explanation to the Siamese but did not put in his diary, "thus the Treaty would be delayed another month." [41]

On Wednesday, "the Prince in trouble wishes me to write him a letter with my reasons for not staying over until Monday. Wrote it and sent it to Mr. Mattoon [the Reverend Stephen Mattoon was an American missionary who had been in Bangkok some nine or ten years and who served as his interpreter while Harris was in Siam]. The reason the Prince wishes this in black and white is that he may show it to the King, as they are such a set of unsanctified liars that the King would not believe him without some proof like this. . . . In addition to what I said yesterday, I wrote that the King's letter to the President could be given to the *consul,* who would forward it in a proper manner. This is the first hint I have given of my intention to appoint a consul." [42]

On Thursday, the treaty was signed with full formalities. "The Prince then delivered to me two copies of the Treaty and I gave him one, at which moment a salute of twenty-one guns was fired from the Prince's battery or fort. All was smiles and good humor." [43] Harris announced Mattoon's appointment as first American Consul to Siam, and the King sent a message asking if Harris would arrange to depart Saturday evening so that he might give him an audience Saturday morning. Harris' reply "proposed that he should give me an audience on Friday night." [44] On Friday "the First King sent me word that he would give me an audience of leave early to-morrow morning, and that his boats should be sent for me at 7 A.M." [45]

At last came Saturday the thirty-first. The King must have sensed long since that Harris' haste was largely from personal irritation with the world, and he apparently saw no reason why he should have to be hurried by this impatient envoy or why he should dispense with the courteous conversation which such occasions demand. It is also just possible that he felt that a small penalty should be imposed for what he considered was a failure in good manners. But whatever the cause, to Harris everything that happened that day was done only to annoy; even the engines of the steamer joined the conspiracy!

"The boats from the King," he wrote, "instead of coming for me at seven o'clock, did not reach me until after eight o'clock. . . . We went to the Hall of Justice where I was kept waiting for nearly two hours before I was admitted, although the King knew that this delay would probably prevent my reaching the *San Jacinto* to-night.

"Was received in the old Audience Hall—a finer interior than the other where I was first received. A very large number of nobles and princes was present. The King was seated on a low throne about two feet above the floor. He asked me how soon I should leave, whether I went to China direct or via Singapore. Spoke about his regret at not having time! to write the President or to prepare presents for him. As to the last, I told him the letter and presents could be delivered to the Consul who would forward then in a proper manner, etc., etc." [46]

When the official audience was ended, the King invited Harris to a private audience. "He gave me a blue velvet envelope which he said contained my *Credentials!* and requested me to open and read them. There were two papers: one a receipt for the presents; and the other an apology for not sending presents and writing a letter to the President, with a short history of the negotiations. The last document must have taken twice as much time as would have sufficed for writing to the President direct.

"So much for his excuse of 'want of time.' I was now delayed over an hour by the most frivolous and pedantic conversation I ever listened to, and satisfied me he was quite as weak-minded as pedantic. He enumerated all the languages he could speak—the various sciences he has a small smattering of—the learned societies of which he was a member, and the various individuals he corresponded with in various parts of the world, and honored me by asking me to correspond with him from Japan. It was now half-past twelve and I was most anxious to get away. But no—I must wait

while he wrote a gossipy letter to Sir John Bowring, informing Sir John that I would show him my credentials, as he
persisted in calling the two papers in the blue pocket. At
last, as there must be an end to all things, I got away a little
past one o'clock. I went down for the steamer in the King's
boat, but, as the tide was strong against us, did not reach
her until two P.M. I omitted to mention that at this interview
I gave the King the *Nautical Almanac* for 1856, 1857 and
1858; and just before I left, he gave me a silver gilt segar
case filled with segars. I shall smoke those and send the case
to the Secretary of State."

Then Harris started for the "San Jacinto," which was
anchored just outside the bar. The King had a small steamer
to convey distinguished personages to and from the anchorage. She was painted sky blue [47] and puffed "as if worn out
by her exertions." [48] "She is about forty tons and has a small,
high pressure engine or locomotive brought out from the
United States. She was otherwise wholly built and set agoing
by the Siamese." [49] It was this steamer they now boarded.*

* A year later Captain Charles Porter Low, the writer's great-
great-uncle, commanding the clipper ship "N. B. Palmer," arrived
in Siam from Singapore. "We anchored off the Menam bar on the
first of June, 1857. The *Portsmouth,* American Man-of-war, was
anchored near us. She was commanded by Captain Foote. . . . As
soon as the ship was anchored I left for Bangkok to report, and
meeting Mr. and Mrs. Telford received another kind invitation to
stay with them during the ship's loading. I accepted for myself and
wife and later we started in the long boat for the city. We were
becalmed in the river and were making slow progress, when a
steamer flying the Siamese flag hove in sight, bound up. It came
close to us and stopped, and Captain Foote hailed me and asked us
to come on board. The King and second King were on board and
the boat belonged to the Kings, a very pretty vessel called *The*

"We went," recorded Harris, "on the little steamer *Royal Seat Siamese Steam Force* for half an hour, when we had to stop to fix the machinery. Then on again for another half hour—another stop and another fix." [50] They arrived at Paknam, about four miles from the entrance of the river, at seven P.M., too late to go out to the "San Jacinto," but next morning they were "up at five, got on board at half past seven o'clock, and at noon precisely got under way."

A little sigh of relief probably escaped the King when Harris finally departed. The King knew Mattoon well. He liked him, and he trusted him as did all the Siamese. He was therefore relieved when Mattoon also "has now assured us to convey our letter and presents designed for your acceptance from us on good opportunity. . . . Now we have liberty to finish our letter [it is dated June 10, 1856] . . . and . . . packing suitable articles of presents which are entirely and wholly manufactured by Siamese blacksmiths, goldsmiths &c."

Mongkut's letter to President Pierce and the presents reached Washington within a year,[51] but for some reason it was not until May, 1859, that President Buchanan sent an acknowledgment and advised that "on the 25th of last month two boxes containing a number of public documents, published by order of the Government of the United States, were sent to Your Majesty and Your Majesty's Royal Brother, the Second King of Siam." [52] As to the presents which the King had sent, "These acceptable gifts," the Pres-

----

Royal Seat of the Siamese Forces, a pretty long name. The Kings had been the guests of Captain Foote on board the *Portsmouth.* We were glad to go on board and to be graciously received by their Majesties. We were soon landed in Bangkok" (Charles Porter Low, *Some Recollections* [Boston, 1905], pp. 144–145).

ident wrote, "which now form a most attractive feature in one of the National Collections * of this, the Capital of the United States, have elicited the admiration of thousands of visitors, and will ever remain a gratifying memento of Your Majesty's liberality and good feeling."

On February 14, 1861, Mongkut wrote:

To His Most Respected Excellent Presidency the President of United States of America, who having been Chosen by the Citizens of the United States as most distinguished, was made President and Chief Magistrate in the Affairs of the Nation for the appointed term of office Viz ÷ Buchanan Esquire who had forwarded an official letter to us from Washington dated at Washington 10th May Anno Christi 1859 . . . with a package of Books 192 Volumes in number which came to hand on the year following; or to Whomsoever the people have elected a new as Chief ruler in place of President Buchanan &c &c &c.[53]

He expressed his appreciation to the President for "forwarding to us the works which will contribute to our enlightenment in various departments of knowledge." At the same time, he thought he should say something about the presents "which were addressed to and intended for your predecessor His Excellent Presidency Franklin Pierce then the President & Chief Magistrate of the United States who had addressed to us an official letter." He was not at all sure that Siamese royal etiquette had been adequately understood by those who headed the astonishing political system that appeared to exist in the United States.

According to the regulation course of things among the various seperate communities & independent nations in the World, it is generally observe that the natural course of affairs among

* They were then on exhibit in the National Institute in the old Patent Office. See Appendix I.

Savage and barbarious tribes is that he who is strongest and bravest by his own might or by the aid of his strong & brave friends & supporters, becomes the Chief whether this be agreeable or not agreeable to the great majority of the people of the land. But in countries where mankind are half civilized, where they are acquainted with some Code of Laws and their manners and customs are good in most of these countries, the one who is most honored and praise worthy and trusted of those whom it is proper to honor, to praise & to trust having excellence & skill in the management of public business, is with one accord, Selected and established as the refuge & Pillar of the state and he becomes Supreme in the land. Having thus obtained authority to administer the Government of the Nation he generally, if he escapes misfortune disease & Violent death and has ability to Govern those who are Subject to him both those who truly fear and reverance and those who are constrained to be loyal yielding assistance in carrying on the affairs of the Country, continues to rule until the natural end of his life.

Because of this, a custom has arisen in countries where such is the established order of things and between which a friendly intercourse has sprung up to communicate one another with letters and Complimentary presents from time to time, and those letters and presents Sent in this way are sent definitely (the name being specified) to the reigning Sovereign or to the one from formerly were received the present & presents and letters. When letters & presents are thus sent, those presented things belong absolutely to the ruler who have received them and he has right to retain them or bestow them upon others, whomsoever he pleases. But Whatever is such as Sovereign rulers only are accustomed to use he retains for his own use till the eve of his dissolution. When he delivers it over to the proper officers in trust for his Successor.

Now in the United States it has been the established Custom from the time of His celebrated Presidency President George Washington down for the entire population of the land with one accord to elect persons who are proper to fill the highest grades of office and establish them as President and Vice President to administer the Government as Chief rulers of the Country for a definite limited term of four years or Eight years, that this Custom should continue for so long a period and no disturbance arise or strife to obtain possession of the supreme power as is constantly occurring in other countries, is very remarkable indeed and the custom is one worthy of all praise.

Nonetheless, Mongkut explained, since the letter from President Pierce was

addressed to ourselves directly as the reigning King of Siam on this account when We would gladly cherish a friendly intercourse and send a letter and respond the presents they were sent directly to President Franklin Pierce according to our Siamese Custom. . . .

But now We have understood from the recent communication that all these our royal presents were deposited and arranged in one of the apartments of state as the common property of the Nation that all visitors may observe them and that they may promote the Glory of both countries.

He was satisfied with this arrangement and took the opportunity of forwarding a sword "manufactured in Siam after the Japanese model with a Scabbard of Silver plated inlaid with gold & its appendages of gold and also a photographic likeness of ourselves holding our beloved daughter in lap": *

These two foresaid articles let them be disposed of in what manner the President and Senate may deem proper whether they shall see fit to deliver them to President Buchanan himself who has forwarded the late letter or to retain them as the National property. . . . We wish only to confirm the existed friend-

---

* See Preface, page xi.

ship between us and the Government of United States of America to be remembered for ever.

Among the government publications sent to King Mongkut by President Buchanan there was probably the very
interesting Senate document giving the "Reports upon the
Purchase, Importation and Use of Camels and Dromedaries,
to be Employed for Military Purposes, according to Act
of Congress of March 3, 1855: Made under the Direction of
the Secretary of War. 1855–'56–'57." [54] But whether or not
this was so and whether or not if so Mongkut actually read
Jefferson Davis' famous report, it is a fact that he was deeply
interested by the American efforts to improve their means
of transportation. The subject came up for discussion when,
as he wrote in a second letter to President Buchanan also
dated February 14, 1861:

A ship of war, a sailing vessel of the United States' Navy, the
"John Adams" arrived and anchored outside the Bar, off the
mouth of the River "Chau Phya." Captain Berrien with the officers of the ship of war came up to pay a friendly visit to the
country and has had an interview with ourselves. . . .
During the interview in reply from Captain Berrien to our
enquiries of various particulars relating to America, he stated
that in that continent there are no elephants. Elephants are regarded as the most remarkable of the large quadrupeds by the
Americans so that if any one has an elephant's tusk of large size,
and will deposit it in any public place, people come by thousands
crowding to see it, saying it is a wonderful thing. Also, though
formerly there were no Camels on the continent the Americans
have sought for and purchased them, some from Arabia, some
from Europe, and now camels propagate their race and are
serviceable and of benefit to the Country, and are already numerous in America.
Having heard this it has occurred to us that, if on the continent

of America there should be several pairs of young and female elephants turned loose in forests where there was abundance of water and grass in any region under the Sun's declination both North and South, called by the English the Torrid Zone,—and all were forbidden to molest them; to attempt to raise them would be well and if the climate there should prove favorable to elephants, we are of opinion that after a while they will increase till there be large herds as there are here on the Continent of Asia until the inhabitants of America will be able to catch them and tame and use them as beasts of burden making them of benefit to the Country. Since elephants being animals of great size and strength can bear burdens and travel through uncleared woods and matted jungles where no carriage and cart roads have yet been made.

Examples we have coming down from ancient times of this business of transplanting Elephants from the mainland of Asia to various islands. Four hundred years ago when the island of Ceylon was governed by its native princes, an Embassy was sent to beg of the King of Henzawatty or Pegu [Burma] to purchase young elephants in several pairs to turn loose in the jungles of Ceylon and now by natural increase there are many large herds of elephants in that island.

We have heard also a tradition that a long time ago the natives of Achen in the island of Sumatra and the natives of Java came to the Malayan Peninsula to obtain young elephants to turn loose in the jungles of Sumatra and Java, and in consequence of this elephants are numerous in both those islands.

On this account we desire to procure and send elephants to be let loose in [*sic*] increase and multiply in the Continent of America. But we are as yet uninformed what forests and what regions of that country are suitable for elephants to thrive and prosper. Besides we have no means nor are we able to convey elephants to America, the distance being too great.

The islands of Ceylon & Sumatra & Java are near to the continent of Asia and those who thought of this plan in former days could transport their elephants with ease and without difficulty.

In reference to this opinion of ours if the president of the United States and Congress who conjointly with him rule the country see fit to approve let them provide a large vessel loaded with hay and other food suitable for elephants on the voyage, with tanks holding a sufficiency of fresh water, and arranged with stalls so that the elephant can both stand & lie down in the ship—and send it to receive them. We on our part will procure young male and female elephants, and forward them one or two pairs at a time.

When the elephants are on board the ship let a steamer take it in tow that it may reach America as rapidly as possible before they become wasted and diseased by the voyage.

When they arrive in America do not let them be taken to a cold climate out of the regions under the Sun's Declinations— or Torrid Zone—but let them with all haste be turned out to run wild in some jungle suitable for them, not confining them any length of time.

If these means can be done, we trust that the elephants will propagate their species hereafter in the continent of America.

It is desirable that the president of the United States and Congress give us their views in reference to this matter at as early a day as possible.

In Siam it is the custom of the season to take elephants from the herds in the jungles in the months of Phagum & Chetre = 4th & 5th generally corresponding to March and April.

If the president and Congress approve of this matter and should provide a vessel to come for the elephants, if that vessel should arrive in Siam on any month of any year after March and April as above mentioned let notice be sent on two or three months previous to those months of that year, in order that the elephants may be caught and tamed, whereas the elephants that have been long captured & tamed and domesticated here are large—and difficult to transport—and there would be danger they might never reach America.

At this time we have much pleasure in sending a pair of large elephant's tusks—one of the tusks weighing 52 cents [per cent] of a picul [about sixty-nine pounds], the other weigh 48 cents of a picul [about sixty-four pounds] and both tusks from the same animal—as an addition to our former presents to be deposited with them for public inspection that thereby the glory and renown of Siam may be promoted.

We hope that the president and congress who administer the government of the United States of America will gladly receive them as a token of friendly regard.[55]

Lincoln had succeeded Buchanan as "Chief ruler" of the country when these two letters were received in Washington. He wrote to King Mongkut:

GREAT AND GOOD FRIEND:

I have received Your Majesty's two letters of the date of February 14th, 1861.

I have also received in good condition the royal gifts which accompanied those letters,—namely, a sword of costly materials and exquisite workmanship; a photographic likeness of Your Majesty and of Your Majesty's beloved daughter; and also two elephants' tusks of length and magnitude such as indicate that they could have belonged only to an animal which was a native of Siam.

Your Majesty's letters show an understanding that our laws forbid the President from receiving these rich presents as personal treasures. They are therefore accepted in accordance with Your Majesty's desire as tokens of good will and friendship for the American People. Congress being now in session at this capital, I have had great pleasure in making known to them this manifestation of Your Majesty's munificence and kind consideration.[56]

Under their directions the gifts will be placed among the archives of the Government, where they will remain perpetually as tokens of mutual esteem and pacific dispositions more honorable to both nations than any trophies of conquest could be.

I appreciate most highly Your Majesty's tender of good offices in forwarding to this government a stock from which a supply of elephants might be raised on our own soil. The Government would not hesitate to avail itself of so generous an offer if the object were one which could be made practically useful in the present condition of the United States.

Our political jurisdiction, however, does not reach a latitude so low as to favor the multiplication of the elephant, and steam on land, as well as on water, has been our best and most efficient agent of transportation in internal commerce.

I shall have occasion at no distant day to transmit to Your Majesty some token of indication of the high sense which this Government entertains of Your Majesty's friendship.

Meantime, wishing for Your Majesty a long and happy life, and for the generous and emulous People of Siam the highest possible prosperity, I commend both to the blessing of Almighty God.

Your Good Friend,
ABRAHAM LINCOLN

Washington, February 3, 1862.
By the President:

WILLIAM H. SEWARD,
Secretary of State [57]

6

The Whale and the Crocodile

THE relations between Siam and the United States never assumed importance to either country until the Second World War; in Mongkut's time the two western powers with which he was deeply concerned were England and France. Just as he had in the case of the British treaty, Mongkut, as soon as the treaty with France was concluded, proposed to send an embassy to the French Court. The French agreed to receive the embassy and to send a warship to take it to France. "Afterward, however, H. I. Majesty the Emperor of France was much engaged in affairs of war in several directions, wherefore the receipt of Siamese Embassy was postponed three years and a little more." Finally, in February, 1861, the French steam frigate "Gironde" arrived at the mouth of the Chao Phraya to take the embassy, and the

King immediately appointed a first, a second, and a third ambassador and dispatched them together with a royal letter and royal presents to the court of Napoleon III. Then he wrote an official letter to Queen Victoria, gave her all the details, and suggested that it would be very nice indeed if she also would receive these ambassadors.[1] He was writing this letter, he explained, because it would be improper if the embassy did not have a royal letter to present to her "for we are your Majesty's distinguished friend by firm and intimate friendship longly existed, and as we have such facility to read and write in your Majesty's vernacular language, so as need not have assistance from any interpreter, when we have no such facility in French language."

Mongkut took this occasion to make "a private proposal" to Queen Victoria. He had heard, he wrote, that the monarchs of various European countries "who are in friendly terms and alliance with your Majesty" had presented her with decorations, and she had then bestowed decorations on them in return. "If this tiding be true," he wanted to bestow a decoration on Queen Victoria which everyone would clearly recognize as Siamese "whenever your Majesty might graciously decorate with it." But in return of course he was anxious to receive a decoration from her. "It will prove greatest honor to us here among Eastern Monarchies. Will the desire occurred to us be proper and agreeable or not?" *

Even today "public relations," as that term is used and the "art" practiced so extensively in the west, is underdeveloped in most Asian countries. It is the more astonishing, therefore, to find throughout his reign how conscious Mongkut was of the value to Siam of an informed and friendly foreign

* Apparently not. The Queen never bestowed a decoration on King Mongkut.

press in molding western opinion and policies. He followed closely both the Singapore and British papers. Even a week before he became king, but when his selection seemed assured, he spent nearly half an hour with Dr. Bradley, as Bradley records, "telling me his history in English that I might get a correct statement in the Singapore papers. His object was to anticipate incorrect statements concerning his relations to the Kingdom which might go forth and be credited as true. He was apprehensive that he might be reported as a rebel inasmuch as he was not a son of the present King." [2] Nor would the new king brook delay. On April 10, Dr. Bradley noted in his diary: "I wrote a letter for one of the Singapore papers in behalf of his Majesty the King as he requested me some days since when I visited him at his temple, and which request he renewed last evening by a note which he sent to me. He desired to see the letter before I should send it." [3]

At a later period we find the King writing a note to John Thomson, who had taken some of the first photographs of the great ruins of Angkor, "I beg to take from you a promise that you should state everywhere verbally, or in books, and newspapers, public papers, that those provinces Battabong and Onger, or Nogor Siam, [Angkor], belonged to Siam continually for eighty-four years ago, not interrupted by Cambodian princes or Cochin China [Vietnam]. The fortifications of those places was constructed by Siamese Government thirty-three years ago. The Cambodian rulers cannot claim in these provinces as they have ceded to Siamese authority eighty-four years ago." [4]

Mongkut was also conscious, of course, of the influence that foreign residents and visitors could exert abroad. Each year on his birthday he gave a great banquet to which all were invited. In the early years of his reign these were very successful and greatly appreciated. Henri Mouhot was in Bangkok in October, 1858, at the start of those travels which brought to the western world its first detailed knowledge of the great ruins of Angkor, now in Cambodia: "I was making my preparation for departure, . . . when I received an invitation from the King of Siam to be present at the great dinner which this monarch gives every year on his birthday, to the European residents in Bangkok. I was presented by Monseigneur Pallegoix, and His Majesty's reception was kind and courteous. His costume consisted of a pair of large trousers, a short brown jacket of some thin material, and slippers; on his head he wore a little copper helmet like those worn by the naval officers, and at his side a rich sabre.

"Most of the Europeans in Bangkok were present at the dinner, and enthusiastic toasts were drunk to the health of His Majesty, who, instead of being seated, stood or walked round the table, chewing betel and addressing some pleasant observation to each of his guests in turn. The repast was served in a vast hall, from whence we could see a platoon of the royal guard, with flags and drums, drawn up in the courtyard. When I went to take leave of the King, he graciously presented me with a little bag of green silk, containing some of the gold and silver coins of the country,—a courtesy which was most unexpected, and for which I expressed my gratitude." [5]

Unfortunately in the last years of his reign these dinners were caught up in the jealousies and rivalries that beset the foreign community. October 18, 1864, was "the Major King's 60th birthday, and he made a great ado to have it universally observed and it was so, being anticipated two days and extending to the 20th. Almost all the houses on the river and vessels were splendidly illumined three nights.

The party of Europeans and Americans at the King's palace was large and the dining table well furnished. But the King in his extraordinary efforts to honor the Consuls, greatly offended the merchants who rose en masse after they had taken their soup and left the place. It appeared that the King did not design to slight them but being absorbed in his attentions to the Consuls forgot the merchants until it was too late to correct the mistake. It produced a great confusion all around so that the Consuls not even enjoyed their dinner and the King felt quite sad about it." [6]

The following year the King arranged that the consuls should be received on the afternoon of the eighteenth, missionaries and merchants the next day at breakfast. Dr. Bradley, who had described the preceding year's dinner, now wrote in his diary: "The King has made this change because the English and French Consuls last year were the occasion of a great disturbance of the pleasure of the birthday party because they insisted that the Consuls of the Western Powers should have a table by themselves. I apprehend that this new plan will make the matter worse rather than better. The second table and that not on a birthday but a day after, will appear a little too dishonorable a relation to bear in regard to those officials." The next day only a handful of foreigners breakfasted with the King. Dr. Bradley could not attend, but he recorded that he "would not have stood much on my dignity in the matter of consuls but I abominate such mean vanity as that which the two consuls have evinced." [7]

Another year went by and the King had the consuls and the Roman Catholic bishop to dinner on his birthday. Not one of the Protestant missionaries, "except Brother Smith an Englishman," would accept the invitation for the party the following day.[8]

Mongkut had one serious failing; there are many references to his quick and sometimes violent temper which alienated not a few of the foreigners in Bangkok. There are also, however, an almost equal number of references to the deep regret which was wont to fill the King when his anger had cooled. This temper was quite possibly the outward manifestation of the constant struggles and contradictions within him between the new and the old, between his efforts to modernize Siam and his own absolute power as the king of Siam. But whatever the cause, the tempers were real indeed, and on at least one occasion had tragic results. In 1856, a year after the Treaty with Great Britain, the King was informed of the ninety-nine year lease of a dockyard by a Siamese to an Englishman, a Captain Phillips. The King was furious, and in a passion ordered that ninety-nine lashes be given the witness to the agreement. Prince Krom Luang Wongsa was distressed at the man's condition and to alleviate his suffering applied strips of cloth soaked in opium to his back. These reduced the pain, but they also affected the system. Three days later the man died. Meanwhile, it transpired that the witness was regularly employed as a writer by the British consul, that the lease was legal under the treaty, and that it was at the direction of the consul that he had signed the lease as witness. As soon as his rage abated, the King was filled with remorse and did all he could to make amends, although Dr. Bradley, who was naturally horrified at what had happened, felt sure that the King's remorse was more for offending Queen Victoria than for having been the cause of suffering.[9]

Whether this was an isolated case or whether there were other and similar instances when Mongkut's temper and his absolute power had tragic results, it is a fact, as pointed out by Professor Hall, that the Siamese memory of him is

not that of a cruel man nor a revengeful one.[10] Had his
temper occasionally reached such despotic extremes this
would have been recorded and remembered.

As already mentioned, the only territories on peninsular
Southeast Asia possessed by European powers at the time
Mongkut was born were Malacca, Penang, and Province
Wellesley. By the time he became king, the island of Singapore had been ceded by Johore, and a flourishing city had
grown up; the British had interfered considerably in the
Malay States, over which Siam claimed suzerainty; the first
Anglo-Burman war had been fought and the Tenasserim
and Arakan annexed by the Honourable Company—while
the second war with Burma was about to commence with
its resulting cession of southern Burma. Gialong, who had
become the first emperor of Annam two years before Mongkut's birth, had been succeeded by emperors who increasingly persecuted their Christian subjects and the missionaries
who ministered to them. Five years before Mongkut came
to the throne, a French fleet had bombarded the Annamese
port of Tourane to secure the release of a French missionary
under sentence of death. During succeeding years this type
of western action was several times repeated—once even
by the United States ship "Constitution," which shelled the
town when an imprisoned French bishop was not surrendered on demand.[11] (He was later voluntarily released
to the French.) Farther afield, but looming larger in importance, was the "opening up" of China following the
Opium War.

The two potential threats to Siam were England and
France, and Mongkut tried at all times to maintain an eq-
uable balance in his dealings with them. He followed this
policy even in the most minor matters. When the Siamese
embassy was in Paris, they promised the Superintendent of

the Imperial Zoological Museum that the King of Siam
would be glad to "send some number of Siamese quadrupeds and fouls." [12] Two French scientists accompanied the
embassy on its return to Bangkok. The "Gironde" followed
a few months later to pick up "the animals required and
selected by those two French Zoographers." Suddenly Mongkut wondered about British reaction. Hastily he wrote the
British consul suggesting that the Royal Zoological Society,
of which he had been made an honorary member, send out
its representatives to make similar choice. Two days later
he was still worried. He was afraid a lot of people in England would know about his present to the Paris zoo and
think that he had suddenly become swayed by admiration
for Napoleon "like the prince of Cambodia who considered
the French Monarch as most and highest of all monarchs
on the surface of the earth." So he thought it best, he wrote
the consul, that he give "equal friendly service" to both
Her Majesty and the French Emperor; and would the consul please write his government, let them know what he intended to do, and suggest that they, like the French, send
a warship for some animals? [13]

But although he walked warily and endeavored to maintain a correct balance between the two countries, Mongkut preferred the English to the French, and increasingly
he felt that France was the greater menace of the two. One
of the principal reasons for this preference was the high
caliber of the men Britain had sent to Siam in the early
days of their new relationship. They were men Mongkut
could admire and trust, and with many he became close
personal friends; whereas the French representatives were
men of quite different stamp. A second factor undoubtedly
was Mongkut's facility in the English language. Not only
was he proud of his ability to understand and speak the

Queen's vernacular, but also he read British newspapers
and books regularly. The third, and ultimately the most
important factor, was the growth of French imperial ambitions and the swelling French desire to carve a great Asian
colony out of Cochin China, Annam, Cambodia, Laos, the
Shan States, Upper Burma, and, many have believed, Siam
as well.

The British were more interested in trade than in colonial
enterprise, but during the decades preceding Mongkut's
accession there were frequent difficulties between England
and Siam concerning several of the Malay states. For centuries Siam had claimed suzerainty over those states, while
the British generally supported the independence of the
various sultans.

In July, 1862, the Siamese made a definite move to secure
their control over the states of Trengganu and Pahang on
the east coast of Malaya by supporting new claimants to the
sultanates. In fact, the Siamese conveyed their men to Trengganu in a Siamese warship, blandly informing the British
that the Trengganu claimant, Mahmud, ex-Sultan of Lingga,
was on a personal visit to his mother. Under British pressure
they promised to remove him, but took no action. Meanwhile, Wan Ahmad, the Pahang claimant, invaded Pahang,
and the British suspected that he was receiving aid from
Trengganu. Finally Colonel Cavanagh, Governor of the
Straits Settlements, sent a warship which shelled Trengganu
in an effort to force the surrender of the Siamese choice.
But Mahmud fled inland, and the ensuing British blockade
of the coast accomplished nothing. The following spring
the Siamese withdrew their man after protesting that the
British bombardment was a violation of Siamese territorial
rights. In fact, however, they made no further move to re-
assert sovereignty. The Pahang civil war petered out. A few

years later when the Bendahara of Pahang died, Wan Ahmad, who was his brother, succeeded him with never a murmur from the British.[14]

The bombardment of Trengganu caused a minor uproar in England, which was opposed to British intervention in the affairs of the Malay States. In Bangkok it created a sensation. And this changed to near panic when presently it was learned that the ships which had bombarded Trengganu had arrived at the mouth of the Chao Phya Menam. How Mongkut met what certainly had the appearance of an impending major crisis in Siamese relations with England is recounted in a letter which he wrote immediately afterward to his nephew Prince George Washington:

On Tuesday the 3rd of the Waning Moon this month, despatches came from Samudprakarn reporting that two British warships had come to the bar of the river and had cast anchor there. The captain of one of the ships, together with some officers came to the port authorities in a pilot boat to inform that their ships were identical with those that had been bombarding Trengganu recently. Since the bombardment of Trengganu had brought no satisfactory end to the affair, as far as they were concerned, they had returned to Singapore and had now come to Bangkok, under the command of one commodore named Lord John Hay, to pursue the affair of Trengganu until its conclusion. It appeared that Lord John Hay had written to the British Consul, who made haste to pass on the information to the Department of Harbour to the effect that Lord John Hay was in command of several British men-of-war stationed in the Indian Ocean. Having brought two of his ships to the mouth of the river, Lord John had now made a request for permission to bring one of them up to Bangkok, for reasons not known to the Consul. It was for the ministers of the King of Siam to decide how to deal with the matter, since it was for the Consul merely to forward the request.

Their Lordships the Ministers received the above report and
the communication from the Consul with some consternation
and began to hold hasty consultation among themselves. Moreover, it was said of the Consul that he had been airing his views
among the traders of the city that Lord John Hay was invested
with higher ranks and greater powers than the Consul himself,
who had no knowledge whatever of the nature of this visit, except Lord John's express demand to bring his warship up to
the city. Since it was not certain whether Lord John Hay might
not do to Bangkok what he had already done to Trengganu, the
merchants were warned by the Consul to take good care of
their own goods and personal safety.

These wild whispers put the more weak-minded part of the
population on the verge of panic, but the situation was not so
serious, since I remained firm. I sent out into the bazaar some
men whom I could trust, to sound the opinions of various people
in business and consular circles. They came back to report to
me that Mr. Knox was the only one who remained aloof from
the general alarm. He had openly stated that he would not
allow Lord John Hay to intimidate Siam into any agreement,
since it was the Consul, and not any commander of war vessels,
who was responsible for the diplomatic relations between this
country and Britain. He said further that if these naval officers
should make any attempt to open negotiations with the Siamese
authorities, he would regard such an attempt as an encroach-
ment upon the power and function of the Consul, and would
make a personal protest against it.

As regards the purpose and the nature of Lord John Hay's
visit, I wrote to my ministers stating to them my conjectures.
There were five of them, one or two of which might prove to be
right.

Firstly, after the bombardment of Trengganu, Sultan Mahmud
or the Sultan of Trengganu himself might have retreated up-
river to join forces with Wan Ahmad, and thence to wage war
on the Bendahara of Pahang, on whom they have placed the

blame for the shelling of Trengganu by British warships. The Siamese man-of-war, which had been sent out to fetch Sultan Mahmud to Bangkok, had probably been waiting for him in Trengganu, owing to his exact whereabouts being unknown. I suspected that the British had known about this, and had come to Bangkok to demand that an expedition be sent by Siam against Trengganu, so that the Sultan of Trengganu and Sultan Mahmud might be arrested.

Secondly, the British might have a suspicion that we were on the side of the Sultan of Trengganu, and had therefore come to demand an agreement on our part to the sending of a British punitive force to Trengganu.

Thirdly, they might have come to ask Siam to pay for the cost of the bombardment of Trengganu, because they thought that we had allowed the escape of Sultan Mahmud which resulted in the Pahang disaster.

Fourthly, they might have come to make us enforce the demand on the Sultan of Trengganu to make good all the losses of British tin miners due to the war in Pahang.

Fifthly, Lord John Hay might have come to deny any personal complicity in the Trengganu affair, and to explain that his warships had only been carrying out the orders of the Governor of Singapore, whose duty it was to attend to all political business; the warships were there to act as mere instruments of the Governor, who must bear the responsibility.

I also pointed out to my ministers another possibility, namely that Lord John Hay might not put forward any demand nor raise any matter for discussion at all, but his real purpose might be to observe our reaction to recent political events. He might have come to find out whether or not we were alarmed, whether we had been intimidated or whether we had felt any resentment towards the British for their treatment of Trengganu.

In all these conjectures, I was certain of the fifth and the sixth. But if the first, second, third or fourth should prove to be right after all, the ministers should reply that although we knew that the British Power—which extended beyond lands and seas around the earth and in whose domain the sun never set— was divided up into separate departments, we had not yet fully understood the various laws and customs peculiar to the British form of government. For this reason, we, a small power, could make no immediate decision on the current political situation. We had, however, submitted to the British Consul our memorandum in which were stated all the pertinent facts as were known to us, with our suggestion that the same be sent to London. . . . Therefore, if Lord John Hay had any communications to make in relation to the same matter, he should first impart them to the Consul, who would hold proper consultation with the Siamese ministers. If there were any urgency measures to be taken, the Consul should make them known to the ministers, who would take appropriate steps to meet the urgency, as far as their powers and abilities would allow them. It must be understood, however, that measures taken at this stage were not to be taken as final and binding. The affair would be considered as concluded by us only after negotiations in London had come to an end. . . .

I wrote all these things down for the edification of my ministers, who agreed with my views. They were of the unanimous opinion that we could not very well refuse permission of entry to the warship, or evade it by sending down a small steamboat to fetch Lord John Hay up to Bangkok, as had been done on the occasion of the visit of Sir James Brooke, as this would lead to another dispute over and above the existing point at issue. Since Lord John Hay was determined to bring his ship up to Bangkok, and since the fortresses at Paknam and Paklat were unprepared and could not be made ready within a single day nor in a single night, it was thought that if any dispute should arise out of our refusal to allow entry to the British warship, the British might make a forced entry into the river, and at whatever fortress they arrived at, they might make their way into it to spike and dismantle the guns in the manner similar to what they had done in China and elsewhere.

It was agreed, therefore, to send Lord John Hay a written permission and to accord him treatment suitable to a visitor from a friendly nation. On the night of the Sabbath, the 1st day of the waning moon, Phraya Pipatkosha and Mom Rajothai were appointed emissaries and received an order to hurry down to Paknam to welcome Lord John Hay, and to deter him from spiking and dismantling the guns or from creating any other unnecessary disturbances, since it appeared in the letter from the British Consul that he had decided to come up to Bangkok on the following Thursday, with or without permission.

On Wednesday morning, a pilot boat was sent out to lead the warship into the river, but Lord John Hay was not yet ready to come in, as he was awaiting a reply from the British Consul. Another day was spent outside the bar, and it was not until the 5th day of the waning moon that the smaller warship named "Coquette" sailed into the river. She was one of those that had been to Trengganu and carried four guns, one of them being of the latest breach-loading Armstrong type, while the rest were ordinary 12 inches guns. The ship arrived at Paknam at 8 o'clock in the morning. Phraya Pipatkosha, Mom Rajothai, Phraya Maha Agnikorn, Phraya Samudniraburaksh and Phraya Amorn Mahady met the ship at the harbour and boarded it there. They were received by Lord John Hay into his cabin. He declined our customary presents, sent down by the provincial authorities, as being contrary to British custom. Phraya Pipat and Mom Rajothai told him that the King's ministers, who were cognizant of his high rank and exalted position, had sent them down to give him a reception befitting his station. Lord John Hay expressed his deep gratitude to the ministers and inquired after the health of the King and his ministers.

After this first greeting, Lord John Hay sailed up-river. He arrived in Bangkok at 2 o'clock in the afternoon and anchored his ship south of the British Consulate. He made a statement to the public officials that he had no particular business in view, that he had been at sea for over three years and was due to return home, and since he had been to every country in this

part of the world with the exception of Siam, it had long been
his desire to make a visit to this country and to pay his respects
to its King.

On the same evening I received a letter from the British Consul intimating to me Lord John Hay's request to call on me, and
asking me to make an appointment at the earliest date possible,
since Lord John had to leave within a short time. I replied that
I would grant him an audience on Saturday the 7th of the waning
moon, and that I would make this audience a State function as
behoved a man in his high position. I mentioned also that the
Second King had been absent from the city for some time, at a
place 150 miles away, and it was not possible to arrange an
audience with him as well, as Lord John was due to take his
leave shortly.

On the following Thursday Lord John Hay, accompanied
by eight naval officers and the British Consul took a boat trip
round the city. They called on Prince Krom Luang Wongsa,
Chao Phraya Suriwongse and Chao Phraya Virawongse. They
made no reference to political affairs during these visits, but
instead, invited those on whom they had called to a dinner to be
given at the British Consulate. On Saturday Lord John Hay, together with Captain Alexander, another officer with the rank
of Sir, the ship's doctor, and some naval officers amounting to
nine persons in all, were received by me in a public audience
amidst a full gathering of royal princes and officials. I offered
them my greetings and enquired after the purpose of their visit.
Lord John Hay replied that he had no other purpose than to
pay his respects to me, whom he had heard to have taken so
great an interest in the British people as to have endeavoured
to learn their language. He told me that he had to be at sea for
another five months, but when he returned to England, he
would make this meeting known to Queen Victoria; this, he
thought, would do much towards the furtherance of the friendly
relations between the two countries.

After the public audience, the British officers called upon me

King Mongkut, from the photograph which he sent to Pope Pius IX early in 1861. (Photograph from the Vatican Library.)

King Mongkut in western uniform wearing the French decoration of the Légion d'honneur of the Second Empire, from a photograph in the possession of M. L. Peekdhip Malakul, the Royal Thai Ambassador, London.

in private, where I received them in the English manner. Lord John Hay said that it had long been his wish to pay his respects to the Siamese Sovereign and his Queen, but it had been his misfortune to be able to come to this country only after the demise of Her Majesty. He asked me whether I had elevated someone to that position, because if I had, he would be very pleased to pay his respects to her. When I replied that I had not yet made such an elevation, the Consul interposed that the younger sister of the late Queen should be prevailed upon to receive Lord John Hay. Lord John then said he would feel greatly honoured, so I had to send for the Princess Barnarai to come out to greet him.

These events seemed to correspond to the report I had received from Phra Bidespanich in Singapore, dated Sunday the 3rd of the 11th month, in which he wrote that a British warship named "Scott" had been calling on the different countries which were not British colonies, or where a British Consulate had been established. It had been to Labuan, Sarawak and some other ports in the island of Borneo. He had heard that the ship was coming to Siam in December, and Sir Richard McCausland, who was then Recorder of Singapore, had said that if he was free at the time, he would take a passage on it, as he would welcome an opportunity to meet me in person. Sir Richard McCausland is a friend of mine. We have been keeping correspondence and he has been giving me from time to time confidential informations and useful personal advices. He was neither in agreement with the Governor on his treatment of Trengganu, nor was he personally involved in that affair. I gather that he is quite a decent person. . . .

During the state of alarm caused by the visit of the warships, I sent out some of my trusted men to observe the general feeling. They had been inside the consulates and had boarded those very warships. Their confidential reports to me were written in English on three small slips of paper. I enclose them herewith. If you think them fit to be submitted to the Second King for his perusal, you may do so. After His Majesty has read them, or after he has shown no interest in them, please return them to me, after you have done with them yourself. No one can say that these men have given me false reports, for the contents of these notes have since proved to be correct.[15]

In striking contrast to their experience with the British was the Siamese experience with the French. For generations Siam had exercised feudal suzerainty over Cambodia and the kings of Cambodia were frequently crowned in Bangkok. In the year following Mongkut's birth, the King of Cambodia, in an effort to preserve the independence of his country by increasing the rivalry among his powerful neighbors, began to pay annual homage to the Annamite Emperor as well as to the King of Siam.

In 1856 a French missionary was tortured and put to death in Annam, and in the following year a Spanish bishop was executed. In the autumn of 1858, French and Spanish punitive forces jointly occupied Tourane but, encountering supply difficulties, abandoned Tourane and seized Saigon in February, 1859. A joint garrison which they left there underwent a seige by the Annamites that lasted from March, 1860, until February, 1861. Then French forces which had been engaged with the British in the China war relieved Saigon and speedily overran the whole of lower Cochin China, the southern part of the Annamite Empire. In June, 1862, the Annamites ceded three of the provinces of Cochin China to the French.

Meanwhile, in 1860 Norodom, who had been educated in Bangkok—he was ordained at Wat Pawaraniwesa while Mongkut was abbot—became King of Cambodia.* A few months after acquiring the Cochin China provinces the

* Norodom was king of Cambodia for forty-four years. He died in 1904.

French suggested that Norodom pay tribute to France rather than to Annam, but for the moment did not press the point. Norodom in his short period on the throne had already encountered a dynastic revolt and fled to Siam. When conditions had improved at home, the Siamese assisted his return. No Siamese troops, however, were sent to Cambodia, yet by July, 1863, the French were able to persuade Norodom to sign a treaty placing Cambodia under French protection to preserve the country from Siam. Torn between his fears of France, Siam, and even Annam, Norodom backed and filled and attempted to please everyone. He started for Bangkok to be crowned by King Mongkut. French troops thereupon occupied his palace, and he called off the journey. Meanwhile the treaty of protection had been ratified by Napoleon III. The ratified copy arrived in Cambodia and was handed to Norodom, who could no longer dodge. On April 17, 1864, the exchange of ratifications took place. Cambodia had become a French protectorate. This was followed by an agreement between the French and Siamese that Norodom should be crowned by the representatives of both Siam and France, but when the coronation took place on June 3 the French refused to allow King Mongkut's representative to place the crown on Norodom's head.

A new revolt broke out in Cambodia. Mongkut wrote one of his brothers: "Prince Kaeo Fa [a Cambodian prince then residing at the Siamese Court, who succeeded King Norodom and ruled as King Sisowath from 1904 to 1928] rather suspects that these insurgents are his own men, and that the trouble is due to their disapproval of Norodom's over-inclination towards the French. It seems that only a small minority of the people in Udong Meechai [then capital of Cambodia] really approve of Norodom's acceptance of his coronation under the auspices of the French; the rest are strongly antagonistic to it. These people say that if Bangkok were to return Prince Kaeo Fa to Battambang they would all come over to him. [Battambang was Siamese territory at that period.] I fear that this business is going to turn out to be complicated in nature and far reaching in effect. Bangkok has now decided to send . . . a small force to Battambang to observe events. . . . Should the authorities require elephants or men for this purpose, would you please see to it that they get what they require?" [16]

On December 1, 1863, during the period between the signing of the French protectorate treaty and the exchange of ratifications, one of Norodom's moves had been to sign a treaty with Siam explicitly restating the vassal status of the Kingdom of Cambodia. An English translation of this secret treaty appeared in the Singapore press in August, 1864. A new French consul had just arrived in Bangkok. He was M. Gabriel Aubaret, formerly a naval officer who had been made Chief Inspector of Native Affairs at Saigon in 1862. As soon as he learned of the secret treaty, he demanded an explanation of what he considered to have been double-dealing by the Siamese. The Siamese agreed to negotiate on the subject, and he so reported to Paris.

Aubaret was also French Chargé d'Affaires at Hué in Annam, and he had to travel back and forth between his two posts. In April, 1865, having received instructions from Paris, he arrived in Bangkok from Hué, opened negotiations, and within a few days signed a treaty with Siam. Under this proposed treaty Siam would have recognized the French protectorate over Cambodia and annulled the secret treaty of December, 1863; but France, on her part, would have recognized that Cambodia, though a protectorate, was an independent kingdom, might continue to pay tribute to Siam if it wanted to, and might continue to have its princes educated in Bangkok if they so desired. Furthermore, France would have recognized Siamese title to Battambang and Angkor and, in addition, to two other provinces to the eastward that Siam had received in payment for its help in restoring Norodom three years before.

Opinion at the French Court was divided between those who wanted to continue the imperial venture in Indochina and those who wanted to curtail it because of the Maximilian venture in Mexico. It was agreed, however, that the proposed treaty was too favorable to Siam, and it was not submitted for ratification. Instead, Aubaret was instructed to seek a revision of the proposed treaty as it related to asserted Siamese territory.

Aubaret had left Bangkok immediately after the signing of the proposed treaty in April, 1865. He now returned in June, 1866, and started conversations with the Foreign Minister. They could reach no agreement, and by December the discussions had become acrimonious. The Foreign Minister wrote to Admiral La Grandière complaining that Aubaret's "angry outbursts and violent and brusque behavior" made negotiations difficult; Aubaret demanded that the Foreign Minister be deprived of authority to negotiate. Then Aubaret tried seeing the King "unofficially" and was badly received, as he reported to Paris.[17] This was a euphemism for some highly irregular behavior on Aubaret's part which led Dr. Bradley to publish in the Bangkok *Recorder* "the particulars of the French Consul's insult to the King, as there seem to be no doubt that all the circumstances were substantially true and because it seemed to be my duty as the only public recorder to publish it."[18] Aubaret promptly sued for libel and won. Mongkut had no intention of giving added publicity to the epi-

sode which might provoke an "incident" or be twisted by
French hotheads and in either event create an excuse for
French aggression or war. He forbade any of his people
to serve as a witness for Dr. Bradley in establishing what
happened. It was noticeable, however, that thereafter the
King went out of his way to honor Dr. Bradley when he
could.[19] This and his subsequent insistence that Aubaret
must be withdrawn from Bangkok would seem to be strong
evidence that Dr. Bradley's account had not been far wrong.

A fortnight after his "unofficial" encounter with the
King, Aubaret modified his demands slightly and proposed
a new formula. The Siamese asked him to furnish not only
his French version of the controversial article, but also an
English version for the King "to look at and compare with
the dictionary. If they are found to agree with each other
the agreement can be entered into immediately." But the
King found discrepancies between the English and Siamese
versions and he wanted to be certain that the French and
Siamese versions were in fact identical in meaning. A few
days later, therefore, his own royal translation of the
Siamese into English was sent to Aubaret with the request
that the French text be conformed to that. "We are acquainted only with the English language," explained the
Foreign Minister.

As Mongkut's translation was more picturesque than
grammatical, Aubaret could scarcely accede, but he expressed himself with customary vigor. "I am a Frenchman,"
he wrote, "and I understand the French language but Your
Excellency tells me to translate my French different from
the Siamese. I really don't understand what Your Excellency means by it. If the Siamese Government has an interpreter who can speak French better than myself, I beg
Your Excellency to send him to me to instruct me. In case

no interpreter comes to confer with me and enlighten me I
am of the opinion this matter cannot be accomplished." [20]

Six days later, on January 11, Aubaret presented his final
draft on a take-it-or-leave-it basis. The next day the Siamese
informed him they were going to send an embassy to Paris
and transfer negotiations there.

The reasons for this move are not far to seek. The
Siamese actively disliked Aubaret,[21] and he had seriously
affronted the King; if further concessions had to be made
there would be less loss of face if made at the seat of empire
than at a consulate and especially to Aubaret; [22] and they
may well have hoped that the division in opinion at the
French Court would work to their advantage.[23]

Mongkut had asked his old friend Sir John Bowring to
represent Siam in the negotiation of certain commercial
agreements with France and other European countries and
appointed him Minister Plenipotentiary for that purpose.
The British consul and others construed this appointment
as giving him now the responsibility for the Paris negotiations. But Mongkut was determined that in political matters
he must always be represented by nationals of his own country and that the embassy to Paris must be entirely Siamese.
It was over the letter to be written Sir John informing him
of this decision that Anna Leonowens reports she and the
King quarreled bitterly.[24]

On March 4, 1867, Mongkut wrote a long letter to the
head of the embassy that he had despatched to Paris analyz-
ing the international difficulties and pressures confronting
Siam:

Your letter sent from Singapore by the steamer "Chao
Phraya" and your additional note have reached me. . . .

I told them [the Prime Minister and the Minister for Military
Administration] that since the uprising in Cambodia had now

assumed increasing proportions and spread towards Battambang and Siemreap, it was difficult for us to forecast the turn of events; and should anything untowards happen in the future, Monsieur Aubaret might again put the blame on us for not letting the facts be known. It was my opinion therefore that it would be best to send him a letter stating the facts. Their excellencies agreed with me, so they had copies of all the reports sent to Monsieur Aubaret. . . . Monsieur Aubaret was at a loss to know what to make of it, since he had not grasped all the facts pertaining to the matter. Only a few days later was he able to compose a reply. . . . It appears from Aubaret's letter that the French Admiral in Saigon [La Grandière] suspects that the Cambodian insurrectionists have obtained their arms and munitions from our provinces of Battambang, Siemreap, Chodok and Sombok. This is to be expected, as it is the intention of the French to put the blame on Siam for this disturbance in any case. Enough for the present about the French.

Now, about the British: when they had no sufficient cause for action, they have remained quiet, for they are not altogether shameless, and when any of their actions is opened to censure, they are not quick to forget. Because Siam's territories are adjoined to theirs, with merging interests as in the case of Chiengmai, Keddah and other states, I would surmise that their attention would be drawn towards whatever direction wherein their interests lie. In former times, when no other country had any cause to meddle in Siamese affairs, the British had remained inactive; but now that they have known of the troubles the Consul Aubaret had started here, you can probably see for yourself what course of action they have taken.

It was during the 8th month in the year of the Dog being the 4th of the decade [July 1862], after the French had assumed power over Cambodia, that one Singapore newspaper published an article to the following effect:—Now that the French have encroached upon the sovereignty of Cambodia, said the article, there is every possibility of differences arising between the French and the Siamese, on account of their adjoining territories. If any difference should really arise between these two nations, then it would be possible for the French to win easy victory all the way through until the boundary of their newly won colony should meet the boundary of the British colony in Burma, from Chiengmai down to Keddah, which is near to Penang. The British should, therefore, take great care of Singapore and Malacca, and the powers of the governors of these provinces should be increased. It is my guess that the article was written by Mr. Reid, but it may have been written by someone else.

Since the year of the Boar [1863–4], the Governor General of Bengal has been asking us every year to send someone up to mark our common boundary with Burma. The request has been made again this year in an urgent manner. I think that the reason why the British have repeatedly urged us to delineate our boundary is because they are afraid of what may happen in the future, when the French power is advanced up to their own territories. If no definite boundary has been fixed by that time, disputes may arise between them and the French and the good relations which have existed between the two countries may thus be marred. They have therefore urged Siam to make the final settlement of the question of boundaries, before the event which they have already expected should take place. Moreover, the British and the French can entertain no other feeling for each other than mutual esteem as fellow human beings, whereas the likes of us who are wild and savage, can only be regarded by them as animals. We have no means of knowing whether or in what way they have contrived beforehand to divide our country among themselves. I have written to Phra Bidespanich expressing the same opinion and he has agreed with me.

Since July [1865] or the eighth month of the year of the Bull to the present date, the outbursts and protestations of Consul Aubaret during the past year must have become a widespread news, for Sir John Bowring has written a letter to me, bragging about his appointment as representative of foreign governments to make treaties with various countries in Europe. He has volunteered to make treaties with foreigners on our behalf. He went on to say that because he was responsible for making Siam well-known to many countries to her own benefit, he still felt bound to her, and would like to see her making still further progress. Although he was getting old, he could still use his wit and ability to the benefit of this country; and should we find any occasion in which we would require his help, we should let him know and he would do his uttermost to help us.

Sir John's letter reached me some time about the 10th month in the year of the Bull being the 7th of the decade, but I did not at the time recognize its full import. I merely thought that Sir John was being polite and friendly to me; I hardly thought that he might have any underlying motive of significance. The Second King was ill at the time I received the letter, so I did not make a long reply, but merely wrote to Sir John a letter of acknowledgement and thanks.

Nearly a year later, when Sir John saw that I took no further notice of his offer, he sent Mr. Knox to advise His Excellency the Minister for Military Administration to make the appointment. His Excellency took the advice and told me to send a letter to Sir John Bowring requesting him to become a Minister Plenipotentiary for Siam, empowered to negotiate with France and other countries on the subject of duties on wines and spirits. I sent a letter to Sir John Bowring with the request, with which His Excellency was persuaded by Mr. Knox into agreement.

From that day on, the activities of Mr. Knox have been very much increased indeed. He even went so far as to have told us, prior to our having received a reply from Sir John Bowring, that Sir John had promised to help us in every way. At first we thought that Mr. Knox was only out to make money from us, but now that our present troubles with the French have come about, we have noticed so vast a difference in the amount of Mr. Knox's activities that we in Siam have begun to guess his true motive. The contents of his letter to His Excellency the Minister for Military Administration alone were enough to give us an insight into his mind.

I, with the concurrence of His Excellency the Minister, have lost all confidence in Mr. Knox, hence it has been my desire to send out to France an Embassy of our own nationals. My misgivings do not seem to go far wrong, for you have said in your letter that the British have been overjoyed at the news of Sir John Bowring's appointment as Minister Plenipotentiary of the Siamese Sovereign, the same news having been published in one newspaper as far back as the 10th November [1866]. Moreover, Sir John Bowring has already written to me twice, giving me strong assurances and saying that even if he should be ill or infirm on account of his great age, he would see to it that his son, Edgar Bowring, who is now in charge of British exhibits at the Paris Exhibition, would take care of our business on his behalf. Mr. D. K. Mason [consul for Siam in London] has also written to tell me that Lord Stanley was very glad to hear of Sir John's appointment. You have already seen for yourself what bitter protests were made by Mr. Knox and Mr. Alabaster [interpreter at the British consulate, Bangkok] after the facts became known that we have decided to send an Embassy to France consisting of our own nationals. You will of course remember how you have been told, on your arrival in Singapore, that the Siamese Consul in Paris will have to act under the orders of Sir John Bowring alone. Mr. Reid has written to me again from Singapore to tell me that you will meet with great difficulties from all directions while you are in France, and that you will be forced to ask for help from those who are against you, for it is not to be believed for one moment that any Frenchman will be willing to offer you his service to be used against the interests of his own country.

All these only go to show that the British want us to solicit help from Britain as soon as possible. They will continue with their intimidation of us until we are afraid to go about our own business. But if we really send Sir John Bowring to France on this occasion, and even if he could accomplish what we desire, it will give the French another cause for resentment against us because we have employed another power to brow-beat them; or if Sir John Bowring should commit any faux pas in his dealing with them, the French would still hold us responsible, as according to the letter of agreement signed by the Foreign Minister and yourself. With France's increasing animosity against Siam, where could she turn? Siam would be driven by the fear of France to seek protection from Great Britain, thereby to continue to be forever under that protection, in the like manner as many states in Hindustan have done and as Burma is doing at the present moment. It is known that as soon as disturbances broke out in Burma, the British Colonel * hurried up to Ava to persuade the King of Ava to submit himself to British protection. The King was told that the British would keep peace and order, and that there would be no more disturbance in his country. When news of British success in Burma reached this country, you can imagine the excitement it gave to Mr. Knox.

If the information received from Mr. D. K. Mason regarding Lord Stanley's agreement to Sir John Bowring's appointment is true, then it is possible that the whole policy on the Siamese situation originated with the British Government and not from Mr. Knox alone. I think that now is the chance for Britain to put into practice her policy of bringing Siam under her protection, since Siam is being harassed by the French on one side, with the British Colony on the other, just as the French Colony used to be on the other side of Cambodia.

As regards the French, they are distinguished for their vainglorious disposition. Their Emperor, famed for his descent from a line of tigers and cobras, would, after his ascent to the Throne, seek colonies that are rich and vast, so that he might exercise his power over them. These lands between Annam and Burma must appear to him to be ownerless and therefore desirable.

* Presumably this reference is to the visit in 1866 of Colonel (later Sir) Arthur George Phayre, Chief Commissioner for British Burma, to negotiate a new commercial treaty with King Mindon.

When Montigny [French diplomat who negotiated the Siamese-French treaty of 1856] came here he tried to turn Siam into a French protectorate by seduction, using as his argument the dangers of British domination. The Siamese were not to be easily seduced however, and he spent some time here employing various methods of allurement. The Cambodians were easier prey than the Siamese, on account of their sensitive nasal organs, for they were led by the Jesuit priests into sensing a sweet aroma issuing from the person of the French Emperor. Due to their constant desire to be rid of the fear of the Siamese and the Annamites, they quickly went over to the French. The Annamites, on the other hand, have been as deaf, dumb and stubborn as the Siamese in previous reigns. Their stubbornness caused them to turn small incidents into serious ones, with the result that their country became a French Colony in the end.

Now that they know that they are unable to win over the Siamese by peaceful persuasion, the French have finally resorted to violence and aggression. I am not certain whether this is merely an idea of Consul Aubaret or a policy of the French Government, for Montigny, Monsieur Ertier and Lord Clarendon have all written to me to assure me that it had never been the wish of the Emperor or the French Government that any harm should befall Siam, but all the troubles that have come about had been due to the fault of the French Agent here. All this may be true, but judging from past happenings, it seems to me that in France the master usually follows the dictates of his own slave and the Prince always defends his servants, however wrong they may be. They seem to hold fast to the idea that all foreigners are animals, and as such they deserve no pity when they are abused. Their only desire is to uphold the glory of France, even at the expense of other countries.

In spite of all this, I do not think that we should as yet go straight to Britain for the solution of our problems, thereby to follow the course of action thought out by Mr. Knox, agreed upon by Mr. Reid, cheered by Mr. Mason and volunteered by Sir John Bowring. What we ought to do is to go first to France and make an attempt at some sort of negotiation, as far as our ability will allow us. Should you be prevented from gaining an audience with the Emperor, or even if you should be forced to give in to all of Aubaret's demands, you must be ready to make sacrifices, so as to bring the whole unpleasant business to a close.

If, however, they refuse to remove Aubaret from Bangkok but insist on keeping him here with full power, then the matter would be beyond my endurance. If you fail to get Aubaret removed, then you may cross over to Britain and ask for whatever assistance that you may think fit from the responsible ministers, from the English lords both in and out of office and from Sir John Bowring. I have my own reasons for this decision.

Since we are now being constantly abused by the French because we will not allow ourselves to be placed under their domination like the Cambodians, it is for us to decide what we are going to do; whether to swim up-river to make friends with the crocodile or to swim out to sea and hang on to the whale. . . .

It is sufficient for us to keep ourselves within our house and home; it may be necessary for us to forego some of our former power and influence.[25]

The Siamese embassy sought the best possible bargain with the inevitable. A new treaty with France was signed July 15, 1867. Again Siam recognized the French protectorate over Cambodia and renounced the secret treaty of 1863; but this time there was no statement concerning Cambodian independence; all Siamese claims to suzerainty in any degree over Cambodia were forever given up; the Mekong and its tributary rivers in Siam were opened to French vessels; reciprocal freedom of travel and trade was promised. But, on the other hand, Siam again secured a renunciation by France, acting on behalf of Cambodia, of all claims to the provinces of Battambang and Siemreap (Angkor), although without the recently acquired territory to the east. Norodom, be it noted, was not consulted on this treaty by his "Protector." Aubaret was transferred from Bangkok a few months later, and for the moment there was reasonable contentment in the Divine City.

But a word as to what happened in Southeast Asia thereafter may not be amiss. In June, 1866, the French had occupied the other half of Cochin China. In the eighties France finally secured control of the rest of the Annamite Empire after heavy fighting which included an undeclared war on China, in the course of which the French captured Kelung in Formosa and the Pescadores.

French ambitions for the westward expansion of their Asiatic empire were a factor in bringing on the third Anglo-Burman war, the dethronement of King Thibaw and Queen Supayalat, and the annexation by Britain of Upper Burma and the Shan States, the most easterly of which they divided with the French.

Meanwhile in the seventies the British began the system of establishing Residents as advisers to the various Malay sultans. In 1895 the Federated Malay States came into being under strongly centralized British control. In 1902 the British expressly recognized that the northern Malay states lay within the Siamese sphere of influence; but in 1909, in exchange for a surrender of British extraterritorial rights in Siam, Siam renounced her rather indefinite rights of suzerainty over these four states which then came under British control. During the recent war Japan arranged the transfer to Siam of two of the Malay states and the Shan state of Kentung, but these were returned by Siam as soon as the war ended.

In 1883 French warships blockaded Bangkok and forced Siam to evacuate the provinces of Battambang and Angkor and also to cede all Laotian territory over which

Siam exercised sovereignty east of the Mekong River. In 1904 a further treaty gave France additional territory, while in 1907, in exchange for a return of some of the territory yielded in 1904, Siam renounced officially all claims to Battambang and Angkor. At the beginning of the last war the Siamese took advantage of the French situation in Indochina to force the return to Siam of these two Cambodian provinces and part of the Laotian territory that she had surrendered under duress; but after the war these were returned, and an international commission, established to examine and determine the border on its merits as opposed to historic claim and counterclaim, confirmed the existing lines.

In retrospect, there seems little doubt that the policy set by King Mongkut was wise. Siam was forced to surrender some of her former power and influence over for the most part non-Siamese peoples, but her house and home were saved.

White Elephants

WHEN the King and Anna quarreled about the embassy to Paris, Mongkut did not link her interest with the official pressure he later felt the British were exerting to secure Bowring's appointment. Bangkok by the last years of his reign had become a mecca for adventurers and scoundrels,[1] and the King was questioning the motives of most foreigners, even sturdy friends like Bowring. Through his secretary he commented on an episode that occurred January 19, 1867:

Mem Leonowens, the governess of the royal children, is becoming very naughty indeed. She meddles in His Majesty's affairs, and has shown herself to be very audacious. On Saturday the 14th of the waxing moon of the second month at about sunset, when His Majesty was presiding over the Council of his ministers, she sent in her son to ask His Majesty for an immediate audience on what she said to be a very urgent matter. But when His Majesty was pleased to grant her an audience as requested, she changed her mind and went away, because she had discovered in the meanwhile that the ministers were with him. His Majesty has deduced from his observation of Mem Leonowens' manner that she had been sent by the British Consul to start an argument with him and to deter him from sending a Siamese Embassy to France. If he was agreeable, then she should ask him to engage Sir John Bowring as his Ambassador instead, so that Sir John might be paid over a thousand or two catties of money. Oh! The King of Siam has a great pile of money! He is very rich and in possession of absolute power and strange desires, but he is at the same time so cowardly, so stupid and vain as to become an easy prey to money-seekers. . . . Those who have written to the King appear to have done so out of their sense of loyalty and devotion towards him, but one occasionally catches a glimpse of their real motive for private gains after an exchange of a few letters.[2]

When Sir John Bowring was in Bangkok to negotiate the treaty of 1855, he was duly shown the white elephant to which Mongkut had referred in his correspondence with him. The last white elephant, one of four secured by King Phra Nang Klao, had died about fifteen years before, "since which time till now there has been no white elephant to stand as a living pledge for the prosperity of the Kingdom. Now since obtaining this one," according to Dr. Bradley, "very lively and sanguine hopes are entertained that the state will prosper. It is now about four months since this young elephant was found, and what is peculiarly hopeful in the history of the case is that it was born about the time the present King ascended the throne three years ago. As yet she is only about half the size of an adult elephant. Her general complexion is reddish, the skin being a greyish dun, modified by sandy or reddish hairs very thinly bestudding the whole body. Her eyes were whitish but not albinous. Her houghs are white and parts of the ears are of the complexion of a common European." [3] Alas, the elephant died a few months later on September 8. Bowring had already, in lieu of a gift from the King of two ordinary but very much alive elephants, "willingly accepted from him a bunch of hairs from the tails of white elephants which had been the cherished possession of his ancestors; and I had the honour of offering two of these hairs for the gracious acceptance of the Queen" Victoria; [4] now the King sent him as a mark of royal favor a portion of the white skin of the recently deceased elephant "with beautiful body hairs preserved in spirits." This gift Bowring transferred to the museum of the Zoological Society of London.[5]

The importance attributed to white elephants in Siam arose from the belief in transmigration. As Anna Leonowens wrote: "Almost all white animals are held in reverence by the Siamese, because they were once superior human beings, and the white elephant, in particular, is supposed to be animated by the spirit of some king or hero. Having once been a great man, he is thought to be familiar with the dangers that surround the great, and to know what is best and safest for those whose condition in all respects was once his own. He is hence supposed to avert national calamity, and bring prosperity and peace to a people." In glowing language she describes the ceremonies after a white elephant is captured:

A wide path is cut for him through the forests he must traverse on his way to the capital. Wherever he rests he is sumptuously entertained, and everywhere he is escorted and served by a host of attendants, who sing, dance, play upon instruments, and perform feats of strength or skill for his amusement, until he reaches the banks of the Meinam, where a great floating palace of wood, surmounted by a gorgeous roof and hung with crimson curtains, awaits him. The roof is literally thatched with flowers ingeniously arranged so as to form symbols and mottoes, which the superior beast is supposed to decipher with ease. The floor of this splendid float is laid with gilt matting curiously woven, in the centre of which his four-footed lordship is installed in state, surrounded by an obsequious and enraptured crowd of mere bipeds who bathe him, flatter him. His food consists of the finest herbs, the tenderest grass, the sweetest sugar-cane, the mellowest plantains, the brownest cakes of wheat, served on huge trays of gold and silver; and his drink is perfumed with the fragrant flower of *dok mallee,* the large native jessamine.

On this raft the white elephant is floated down river to Ayuthia, where he is met by the king and his court and towed in state to Bangkok. Presently he is

conducted with great pomp to his sumptuous quarters within the precincts of the first king's palace, where he is received by his own court of officers, attendants, and slaves, who install him in his fine lodgings, and at once proceed to robe and decorate him. First, the court jeweller rings his tremendous tusks with massive gold, crowns him with a diadem of beaten gold of perfect purity, and adorns his burly neck with heavy golden chains. Next his attendants robe him in a superb velvet cloak of purple, fringed with scarlet and gold; and then his court prostrate themselves around him, and offer him royal homage.

When his lordship would refresh his portly person in the bath, an officer of high rank shelters his noble head with a great umbrella of crimson and gold, while others wave golden fans before him. On these occasions he is invariably preceded by musicians, who announce his approach with cheerful minstrelsy and songs.

If he falls ill, the king's own leech prescribes for him, and the chief priests repair daily to his palace to pray for his safe deliverance, and sprinkle him with consecrated waters and anoint him with consecrated oils. Should he die, all Siam is bereaved, and the nation, as one man, goes into mourning for him.[6]

"One day," one of the American missionaries wrote, "a strange procession passed down the river in front of our house in Bangkok. There were eight large barges, six of them with curtains of crimson and gold cloth, each manned by about thirty boatmen dressed in red trousers, jackets and caps. They had a brass band, which made very mournful music, for it was a funeral occasion. The first impression was that some personage eminent for rank was being born to sepulchre; but no, this procession was simply doing honor to the dead body of a light-colored elephant.

"The third and fourth boats had no gay curtains, but they had the five-storied umbrellas which denote great rank, and between these two boats the corpse was fastened and floated on the water. There was a canopy of white cloth over it to protect it from the sun. Phya is a title given to a high order of nobility in Siam, and this distinguished elephant was named Phya Sawate." [7]

On June 11, 1860, "a new white elephant was escorted this day into the city by a royal procession"—a male elephant from Korat province.[8] Bradley recounts nothing further about him, but early in 1864, a third white elephant was discovered in the jungle not far from Bangkok. It was captured sometime in April. "He was pronounced by the best judges to be the whitest elephant Siam has been possessed with for hundreds of years," Dr. Bradley recorded. "The King and his Ministers have spent many weeks in the Old City [Ayuthia] to prepare the creature by many ceremonies and superstitious observances for removing down to his palace in the Fall. One hundred catties [about 225 pounds] of gold was ordered to be wrought into various ornaments for him to wear on the occasion." And then the sympathetic entry on July 14, "The King of Siam has met with another sad bereavement in the death of the new white elephant." [9]

Mongkut was naturally eager at all times to secure a white elephant. In a letter to his brother Prince Mahamala, he wrote:

I approve your plans for the hunt, and should the elephant not be found this time, I am also in agreement with your plans for further hunts to be made for it in Dong Nakorn forests and in other places. Endeavour to keep on with the good work. If you lack supplies or should require anything especially, please let me know and I will see that they are despatched to you with all possible speed.

There is no news of any importance from Bangkok. . . . All the members of the nobility who are at present in the Capital are in good health. The Second King has left for Ban Sritha [a new palace about 160 miles north of Bangkok whither the Second King had moved] since Friday the 11th of the waxing moon this month, it being now a festive month in the Lao country. It is customary for the Laos to make merry after their crops have been harvested. You too have a great number of Laos under your personal control. Will you take care not to allow yourself to be led into too much gaiety? It is far, far more beneficial to acquire white elephants for the State.

It has been said in some circles that the Lao country is a veritable paradise, since all its male and female inhabitants are merry from evening till late at night, forever singing and dancing gayly. In more roguish circles, it has been said that there is no need to make merit for the sake of going to heaven at all, since the Thai country is already in possession of all amenities supposed to be found there. Among the amenities are the heavenly nectar, which is liquor; angelic food, which is opium that produces a happy state of coma; and the celestial Tree of Wealth, which is the gambling house. These things are to be found all over the country on land and water.

I do not support the above theories at all. If the Lao and Thai countries are really heaven, it is, to my way of thinking, a most untidy one, as evidenced by the ruinous fires that frequently burn down the heavenly edifices.[10]

In a later letter to his brother he reverted to the serious matter of white elephants: "To try to find an elephant of such excellence in the forest as you are now doing is as difficult as to dive for fish in deep water. Glowing reports of elephants of good qualities often reach me, but as soon as I start the hunt for them, the elephants seem to disappear. There has been one exception, however, when a white elephant was actually found and captured in the year of the Rat last [1864–5]. I admit that that success has spurred me on to further hopes. Whenever I hear of a new white elephant, I cannot help but to organize a hunt for it." [11]

8

The Inner Palace

MONGKUT had spent twenty-six years in celibacy while in the priesthood. He became king early in April, 1851. By mid-August he already had thirty young wives.[1] Children began arriving early in 1852. Three years later, when Bowring had a private audience with the King after the signing of the treaty, he asked the King how many children he had. "Eleven since I was King," Mongkut replied, "and twelve before—plenty of royalty." [2] In 1863 the King authorized the *Bangkok Calendar* to publish a list of the sixty-one children he then had had and the further information:

There have been altogether 27 royal mothers in the King's family: one of them had 7 children, two of them each 5, another 4, two of them 3 each, four of them 2 each, and all the others but one each. His Majesty has at the present time 34 concubines. . . . Besides these 34 concubines there are 74 daughters of noblemen who have been presented to the King by their fathers, with the view to serve as maids of honor. . . . When any of them desire to exchange their situation for one out of the palace, with freedom to marry or otherwise, they may obtain the privilege by requesting it of the King. His Majesty has granted many such requests since he began to reign. There are also in the female department of the 1st King's family 27 persons, being aunts, sisters and nieces of His Majesty. . . . There are also 5 official ladies in the royal palace.

All those listed were on official salary.

At the end of this notice the missionary editor of the *Calendar* added a statement about the Second King.

He has now about twenty Laos and five Siamese wives. The whole number of his children is about 60, of whom only 30 are now living. . . . Thus it appears but too plainly that the present kings are great polygamists. But it should be noted somewhat to their praise that they have not a quarter as many concubines as their regal predecessors. . . . Would to God the Kings of Siam would go further and put down this pernicious custom of polygamy by their own example to the full extent and by the power of righteous law. Virtue can never have much sway in Siam, nor any true prosperity, until polygamy is made a crime by the Government.

A correction appeared in the following issue:

His Majesty the First King appears not to have been well pleased that the Editor of the Bangkok Calendar should have represented him, in the number for 1863, as having more wives than his brother the Second King. The statement was made according to a MSS said to have been prepared for the press under the direct supervision of the King himself. Indeed much of it was in his own handwriting, particularly that part relating to the Second King's family. But it seems that the Editor misunderstood a

sentence or two of the statement, and hence, soon after the issue
of the Calendar for 1863, His Majesty was pleased to make the
following correction of it—

"What number of the Second King's wives given here as 5
Siamese and 20 Laos, is only those that are the most-beloved
to him at the present days. Those 25 wives accompanied him
always to Seetha [Ban Sritha]. In fact his Laos wives more than
60, his Siamese wives more than 60. For instance on the year of
enthronement, he has 48 wives accompanied him to Second
King's Palace. Since that time his wives increased every year.
He endeavor always to obtain wives especially from the Laos.
Now he has 120 wives at least."

And again the irrepressible Reverend Dr. Bradley added
his own comments:

Does it not show a great stride towards reform in that most
pernicious sentiment, that the honour and glory of princes is
enhanced by the number of their wives? Do not the few lines of
His Majesty evince a desire on his part to be published in the
Calendar as being in advance of his brother in reformatory efforts against the sentiment that polygamy is honourable? [3]

During the seventeen years that he was on the throne
Mongkut had eighty-two children. As one of his great-
nephews remarked, "This after twenty-six years spent in
the monastery was no mean feat." [4] Mongkut's first child
was born in 1823; his last in 1868. Sixty-six of his children
were living shortly before he died. [5]

Occasionally the multiplicity of children produced situations which the the monogamous are not apt to encounter.
He wrote one of his Ambassadors in London:

The second box, contained several rings addressed to various
people, to whom they have been forwarded according to directions. There were two more rings, one of which was a present

from you to Yingyowalaks, to whom it has been given, but the second ring was, according to your note, to be given to my new-born child. As ten more children have been born to me since you left, one girl, a grand-daughter of the Somdetch Ong Noi,* having died, leaving nine, to which one of these nine children shall the ring be given? Since I have mentioned only two of these children in my last letter to you, namely the birth of the boy who is younger brother to Taxinsha and to whom I have given the name of Kashemsri, and the birth and death of the girl who was grand-daughter of the Somdetch Ong Noi, I presumed that it was your wish to make a present to the boy Kashemsri. . . .

The following are the eight children born after your departure and of whose births you have not been informed, viz. a girl named Samoe Samai born of Malai, a boy named Srisiddhi Thongchai born of Bua, a boy named Tong Taem born of Sangwal, a girl

---

* The Somdetch Ong Noi was Chief Councillor. At the time of his death in February, 1858, Bradley wrote: "No man in the Kingdom has so great power as he, the King only excepted. He has always been opposed to such changes in the government as would enlarge commerce and foreign influence. But the King's power was too much for him and he could do little more than hinder and embarrass the policy of His Majesty to come into more intimate contact with the great western nations. He represents old Siam which is fast departing." [6] Many of the King's marriages were of course motivated by political considerations. Family alliances were important in his dealings with his nobles. Three years before the death of the old Chief Councillor, Mongkut had written Dr. Bradley about one of his children who was very ill. "Though there are now my children many, totalling twelve souls, yet I very wish this male infant for his being the grandchild of His Excellency Somdit Chao Phya Ong Noi who earnestly desire his family be connected with the royalty by birth of such a royal infant. Please do your kind attention carefully." Alas, five days later the diary records: "My royal patient died a little after noon to-day." The cause of death was lockjaw.[7]

named Kanokwarn born of Thaing, and three more girls born of nondescript mothers.

I have given these last three to be adopted children of my sister Yai, His Honour Sri Suriwongse and the Minister of Harbour respectively. They are very pleased indeed with them, for His Honour Sri Suriwongse has no other children than Phra Nai Wai and Klang, the wife of Phra Phromboriraks, while the Minister of Harbour has been constantly awaiting the birth of a child from Bua, his Lao wife, who has been expectant for the past thirteen or fourteen months. He is so pleased when anyone tells him that his wife is truly pregnant that he usually rewards them with sums of money varying from eight to seven taels. He is so happy now that he has received one of my children in adoption that he very frequently comes to dote on the child, and has already bestowed on it large sums of money amounting to many catties.

All news of any importance has been given in my last letter to you. Do not take it amiss if I have given the ring to the wrong child; I will make it up to the right one later when I know your true wish. Please tell Phraya Montri Suriwongse that I am very pleased with the pipe and buttons which he sent me. I will use them myself and promise not to give them away to any one.[8]

In 1855 Bowring was informed that there were about three thousand women in the Inner Palace of whom perhaps six hundred were said to be wives and concubines although it is obvious this latter figure is not so. Anna Leonowens, a few years later to be sure, spoke of the number of women as nine thousand. Whatever a census would have shown, the Inner Palace was in fact a city of women where no man but the King might enter except the priests or an occasional doctor, all of whom were under suitable female guard. In the Inner Palace lived the princesses of the blood, the wives and concubines of the King, and the slaves and attendants that each possessed. Also there were the lady officials comprising the administration of the city. The senior administrative personnel were ladies of high rank and were directly responsible to the King. Below them were the ladies who served as clerks and treasurers and the women who filled the menial posts. In addition there was an Amazon guard—the police force of this strange city. Unlike other oriental harems the practice of employing eunuchs was unknown in the Siamese harem.

The community of women in the Inner Palace was subject to frequent change. New women were constantly coming, and many, in the lower ranks particularly, were leaving to be married or to take other employment. Some of those arriving were presented as gifts to the King or to a princess by willing parents or relatives; if the girl were successful in finding favor the whole family would benefit. Others came of their own accord hoping to secure a pleasant life. Still others came to seek employment. Furthermore, as the Inner Palace was the only place in Siam (other than the Inner Palace of the Second King) where a girl could receive a suitable education and acquire the manners and accomplishments required of Siamese ladies of high birth, the noble families were apt to send their little daughters to the palace to remain there for a few years until ready for marriage.

All these women were called *Nang Nai* or Ladies of the Inner Palace. Only the royal wives and concubines and the princesses of the blood were regarded as *Nang Harm* or Forbidden Ladies. Princesses of the blood were prohibited from marrying; sons-in-law and brothers-in-law might become too powerful.[9]

In addition to his own vast family, the King was head of the entire royal family, consisting of the widows, children, grandchildren and great-grandchildren of former kings. The royal family had begun modestly enough with General Chakri only seventy years before Mongkut ascended the throne, but already it was a large group and by the end of Mongkut's reign it was a vast congregation ranging in caliber from men of outstanding ability and sense of public responsibility to wastrels and ne-er-do-wells. Siam does not have the law of primogeniture as in monogamous England, where titles usually descend only through the oldest living male descendant. The problem of a nobility increasing in geometric progression was solved by diminishing their rank in each new generation. From King to commoner is a matter of five generations in Siam. Sons of the King and a queen are *Chao Fa,* of the King and a nonroyal mother *Prong Chao;* sons in succeeding generations are entitled respectively *Mom Chao, Mom Rajawongse,* and *Mom Luang.* The fifth generation are addressed, as are all other commoners, as Nai, the equivalent of Mister. Commoners may be elevated to the nobility, but their titles are not hereditary.

Although Mongkut was in theory an absolute monarch, in practice he was bound by the palatine laws handed down from the remote past which rigorously prescribed the daily life of the King. According to these laws his daily routine should have been as follows:

7 A.M.   The King rose from bed.

8 A.M.   He partook of a light repast consisting of rice gruel.

9 A.M.   He gave audience to the officers of the Royal Guards.

10 A.M.   He took his morning meal and retired again to bed.

11 A.M.   He was attended by the ladies of the palace.

1 P.M.   He went out on an excursion.

2 P.M.   He gave audience to his children and members of the Royal Family.

3 P.M.   He presided over a council of his ministers and gave his decisions on affairs of state.

4 P.M.   He went out on an excursion.

5 P.M.   He went to the Royal Chapel.

6 P.M.   He decided on the affairs of the Palace.

7 P.M.   He studied the Art of War.

8 P.M.   He studied Politics.

9 P.M.   He studied History.

10 P.M.   He was served a meal.

11 P.M.   He conferred with astrologers and pundits and discussed Religion and Philosophy.

Midnight   He listened to musicians and singers.

1 A.M.   He listened to story-tellers.

2 or 3 A.M.   The King retired to bed.[10]

In two respects at least, it is known that Mongkut deviated when he could from the lawful procedure. He was wont to discuss official business with his ministers instead of discussing religion and philosophy with the astrologers and pundits. And he preferred to dictate far into the early morning hours instead of listening to music, minstrels, and story-tellers. Also, he carried on his priestly tradition and generally started his day, according to Anna, two hours earlier, rising at 5 A.M.

Bishop Pallegoix reports an interesting aspect of the ancient laws governing the palace. "If, during an audience, the King becomes exasperated with any of the mandarins, and orders the sword-bearer to deliver his sword into his hands, there is the penalty of death attached to the sword-bearer should he obey his Sovereign; because he is not to be the instrument of the King's anger, but, at any risk, must refuse to place in his master's hands the means of gratifying his passion." [11]

There were other limits too to Mongkut's absolute power. One of the medical practices that was widespread in Southeast Asia and which, indeed, survived in some rural areas into the twentieth century was the "roasting" of the mother after a child was born. A brazier of lighted charcoal was brought to the bedside and kept as near the patient's stomach as she could bear. According to Dr. Malcolm Smith, who was for many years physician to the then Queen Mother, Saowapa, one of Mongkut's daughters, this practice "was said to 'dry the womb.' Often it raised huge blisters, and when the skin was covered with them and the patient could stick it no longer, they turned her over and blistered her back. This treatment went on for two or three weeks. It caused great suffering but it was the 'custom,' and custom to them was sacred. That anyone should dispute it would never have entered their heads. Altogether the woman had a rough time and she paid the penalty. The maternal mortality rate was high." [12]

On January 28, 1852, as Dr. Bradley recounts, after being "sent for in the morning to visit one of the King's wives who had been recently confined, I was admitted in the inner palace, the apartment of the royal females into which no European man ever before was allowed to enter. . . . The case was committed entirely to my care by the King. He had been much alarmed for her life. . . . I went boldly forward and had the fire removed at which the poor woman was lying when I first saw her, and which Siamese custom would require her to do for a full month. I also opened the window which had been so much closed that there was very little ventilation in her room. I put her on homeopathic treatment. She soon began to mend." [13]

The next day Dr. House accompanied him. Dr. Bradley recorded in his diary merely: "Spent all last night in the inner apartment of royal palace and had Dr. House for my companion besides several royal physicians, the latter of whom were only spectators of my procedure." [14] But Dr. House wrote in his diary: "An old lady of rank waited to carry up my opinion of the case to the 'Sacred Feet.' At midnight, finding our patient had no new paroxysms, as we feared she might, we proposed going home. 'Go, how can you? You must stay till morning; you are locked in and the key sent to the King, so stay you must; no one goes out till daylight!' " [15]

Afterwards Mongkut wrote touchingly to Dr. Bradley: "My mind is indeed full of gratitude to you for your skill and some expense of medicine in most valuable favour to my dear lady, the mother of my infant daughter, by saving her life from approaching death. I cannot hesitate longer than perceiving that she was undoubtedly saved. . . . I trust previously the manner of curing in the obstetrics of America and Europe, but sorry to say I could not get the same lady to believe before her approaching death, because her kindred were many more who lead her according to their custom. Your present curing, however, was just now most wonderful in this palace." [16]

A few months later tragedy struck when the seventeen-year-old Queen was stricken, gave premature birth to an heir—he died a few hours later—and herself died after a severe and lingering illness, having been queen only nine months and a few days. Deeply attached to her, Mongkut not only made proclamation in Siamese but also circulated among their English friends, "so that they may know accurately about her," a pamphlet giving in English "an account of the most lamentable illness and death of her young and amiable Majesty." * This detailed recital discloses all

* This pamphlet is reproduced in Appendix III.

too pathetically the struggle between the old and new ideas of treatment, and that once even Mongkut in his despair surrendered momentarily his confidence in western medical theory.

According to Dr. Smith, King Mongkut never succeeded in stopping "what he called 'the senseless and monstrous crime of having lying-in women smoked and roasted from 15 to 30 days.' 'Could he have his way,' he said, 'he would effect reform in his own families on the subject.' But the women would have nothing to do with his new ideas. They were having the babies they said, not the King." It was not until his own daughter, Saowapa, became queen and broke away from accepted practice that the custom was abandoned at court.[17]

Of the wives of the King elevated to queenly status, the young, royal Princess Somanass Waddhanawadi was the first. His second queen—Queen Debserin—was the Princess Ramperi Bhamarabhirami, a granddaughter of Mongkut's half-brother, Rama III. She was the mother of Mongkut's successor, Chulalongkorn, who was born September 21, 1853, and died October 23, 1910. It is she who stands beside the King in the daguerreotype sent by the King to President Pierce. Queen Debserin died in 1861. Mongkut's third queen—Queen Piyamawadi—was not a royal princess, but the daughter of a nobleman and a palace dancer. Anna Leonowens described her: "Hardly pretty, but well formed, and of versatile tact, totally uneducated, of barely respectable birth,—being Chinese on her father's side,— yet withal endowed with a nice intuitive appreciation of character." [18] Her three daughters, Sunanta, Sawang, and Saowapa, became the three queens of their half-brother Chulalongkorn. A son, Prince Svasti, became the father of Queen Rambai Barni, widow of King Prajadhipok. It was Queen Sunanta who drowned when those nearby were forbidden to aid her.

Notwithstanding the routine of the palace, the vast congregation of women with which he was surrounded, and the total lack of privacy in which he lived, Mongkut established a sense of intimate family relationship with at least some of his wives and children. "Little Turtle," he wrote to Lady Phung a year after he came to the throne, "I have consulted the American doctor about the illness of your boy. . . . The doctor informs me that the case is hopeless and that he can be of no use. It grieves me to lose the child, especially when it is a boy, but I am even more concerned with your great sorrow. Do not take it too much to heart, since death is only natural in this case and it cannot be helped." [19]

Some of the problems inherent in life in a harem appear in a gossipy family letter to Lady Phung written two years later. "My own Turtle," he wrote:

This is to show how much and truly I am thinking of you. I left the Water Palace last Sunday before dawn and arrived at Wat Khema in Talat Kwan at about 7 o'clock in the morning. There, we noticed a very fast boat which was being paddled at full speed towards the Royal Barge. At that moment it had already passed the boats carrying the guards and all the other boats in the retinue. It gained upon us, and finally it caught up with the Royal Barge and was actually running parallel to it. At first I thought that Ramphoey's * little girl was in the boat, possibly crying to be put in the Royal Barge so as to be with me, and that they were trying to do so to please her. I shouted at them to inquire whose boat it was, but there was no answer. The cabin of the boat was heavily curtained and many women were to be seen in the stern. The guards told me later that they

* Princess Ramperi Bhamarabhirama, who became Queen Debserin.

thought the boat had come in the retinue and therefore they had not stopped it at the beginning. My Chamberlain, Sarapeth, challenged it many times; I myself repeated my question again and again, but instead of any reply, the women in the boat all laughed merrily and with the utmost abandon, so that the people in my barge were getting quite annoyed for being laughed at.

I thought of ordering my men to open fire according to the Law; but on second thought I was afraid someone might be shot dead. It would then be said that I was a cruel and irresponsible Monarch, to have caused death to people so easily.

By now the boat was having a race with the Royal Barge itself. This went on for some time until I thought it was really out of the ordinary and had to be stopped. Only then did I order the guards to give chase and stop the boat. They had to chase it for quite a distance before they could bring it back. It was found that the boat belonged to Prince Mahesavara's mother [Prince Mahesavara was the King's eldest son, born before he entered the priesthood] and she herself was in it. She appeared to be in a brazenly playful mood and had a most unseemly desire to tease me in public. I ordered Phra Indaradeb to take the boat down to Bangkok. I have also ordered the owner of the boat to be held within the Inner Palace, while all her servants who were with her were to be kept in custody. I have written to inform her son of the incident, and have given my instructions to the Ladies Sri Sachcha and Sobhanives accordingly.

I have heard that some women with connections to Princess Talap and Princess Haw were in that boat. These two women are related to your aunt. Do not go and see them or say anything to them, for they would only be rude to you and make you ashamed. The chief culprit does not acknowledge her own wantonness. She still regards herself as my favorite and would follow me just to ridicule me in front of my new young wives. She claims to be a great lady, for when she was arrested she cried out that she intended to accompany me to Ayuthia.

I have sent you five hives of honey. You may call for them at Lady Num's. Should honey disagree with you in your present state, so soon after child-birth, do not eat it but give it to your mother or to your aunt. Will you all take good care of my child? I am worried about his health and do not want him to be ill. I have asked Prince Sarpasilp to keep an eye on him also.

The water level is very high this year. Beyond the Royal Pavillion there is a great expanse of water. It is full of lotus, water lilies and water chestnuts. Those who have accompanied me here cannot contain themselves for the desire to go out boating. This they can already do at the back of the pavillion within camp. Everything is as it should be at present. Princess Pook, by being absent, is not able to make a nuisance of herself as usual. There has been only one accident so far; a golden receptacle is lost. It has probably fallen into the water when one of the boats carrying my servants was sunk to-day in a collision with another boat. They are diving for it now, but I am not so sure whether it will be found.

I have told Lady Num to give you also some pressed new rice, but as I have sent this present to a number of other people as well, you may have to take your share of it only.[20]

A vivid portrait of Mongkut as a father is found in another letter:

This is to let you know that on Tuesday the thirteenth of the waxing moon of the tenth month, there was an accident which caused great alarm inside the Royal Palace. On that date, I went out in the afternoon to inspect the rice cultivation on the Royal Plaza. On our way out, I was riding on a horse, while four of my children who accompanied me, namely Yingowalaks, Taxinsha, Somavati, and Chulalongkorn, were taken there in a carriage which I was wont to drive myself. We arrived there safely and spent the afternoon looking around the paddy fields and the orchards until it was time for us to return to the Palace. I made the return journey with the children in the carriage which I drove as usual. We did not come back directly to the Palace, but went on to inspect the almshouse and thence to the Indrarangsarn Fortress to see how the construction of some cannon bases there was progressing. We spent a long time at the last place mentioned and it was getting nearly dark when we started on our journey home.

The carriage was so crowded, what with the four children and all the various little things children love to bring back with them from these outings, that I hardly found any room to sit or stand securely on it. I had to drive in a most uncomfortable position, with my back half leaning on the back of the seat and with my feet pressing down tightly on the front part of the carriage.

Because the route back to the Palace went only towards the right, none of us noticed that the left rein was getting loose. This was due to the rotten state of the gut with which it was sewn to the bit. When we came through the Visejaisri Gate, the horse quickened its pace and I pulled it in slightly by drawing in both reins. When we came to the turning towards the Temple of the Emerald Buddha, the guards who accompanied us wheeled towards the Temple and stopped, while I drove straight on. However, when we passed the Hall of Priests there were the customary fanfares of trumpets and drums, which caused the horse to break into a gallop. I pulled in the reins a little bit more, because I was afraid the speed might cause the children to tumble out of the carriage, but the horse merely swerved to the right instead of slowing down. When I tried to correct this by pulling in the left rein, the far end came off and I knew at once that it had broken.

I called for help but it was too late, for by that time the carriage had already collided with the seat under the acacia tree there, and with one wheel over the seat it was running into a fence. By that time I had lost control of the horse altogether, and owing to my insecure position on the carriage from the beginning I could do very little when the carriage finally overturned, throwing me and the children on the ground. The carriage fell on top of us. I tried to protect the children and myself from being crushed to death by its weight by holding it up from our bodies with my right arm. I could not, however, prevent it from running over my right leg. My left arm was pinned down under my body and the whole of my left side thrusted along the brick path by the carriage.

I was bruised and cut in many places on the left side. My right hip was also badly hurt and there was a pain underneath my right ribs where Somavati had fallen on them. As regards the four children who all fell down with me, Chulalongkorn had three small cuts on his head, which was a little bruised as well. Yingowalaks sprained her ankle and could not stand up. Somavati had a few bruises and some minor injuries on her back; but Taxinsha was seriously hurt. Her right foot was badly crushed by something and a great deal of blood was flowing from the wounds at the time.

The children were all crying and screaming after the accident; but luckily and with the help of the merciful gods, the horse stopped where it was. Some men ran forward to raise up the carriage and to pick up the children. Taxinsha was in an alarming condition. Her bleeding did not stop until an hour after medical aid had been given. The doctor said, however, that no bones had been broken and that there were only flesh wounds. That night she suffered from shock which brought on a fever. She is better now after treatment. Yingowalaks recovered after a massage with some ointment. Somavati was sick on the same night, but Chulalongkorn only had three small wounds on his head and nothing more.

Although I had many cuts and bruises and felt a pain under my ribs, I did not take a sick leave after the accident but appeared in public daily at the appointed time, for I did not want people to be unnecessarily alarmed. As a thanksgiving for our escape from serious harm, I made merit by ordering a religious service to be held, at the end of which I offered food to the priests. Moreover, I had a statue of Buddha cast in commemoration of our safe delivery, and a theatrical performance was held in celebration. I attended all these ceremonies and celebrations in person, having put on a coat with long sleeves to hide my wounds and bruises. Fortunately I had none of them on my head.[21]

There was one aspect of harem life that troubled Mongkut deeply. In the most dramatic of all the reforms that he initiated, he broke with age-old royal tradition. To all his wives and concubines, who once they had become *Nang Harm* had heretofore been immured for life in the Inner Palace, he granted the right to resign and, with the exception of the mothers of royal children, the right to marry other men.

His Majesty King Phra Chom Klao is graciously pleased to pledge His Royal Permit, bound in truth and veracity, to all Lady Consorts serving in the Inner Palace, Middle Palace and Outer Palace, excepting Mother Consorts of the royal children, as well as to Forbidden Ladies of all ranks, Ladies Chaperon and Chaperons and all Palace Dancers and Concubines as follows:

Whereas it is no longer the desire of His Majesty to possess, by means of threat or detention, any of the ladies above referred to, and, having regards to the honour of their families and their own merits, it has been His Majesty's pleasure to support them and to bestow on them annuities, annual gifts of raiment and various marks of honour and title befitting their station.

Should any of the ladies, having long served His Majesty, suffer discomfort, and desire to resign from the Service in order to reside with a prince or to return home to live with her parents, or to dispel such discomfort by the company of a private husband and children, let her suffer no qualms. For if a resignation be directly submitted to His Majesty by the lady accompanied by the surrender of decorations, her wishes will be graciously granted, provided always that whilst still in the Service and before submitting such a resignation, the lady shall refrain from the act of associating herself with love agents, secret lovers or clandestine husbands by any means or artifice whatsoever. . . .

The Mother Consorts of the Royal Children can in no case be permitted to resign in favour of matrimony because such an action will prejudice the dignity of the royal children. In this case resignation is only permissible if the purpose is restricted to residence with the royal children unaccompanied by matrimony.

The said royal intention, in spite of repeated declarations to the same effect as above stated, seems to make little progress with popular credence, it being mistaken as a joke or a sarcastic remark. Since in truth and veracity His Majesty bears such an intention in all earnestness, His Pledge is hereby doubly reattested by being declared and published for public perusal. Such a course of action has been taken in order that all manner of men and women will be completely reassured that His Majesty harbours no possessive desire in regards to the ladies, nor does he intend to detain them by any means whatsoever, and that previous declarations do represent His true and sincere purpose.[22]

This decree was issued in the year of the Tiger when Mongkut had been on the throne for three years. Four years later some of his concubines plucked up enough courage to take him at his word. A further decree was issued giving their names, but the references given to the departing ladies can scarcely be considered gallant: "Twelve ladies," it was announced, "have been granted leave to resign by Royal Permit without the benefit of a grant of annuity." The first four, who were mostly in their late thirties, entered the Service in the reign of His Majesty, King Phra Nang Klao. The two first named were promoted to the rank of Lady Consort attached to the Royal Bed Chamber. The third lady, however, remained without any special assignment. The fourth lady served as one of the Miladies of the Lamp. In the present reign the first two were moved down to serve as Miladies of the Lamp and Tea Service. The third lady was moved up to the Royal Bed Chamber, whilst the fourth remained in her former post. The four having expressed their wishes to seek physical and spiritual comfort outside the Royal Palace, were granted leave to resign.[23]

Then followed the names of the other eight—all but one fifteen or sixteen years old.

The eight ladies above referred to entered the Service in the Present Reign. The first lady served as Milady of the Royal Sword, but had to resign on being stricken with a nervous breakdown. The second and third ladies entered the Service after the death of their father for the purpose of getting a larger share in the inheritance of the deceased for the reason of having entered into His Majesty's Service. Having been awarded their duly increased shares of the inheritance, they resigned.

The rest on the list are gifted dancers. A difference of opinion arose with regard to the fourth and fifth ladies. Their respective fathers wanted them to remain in the Service, but the ladies themselves and their respective mothers decided in favour of resignation. Wherefore, His Majesty gave them leave to resign. The sixth lady was much feared in the Palace for her dangerous eye and ear. After a violent quarrel with her friends in the Palace she was permitted to resign on the approval of her parents. As for the seventh on the list, the lady was possessed of doubtful beauty. Her mannerism was altogether over-cultivated. Considering that she might be desirable in the eye of someone who desired her, His Majesty graciously granted her leave to resign. The eighth and last lady on the list was afflicted with the malady of fast hand, and having been found by responsible persons in the Palace to be untrustworthy with valuables and such like, was advised to resign from the Service.

The twelve ladies above named are now resigned from the Palace and are wholly free to pledge their services to any prince or noble. Should there be any such a prince or noble who would desire any of them in marriage, His Majesty would gladly and sincerely offer them congratulations. That a man should be free to choose a woman of his heart's desire is the wish of His Majesty, and so happy He will feel to know that the satisfaction of any such man is shared by any of the ladies who recently resigned. In fact, His Majesty might have gone one step further by graciously giving the said ladies away in marriage; but he was restrained by the consideration that He might have erred in His choice to the dismay of the parties concerned. Wherefore, the present middle course has been adopted in the hope that the honour and liberality of His Majesty will be firmly established in the newly founded custom.

9

"However Differently Perceived and Worshipped"

EXCEPT for one short period when he thought—wrongly as it turned out—that one of the missionaries had been responsible for a slanderous article in the *Straits Times,* Mongkut maintained pleasant and friendly relations with the missionaries. As a devout Buddhist he was naturally given to religious tolerance. At the same time he doubted —in this he was correct—that the missionaries would make many converts among Buddhists. He thought it just as likely, he once observed, that the Buddhists would convert the missionaries.[1]

He was entirely willing that the missionaries should preach the Christian religion. When one of his own disciples became a Roman Catholic, there was murmuring against a priest who would abandon the religion of his country; but Mongkut, who was still Abbot, protected him, maintaining that everyone should have freedom to follow the religion that he desired.[2] He gave the Reverend Caswell a room in his temple where he might preach Christianity and authorized his priests to attend his sermons. He even invited the American missionaries to attend a cremation ceremony and to distribute religious books among the head priests from other temples who would be assembled there and to preach to them on the new religion.[3] After he became king, he gave a plot of land for a Protestant cemetery, and he purchased and made available at a very low rent land on which some of the American missionaries could build their compound.

Mongkut was always anxious that the missionaries should understand clearly his position. He had considered carefully the Christian religion. He recognized that there was great good in Christianity, for its ethics and those of Buddhism are very similar, but he would not accept the miracles related in the Bible nor would he accept divine revelation. These appealed to his reason no more than the demons and gods of the Buddhist scripture. He is said to have told Christian friends more than once: "What you teach people to do is admirable; but what you teach them to believe is foolish." [4] In exasperation he wrote on one occasion, "Though you should baptise all in Siam I will never be baptized." [5] Having reached these conclusions, his interest in the missionaries was their knowledge of western science and the English language which was the key to that science. Some months after the Reverend Caswell began coming to his wat to give him English lessons, Mongkut wrote Captain Brown of the steamer "Express" explaining that Mr. Caswell seemed to think that he and his disciples were seeking to become Christians and were studying the English language for that reason. He had, he explained, no intention whatsoever of abandoning Buddhism, and if Mr. Caswell does not yet understand will Captain Brown please give him to understand it. "There is too much reason to fear," commented Dr. Bradley "that he and his party have no other object as he says than to acquire the English language and get hold of foreign science." [6]

Years later Mongkut sanctioned the statement:

The American missionaries have always been just and upright men. They have never meddled in the affairs of government, nor created any difficulties with the Siamese. They have lived with the Siamese just as if they belonged to the nation. The government of Siam has great love and respect for them.[7]

Nevertheless, although clearly he liked some of them, he appears not to have had too high an opinion of the majority. In a letter written to an American acquaintance while he was still Abbot he stated his view that many of the missionaries had come to Siam because they could find no religious employment at home, but were able to make a living by collecting funds from "gentle and induligent pious people" who were "glad to pay for spreaching of their most respected religion to other countries which they think very benighted." [8] Particularly he felt that a special effort, which he clearly resented, was being made to convert him on the theory that as he was a high prelate, as well as royalty, his conversion would render easier the conversion of others, a policy, he pointed out, that had been followed by the missionaries in the Hawaiian Islands.

This last feeling was quite justified. In later years the missionaries published periodicals, both in Siamese and in English. In addition to news items, they often included attacks on the Buddhist religion and on the King himself: "An article . . . to expose the falsehood of Buddhism and the great excellency of the Christian religion as contrasted with it." [9] "I felt that I must deal faithfully with the King on the subject of polygamy and wrote an article for the English paper on that subject." [10] "40th number of English Recorder today. Have felt constrained by the spirit of God to bear heavily on the subject of idolatry and to lay the whole responsibility of Buddha's idolatry in Siam upon the King himself and to show that he has no excuse for refusing to retire from its support. Which if he would but have the boldness to do would lead all his princes, nobles, lords and priests off with him." [11] These are typical entries in Dr. Bradley's diary.

The King with characteristic tolerance would ignore these attacks or would joyfully enter into theological debate with the editors, sending them rejoinders under such signatures as "Buddhist Champion," [12] and these in turn would provoke further missionary replies: "In my English issue I published my concluding articles in answer to the King's objections to the Bible." [13] "Received another paper from King in reply to my last article in the Recorder on his puerile effort to upset the Bible." [14]

Not all the articles, of course, were on religious subjects:

In the Siamese issue [of the *Recorder*] I had an occasion to write an article on the disgraceful conduct of one of the King's brothers, being requested to do so by the Deputy Mayor of the city. The Prince has become a notorious drunkard and goes about daily begging something to drink and something to eat, sometimes a little money and sometimes one thing and sometimes another. In this way he has become a public nuisance and being so high in rank no one dares to deny him, and none to report him to the King.[15]

In May, 1865, the *Bangkok Recorder* published the proposed French-Siamese treaty concerning Cambodia, signed the preceding month, together with editorial comment about the treaty and about M. Aubaret. Aubaret became furious and demanded that the King suppress the *Recorder*. The King limited his request to the editor to "suspend for the present further comments on the Consul's procedure as enough appears to have been said for the object desired." [16] Then the next day he sent a message asking the editor to keep a complete file until the end of the year and then have the volume bound for him as a book of reference—a charming method of letting him know that he had no intention of suppressing the paper.

According to Reverend Sammy Smith on a number of occasions foreigners had pleaded with Mongkut for one reason or another to muzzle the press. He resolutely refused. [17]

But the missionaries did not confine their lecturing of the King to articles in the press. These upright men were earnest and deadly serious. They did not hesitate to make frontal assaults. In their seriousness they sometimes missed the gentle teasing which their earnestness provoked. Dr. Bradley solemnly records in his diary: "Received a letter from the King inquiring about a Mormon missionary. . . . [Another missionary later wrote: "In 1854 a Mormon missionary found his way to Siam, but, meeting no encouragement, soon withdrew. The Siamese did not need any urging to the practice of polygamy."] [18] Before I opened it I supposed it very likely that it was a letter to resent a word that I sent to him a few days before declining his invitation to attend a theatrical performance of his wives. The reason I gave was, I believed it was a wicked amusement and did not like to afford him any countenance in his sin. I have

been creditably informed that my message was carried to
him just as I had dictated it. Of course I was glad to receive that he took it in good part and was not angry for
my being faithful to tell him his sins." [19] A few months later
arrived the invitation to the dinner which Mongkut gave
annually for the foreign colony on his birthday. "One remarkable clause in the invitation," noted Bradley, "was
that whosoever of the Mission feels in his heart that the
King of Siam is too great a sinner to be the recipient of the
blessing from him, let such a one stay away. So it would
seem as if the King was going to make that dinner party a
testing ceremony to see who, if any of the missionaries,
have lost their affection for him." [20] Bradley accepted
gladly. And then a few months later, we find him writing:
"We found the King seated in the Elephant's Stall [they
had been invited to see the White Elephant] amusing himself with theatrical performances adjacent thereto. . . .
He came to us and greeted us as usual with a shake of the
hand and said 'You cannot look at the play without sin,
but you may look at the elephant and not sin.' " [21]

A decade later Dr. Bradley finally sinned! He took a
Miss Atkins, newly arrived missionary, and "called upon
Mrs. Leonowens who took us into a royal theatrical performance to show Miss Atkins the heathenism of Siam.
She there had such a view of it as quite horrified her and
made her feel that it is almost a hopeless work to preach
the Gospel to such people." [22]

Early in Mongkut's reign all the European merchants
and shipmasters and missionaries were invited to a festival
at which one of the leading princes was to receive a new
name and new honors from the King. Before the conclusion
of the ceremonies the foreigners joined together in composing and signing a letter of congratulations to the Prince,

which included this happy blending of interests: "May gambling, opium smoking, spirit making and drinking, and high taxation flee from before you. And may agriculture and commerce, the arts and sciences, and the true religion ever find in you a powerful patron." [23]

Heathenism, polygamy, theatrical performances, gambling, opium smoking, drinking. But never a word about slavery! It was Mongkut—without the exhortation or encouragement of the American missionaries—who took the first small steps against slavery in Siam.

Mongkut exchanged greetings with Pope Pius IX in 1852. In 1861 he addressed a second letter to the Pope. This, together with his photograph * and a number of presents, he entrusted to the embassy that he was sending to Paris in the hope that they "would by some means or other, through the kindness and good offices of the King of France, find their way to their holy destination." [24] The salutation in this letter is interesting. It reads: "These presents from His Majesty Phra Paramendr Maha Mongkut &c &c, Phra Chom Klao, King of Siam, Lord of the Realm who, by the blessing of the Superagency of the Universe, however differently perceived and worshipped by its populations each in accordance to their own peculiar faith, upbringing and education, is made the fourth ruler in the reigning Dynasty of and maintained as well as strengthened in his peaceful and beneficent reign over the Kingdom known as Siam, bear greetings to His Holiness Santus Papa Pius IX, Holy Father of all believers in the Roman Catholic Faith, residing in the City of Rome, Italy."

In this letter Mongkut spoke of his close and affectionate friendship with Bishop Pallegoix; he recalled that nearly

* This photograph is reproduced in this book.

two centuries before the Holy Father had sent King Narai a letter of greetings "commending the Roman Catholic Faith and its believers in the Realm to His Majesty's grace and protection"; and he wrote: "Never, in the long and continuous history of Siam, had any of its kings ever constituted himself an enemy of any religious faith in this Kingdom. Although numerous other faiths were professed all at variance with Buddhism, which was for the Capital the centre of unity and the object of veneration for all its kings, all such other faiths had always been tolerated and sustained, making it possible for those who professed them to continue in their own religious practices and spread their respective gospels among the people of this country. Particularly speaking, no hostility to Christianity has ever been manifested here in this Kingdom as in the cases of the Emperor of China, the King of Annam and other heads of states. This tradition is considered to be well-founded by Siam and it breathes a spirit of happy tolerance among the people of the Kingdom. For in as much as it is difficult to foretell the shape of the life to come hereafter, it is only just to allow every person the right to seek happiness therein in his own way."

This last sentence typifies the spirit of religious tolerance which, reflecting his beliefs as a devout Buddhist, was part of Mongkut's very essence.

Even though he had been the leader of the great Buddhist reform movement and was sincerely opposed to many of what he considered to be superstitious accretions to the teachings of Gautama, he never used his position as king to discriminate in favor of his own followers or to discriminate against others.[25] There existed, however, one extraordinary and totally un-Buddhistic practice in Siam. "Now and then," Bowring wrote, "a fanatic is known to cover his body with resin and oil, and offer himself to be burnt as a living sacrifice to Buddha." [26] Mongkut's tolerance would not accept this.

"Whereas no just ruler," he proclaimed, "restricts the freedom of his people in the choice of their religious belief wherewith each man hopes to find strength and salvation in his last hour as well as in the future beyond;

"And whereas there are many precepts common to all religions, such for instances as the injunctions not to kill, nor steal, nor commit adultery, nor speak falsehood, nor partake of intoxicating liquor, and the advices to forbear anger, to be kind and truthful, to practise gratitude and generosity and to perform innumerable other merits which mankind of whatever race and language hold to be good, true and righteous;

"Wherefore, in the exercise of the said freedom of religion some persons do commit acts which are inconsistent with policy." He then listed by name some of the fanatics— a nun included—who had committed themselves to the fire. "Just rulers and wise men," he continued, "in all lands and religious faiths find in such self-destructive acts nothing but an expression of worthless credulity.[27] . . . None should be taken as meritorious under the Buddhist teaching. Search as one might in the Book of Precepts whether given by our Lord the Buddha or by His Disciples, one would never find a single passage to support the practice. True, tracts may be found in some translation of the Pali made by some careless priests referring to the gruesome sacrifices aforesaid, but upon studied examination of the difference in style one cannot but reach the inevitable conclusion that they were made by ignorant and superstitious priests to deceive ignorant and superstitious people. . . . Wherefore, the said acts are not meritorious under the

Buddhist Faith, but are inconsistent with polity, and are deplored by all religions. As such, they should never be encouraged." [28]

In the same proclamation Mongkut also stated his firm resolve "to preserve the purity of the Holy Order, so that it may continue to be a help and guidance to His people, for whom He ever wishes a long life in coolness and felicity." [29] He reduced the number of monks at some of the wats—there were, for instance, over five hundred priests established at what is now Wat Arun [30]—and he made a drive on some of the abuses which obviously he had witnessed at first hand:

Women who for a long time have been divorced from their husbands or whose husbands have long been dead, including spinsters who have never met their mates are prone to choose bachelors for their husbands. As the masses of laymen are occupied in matrimony, the only field left open for such women to exercise their energy is the monastery. The institution is a place where the priests are confined to long celibacy, thus capable of providing the ladies with brand new husbands. Even more so are the priests looked upon as a fattened hog, for indeed many of them have grown great in fame and wealth, having been promoted to the rank of Head Priest with the title of nobility, awarded their degrees and royal grants, and what with a worldly offering here in a sum of money at a public preaching and another such offering there at a cremation or official function, such a pile of feungs, salungs, taels and bahts as accumulated by them may be had for the taking after their being lured into matrimony.

That the priests are expected to fall easy victims is because they are likely to be driven crazy by their newly found love. For this reason the artful ladies would place their son in the custody of their prospective catch, or assign a grown kinsman or neighbour to wait in attendance on the priest, whereby their line of communication and intelligence being firmly established, they would feed through that channel all the toothsome tidbits and choice delicacies calculated to break down the resistance of the holy brother they intend to victimize.

The result is invariably as might be expected. For the priest, having been favoured with such kindnesses, would begin to show signs of weakness, first by getting on terms of civil intimacy with his benefactress, calling her Milady Benefactress at the House, at the Boat-House or at the Building up North or South, as the case may be. Later, having divested himself of the yellow robe, the man would be wedded to the benefactress under consideration, or to her sister or daughter as suits the convenience. Worse still, sometimes the said civil intimacy oversteps its bounds. . . .[31]

Less than three months after he became king, Mongkut asked the three Protestant missions in Bangkok "to furnish a Preceptress for the Royal females," as the *Calendar* recorded the event, "which request, duly considered in a united meeting of the resident missionaries, was granted." [32] For some reason Dr. Bradley did not inform the King until some six weeks later, when Mongkut wrote inquiring their decision. On learning that the missionaries had designated Mrs. Bradley of the American Missionary Association, Mrs. Mattoon of the Presbyterian Mission, and Mrs. Jones, who later married Reverend Sammy Smith, of the Baptist Mission and that they "would endeavour to comply with his request," he lost no time. Early next morning he sent word "that this day was a favorable one to begin the exercise of teaching a class of ladies in the royal palace and that he would like Mrs. Bradley to proceed forthwith to the palace and make a beginning. She did so." [33]

For three years these three ladies each gave two mornings a week to their task; the opportunity to proselytize seemed heaven-sent. Twenty-one [34] young wives—"pretty, bright young girls," wrote Mrs. Mattoon "worthy of a far better and happier fate than they could possibly find in the harem of any king"—and several royal sisters comprised the class. "As was expected, these royal ladies dropped away from the English class, and ere long none were left excepting a few young wives of the king who were ambitious to please His Majesty and to be able to converse with him in English. As the ladies left the English class, they wished us to visit them in their homes; which we did." [35] There the three ladies brought Christian tracts written in Siamese and discussed religion. They even discussed that fearsome topic, polygamy. According to the good Dr. Bradley, however, "the sisters were, as I have every reason to believe, sufficiently cautious how they handled that very delicate subject. It was almost always brought up by the pupils asking them questions directly on that point, inquiring, if it is right or wrong to practice polygamy." [36] One day in 1854 the teacher on going to the palace found the gate closed. The next day the next teacher found the same. The class just stopped. "It was thought," wrote Mrs. Mattoon, "that some of the ladies were becoming interested in Christianity but of this we could not be sure." [37]

Two years later a more probable reason came to light. One day Prince Krom Luang Wongsa sent for Dr. Bradley and two other missionaries so that he might convey a message to Dr. Bradley from the King, to be delivered before witnesses. "And that message was," as Dr. Bradley wrote in his diary, "to ask me if, when Mr. Harris [Townsend Harris, the American envoy] comes to negotiate a new treaty it would not be well to have an article stating that the King of Siam should hereafter be allowed to have only one wife. And another, that the wives of the missionaries should be allowed to visit the Royal Harem and teach the wives of the King that it is wicked for the King to live with more than one wife and hence they must leave him. The Prince wished to know what reply I would make to this message. I promptly replied that I was glad to perceive that his Majesty had some conscience of wrong doing, that he could not let the subject of his polygamy rest, that I had feared he would become calloused to that sinful practice. 'Don't,' said his Highness, 'send him such a reply for it would make the matter worse. Sir John Bowring has told him that polygamy does not particularly affect his reputation in the estimation of European nations as they well know that it has been an immemorable practice with oriental Kings to have many wives.' " Dr. Bradley concluded in his own mind that the three missionary wives must have produced some commotion in the Royal Harem "in regard to the Marriage State," and he thought it even possible that it was because of their work that the King had recently issued his proclamation giving "all discontented royal concubines an honorable discharge from the royal family." [38] Whatever the cause of their ending, the classes were never resumed.

Mongkut had encountered western ideas only when he was already adult, and they reached him by haphazard contacts. He now decided to wait until the first of his children were old enough and then arrange that they—chiefly Prince Chulalongkorn—should meet western ideas while still young and that these should come to them in organized form. Accordingly, some years later, in 1862, he sought an English governness with—mindful of his previous experience with the three missionary wives—the strict proviso that Christianity should have no place in her teaching.

Typically, he dealt with the subject as a business matter

in the middle of a business letter to the Manager of the Borneo Company in Singapore:

I . . . am glad to learn that the small cannon . . . was alreadily ordered through your agent of London. I hope it will be sent down here & reach my hand as soon as about middle time of present year.

I was informed that a breach loading brass cannon . . . brought to Sarawak by the Rajah Sir James Brooke for his own use . . . was deposed for sale, is this information True? . . . How much price required for same?

There is a necessity for cough lozences moreover than an only one bottle you have had sent me lately. There are many here who required me for their good remedy. Can you obtain half dozen or 6 bottles thereof? . . . I wish but those which are genuine.

My faithful agent Mr. Tan Kim Ching has told me in his letter to me that you & your lady has introduced Ms. Leonowens to him with an application that she will be English School Mastress here under the salary of $150 per month & her residence shall be near of Protestant Missionary here. For this we were hesitating on the subject considering that our English school will be just established & may be very small so the required salary seemed to be higher than what we proposed although proper because every thing here cheaper than at Singapore, also we wish the School Mastress to be with us in this palace or nearest vicinity hereof to save us from trouble of conveying such the Lady to & fro almost every day also it is not pleasant to us if the School Mastress much morely endeavoured to convert the schoolars to Christianity than teaching language literature &c &c like American Missionaries here because our proposed expense is for knowledge of the important language & literature which will be useful for affairs of country not for the religion which is yet disbelieved by Siamese schoolars in general sense.

But now we have learnt that the said Lady agree to receive

an only salary of $100 per month & accept to live in this palace
or nearest place hereof, I am very glad to have her be our School
Mastress if the said information be true. I can give her a brick
house in nearest vicinity of this palace if she would decide to
live with her husband or maidservant, and I will be glad if she
would make written best arrangement with my faithful agent
Mr. Tan Kim Ching before she would come up here.

When the said Lady came here & on being the Mastress of
our English School would do good & be so active as her schoolars
might become in facility of language literature quickly & the
study of School might so increasing as I would see her labour
heavier than what we expected, myself will reward her some
time or add her salary in suitable portion.

My friend Sir John Bowring . . . has requested me to send
some things which may be remarkable product or industries of
Siam . . . to be exhibited on May next. . . . I . . . do not
know how much price for freight &c of what weight or extension
of article. Can you tell me about this purpose? [39]

"Mem" Leonowens came to the Court of the King of
Siam, where she served for five years as teacher and as a
foreign-language secretary to the King.

10

"Thus Have I Followed the Teaching of Buddha"

OF all the sciences, astronomy appealed most to Mongkut. He loved to compute eclipses, and while still in the monastery he published calculations of the eclipses of 1850 so that his foreign friends "may know that he can project and calculate eclipses of the sun and moon, occultations of planets, and some fixed stars of first and second magnitude, of which the immersion in and emersion from the limb of the illuminated moon can be seen by the naked eye, for every place of which the longitude and latitude are certainly known by him." [1]

This interest in astronomy continued all his life. When Sir John Bowring was received by the King in 1855, Mongkut inquired about the discovery of the planet Neptune. He also demonstrated his knowledge of English by pointing out correctly, "You have two terms,—one, the vulgar—leap-year, and another, the classical—bissextile,—when February has twenty-nine days." [2] A few years later he was writing Schomburgk, the British consul: "There is our necessity of a tract entitled Chronometer Companion, in which there are many tables for the purpose of observation of heavenly bodies in taking latitude &c. Can you obtain one of such the tract newly edited from the Admiralty? . . . I am very glad," he added concerning a trip to the north planned by Schomburgk, "that you will take useful observation and survey of a part of our country, in which accurate surveyance has not been done by any one before." [3] Wistfully he indicated that he wished he could take time off to make such a journey and carry out the "observation and surveyance myself. On this occasion I will wait on you to have some truly observed and surveyed map." Then turning to another area he asked the Consul's assistance: "I have not yet possessed a small chart of Gulf of Siam which was surveyed by Captain John Richard R.N. master commander of Her Britannic Majesty's Surveying Schooner 'Saracen,' though I have received a small tract from the Hydrographick office through you lately, it was only the tract without accompanied map or chart."

But the peak of astronomical interest was always the total eclipse of the sun, and on August 18, 1868, there was to be a total eclipse whose path would cross southern Siam. Mongkut made his own calculations although he admitted that his "knowledge of algebra, etc. is not sufficient for accurate calculation." He could determine, however, that the maximum duration "will be fallen at about the middle of the Gulf of Siam, . . . where there is no land, to be standing steadily and see" although this would be only two or three seconds longer than at Bangkok. "But to point directly the place of most durable point of land," he confessed, "my knowledge is not sufficient." [4] It was generally agreed, however, that the best point of observation on land would be a promontory known as Hua Wan, just north of a long white beach at Sam Roi Yot, a lonely spot on the Gulf close to the present Malayan border.

Mongkut invited a French astronomical mission headed by M. Stephan, the young director of the Marseille Observatory, to witness the eclipse. He issued proclamations concerning the forthcoming event. The astrologers were convinced he was wrong. The lay public was willing to accept the King's judgment, but they were deeply stirred, believing that the phenomenon must portend some national disaster. Mongkut issued more proclamations in which he criticized the astrologers and tried to calm the people by scientific reasonings.[5]

At the appropriate time the King sailed for Sam Roi Yot with a small fleet of steamers. He was accompanied by Chulalongkorn and other princes, by a large retinue including the unbelieving astrologers, by as many foreigners in Bangkok as were able to accept the invitation to be his guests ["but he seems not to have left any one in charge of seeing that they get berths," complained Dr. Bradley [6]], by the French astronomical mission, and, to maintain as always a suitable diplomatic balance, by Governor Ord of the Straits Settlements and his wife. A herd of fifty elephants had been brought overland from Ayuthia, as well as horses and cattle. Nearly a thousand people were housed along the beach. The telescopes were installed on Hua Wan.

The whole occasion was a gala affair. There were numerous entertainments. Dr. Bradley conducted religious services. "The King and his nobles broke through the trammels of Siamese etiquette for the purpose of doing honor to their guests," wrote one of Governor Ord's suite in the Bangkok *Calendar*. "On no previous occasion had the Court been so completely revolutionized; the royal apartments were thrown open, and the ladies of the household brought prominently forward, whilst the younger members of the royal family were allowed to mix with their English visitors in the most friendly and sociable manner." [7]

At last the great day arrived, and a wet monsoon was blowing. The sun was invisible. And then twenty minutes before totality the sky began to clear, and ten minutes later the sun burst through a great opening in the clouds. The totality in all its glory was seen under perfect conditions. The Prime Minister was so excited that he "left his long telescope swinging on its axis and walked into the pavilion and addressed several of his wives, saying 'Will you now believe the foreigners?' " [8]—by which one must assume, since clearly he would not be guilty of *lèse-majesté,* that he meant foreign science. The King, of course, was in excellent humor. The eclipse had taken place as he had predicted, and not only were his calculations proved correct, but it was currently reported "that he was more correct in his calculations about the eclipse than the French astronomers by 2 seconds." [9]

But if the King was right, so also were the people.

Although the party left as soon as the eclipse was over, malaria struck deeply among those who had attended. Chulalongkorn and a number of the princes were taken ill; eight of the ten French scientists contracted the disease; the ships' crews suffered heavily; and hundreds of laborers who had prepared the camp were stricken. Shortly after he reached Bangkok, Mongkut himself developed chills and fever and had to forego giving his daily official audiences.

Instead of getting better, however, his condition grew steadily worse. Chao Phraya Mahindr, faithful attendant on the King, recorded in his diary the poignant details of King Mongkut's last illness and death.

Tuesday, the 6th of the Waxing Moon of the 11th Month [September 22, 1868].

The King sent for his brothers Prince Krom Luang Wongsa and Prince Krom Luang Devesr, together with Chao Phraya Sri Suriyawongse, Minister for Military Administration. When all of them were present in the royal bedchamber, the King entrusted to them the care of the State and enjoined them to consult with each other in matters concerning the welfare of the people, and that the trials of cases in the law courts must not be delayed but must be attended to with the usual prompt despatch.

Thursday, the 8th of the Waxing Moon of the 11th Month.

The King wrote a letter and told his daughter, the Princess Somavati, to take it to the council of princes and ministers. The Princess took the letter to the Ananta Smagom Hall where it was read in council. The letter ran as follows: "It is the King's wish that the person who shall succeed him to the throne, be he a royal brother, a royal son, or a royal nephew, shall do so only with the full approval of the ennobled princes and ministers of state in council. The princes and ministers shall place their choice upon a prince, endowed with the most ability and wisdom, who is best qualified to preserve and further the peace and welfare of the Kingdom." [10]

On September 27, three days after he had written the Council:

The King saw Phraya Purus and told him that since his illness seemed to be beyond the power of the court doctors to remedy, he felt that if any harm should come to him, those who were faithful to him might be aggrieved by the fact that they had been given no opportunity to serve him in his hours of need to

the best of their abilities. The King therefore gave leave to all
to administer to him whatever remedies they thought best. . . .
The Chief of His Majesty's Inner Treasury obtained leave to
administer to the King a remedy of his own concoction, consisting of the bulb of the Zingiberaceae [root of ginger] and some
salt mixed together according to a magic formula. The King
showed no sign of improvement after he had taken the remedy.
Although His Majesty became resigned after this episode, he
tried very hard to partake the foods that were offered him. . . .

At about 7 o'clock in the evening, His Majesty called Phraya
Purus to his bedside and said: "Although you and I are not
related by blood, I have brought you up from childhood and I
feel towards you as though you were my own son. You have
not been conducting yourself well in the past and have thereby
given to your betters and elders a cause for taking an objection
to yourself. After I am gone, you will not be able to look after
yourself if you do not change your behaviour. In whatever you
do you should first pay attention to the views of your elders and
betters. Be not proud of the fact that you are a rich man. I am
reproving you now like my mother used to reprove me and my
younger brother. I can still recall the remark she made to me
that rich children owed their wealth to the labours of their
parents. Take good care of yourself after I am gone. . . . When
you returned from London," the King went on, "you brought
back a sword which you gave to me as a present. I want to return this sword to you, so that you may keep it ready to be
presented to the prince who shall come to the throne after me,
thereby you may hope to gain his favour and protection."

Two more days elapsed. The King then sent Phraya
Purus to Chao Phraya Sri Suriyawongse.

"Give him my compliments and tell him that since I have many
young children, like a tree that has many, many roots in the
ground, and since Chao Phraya Sri Suriyawongse has always been
a benefactor to me it is my wish that he continue to be a bene-

factor to my children and see that no harm should befall them. . . ."

When Chao Phraya Sri Suriyawongse heard the King's message, he consulted with Prince Krom Luang Wongsa, and between them they decided that, for the peace of his mind, the King must be told the measures taken at this critical time for the personal safety of His Majesty and the Heir to the Thone, Prince Chulalongkorn, who was also seriously ill. Phraya Purus was requested to inform His Majesty that for the purpose mentioned extra guards had been posted at the Grand Palace and at Suan Kularb Palace, where Prince Chulalongkorn was lying.

After Phraya Purus had returned, . . . His Majesty seemed to have more strength and to be more lively. He said, "Dear little Soma, give your father a drink of water." After taking the drink of water the King was silent and pensive for a while. Then he said to Phraya Purus: "Go back to Chao Phraya Sri Suriyawongse and tell him that I do not wish my son to become King, because he is too young and inexperienced. He is not old enough to bear the whole burden and it may be harmful to him. [Prince Chulalongkorn was just fifteen years old at the time.] Will you go and tell him now?"

When Phraya Purus returned "the King asked what Chao Phraya Sri Suriyawongse had said to his second message. Phraya Purus replied that the Minister said nothing but only heaved a deep sigh."

On the following morning:

His Majesty sent Phraya Purus to bring Phraya Sri Suriyawongse into his presence. When the latter had arrived, the King told him to sit on his bed and asked, "How is Chulalongkorn?" Phraya Suriyawongse replied, "He is much better, Sire." The King then said to him: "You have been of great service to the State but you have not been sufficiently rewarded for your merit. I have, therefore, ordered them to take you a sword, as a personal reward from me. Have you received it?" When Phraya Suriya-

wongse replied in the negative, the King said, "Little Soma, go
and order the Treasury official to take the sword to Phraya
Suriyawongse." The King then turned to Phraya Suriyawongse
and asked, "How are they carrying on with the official business?"
Phraya Suriyawongse replied, "Now that Your Majesty is in a
critical condition, my father has consulted with the members of
the royal family and the high officers of the Realm, and they are
all of one opinion that, should anything happen to Your Majesty,
Prince Chulalongkorn is the only royal personage fit to succeed
to Your Majesty on the throne. In accordance with this con-
sensus of opinion therefore, my father has issued orders for
extra guards to be posted at Suan Kularb Palace in case of
emergency." The King said, "No, my son is too young, with
not enough experience to enable him to perform his duties. How
can he become King? There are other princes," the King continued, "who have experience and wisdom, and it is for you to
choose one of them. My son is so young it is not fair to place
him thus in the way of danger!"

To this Phraya Suriyawongse replied: "It is our opinion, Sire,
that if Prince Chulalongkorn is not elevated to the throne a
secure and stable future for this Kingdom cannot be ensured.
His Royal Highness is already recognized as your rightful heir
in all foreign countries, as evidenced by the royal letter of felici-
tation and royal gifts sent to him by the Emperor of France.
It is our belief that no other successor to the throne except His
Royal Highness will be recognized in Europe. We therefore think
that, for the security of the State and for the peace and prosperity of the people, Prince Chulalongkorn should be proclaimed
King after your demise." The King was silent for a while, then
said: "Let it be as you wish."

After a short pause the King went on to say to Phraya Suriyawongse, "I can still recall the events that took place before the
death of King Phra Nang Klao. Your grandfather was still alive
then, but the King did not call your grandfather to his deathbed
to give his final instructions regarding affairs of state, he gave

those instructions to your father instead. I will now do what the late King has done; I will not give your father my last instructions but will give them to you. Should you find any difficulty in carrying them out, you may consult with your father. Since my son, Chulalongkorn, is also your son-in-law, I will leave him under your care. I am pleased that you have all agreed to offer him the crown, but you must all take care that there should be no political disturbance or assassination at the change of reign, as there has often been in the past. To allow such things to happen would incur a great loss of national prestige."

That evening:

His Majesty had the chest containing royal regalia brought to him. He took from the chest a diamond ring and a golden rosary that used to belong to the first King of the Dynasty. These he sent to Chao Phraya Sri Suriyawongse by Princess Somavati, to be forwarded to Prince Chulalongkorn at Suan Kularb Palace. The King then made various gifts to his secretary, Phraya Sri Sunthornvoharn, and to his brothers, the Princes Mahamala and Vorachakr.* To each of his children who has not yet built a home of his own, he gave 30 catties of money for the purpose.

On Thursday, October 1, 1868, the fifteenth of the waxing moon of the eleventh month:

At 8 o'clock in the morning the King said to Phraya Purus: "The fateful day has come; do not leave my bedside to-day. . . . I have known for a long time that death will come to me to-day." . . . Phraya Purus did not take His Majesty's words

* Prince Mahamala was founder of the Malakul family. He was the great-grandfather of M. L. Peekdhip Malakul, Royal Thai Ambassador at London. See Preface, page xii. Prince Vorachakr was founder of the Pramoj family. He was the grandfather of M. R. Seni Pramoj and M. R. Kukrit Pramoj, to whom this book is dedicated.

seriously, for the King's condition appeared to be normal and there was no outward sign of its taking a turn for the worse.

At 9 o'clock in the morning, the King saw Phraya Rajkosha, the Master of the Robes, and gave him final instructions as to how his body should be dressed after death. The King was very particular that only the gold and jewel ornaments belonging to him personally should be used. On no account must the jewels belonging to the Crown be taken for the purpose. It was one of His Majesty's wishes that his cremation ceremony should be performed with strict economy.

At 11 o'clock in the morning, the King sent for his brother Prince Krom Luang Wongsa, Chao Phraya Sri Suriyawongse, Minister for Military Administration, and Chao Phraya Bhudarabhaya, Minister for Civil Administration. The three personages arrived at about midday. When the King saw them, he called each one of them by name and invited them to sit close to his bed. He asked them to give him their hands and in turn took each man's hand into his own and pressed it. He then said: "The moon will be full to-night. To-day being my birthday,* I feel sure that the end of my life has come. You and I, dear friends, have laboured together in perfect harmony for the welfare of this country. Now it is time for us to part. I will take leave of you. I leave my children under your care. Protect them from harm." When the three men heard this, they broke down and wept. The King said softly to them: "Do not cry, my friends. Death is not after all very strange. Sooner or later it must come to each one of us. Since it is now my turn to go first, I have called you in to say farewell." . . . The King took a long look at the faces of his brother and the two ministers and said: "I would like to speak to you on official business, but I have not yet made a vow to keep the Five Precepts. He then raised his hands

---

* He was born October 17, 1807, but that was the full moon of the eleventh month according to the old calendar.[11]

in the attitude of prayer and recited aloud the three stanzas in veneration of the Buddha, after which he made a vow to keep the Five Precepts. When he had finished, His Majesty spoke long sentences in the English language. He later said in Siamese: "I spoke in English because I want you to realize that I am still in full possession of my senses. If I can still converse in a foreign tongue, I must be capable of talking business with you. You and I have helped each other for a long time in our work for the welfare of the people in this country. I have always been happy with you up to this very day when my life will end. When I am no more, please go on with our good work in the interest of the people. Be just to them, and see that they are happy and contented. First and foremost, you must see that their petitions are received and attended to in the same manner as I have always done. Moreover, you must be unanimous in your choice of the next sovereign. Use your own judgment as regards his wisdom and ability; make your choice according to your conscience and with a view to the furthering of the welfare of the people. . . .

Past 5 o'clock in the afternoon. The King said to Phraya Purus: "Go and bring grandpa Fak [Phraya Sri Sunthornvoharn] here. Tell him to bring his abominable notebook and pencil, but make him wait until I feel a little better." His Majesty then turned to Luang Rajo, the court masseur, and said, "Doctor, I still have some work to do; would you kindly massage me a little to relieve the pains in my chest and abdomen?" At this request, Luang Rajo began to massage His Majesty until his pains were relieved, and the King was told that the King's secretary was awaiting his pleasure. The King told Phraya Sri Sunthornvoharn to come in and began to talk to him in the Pali language for a long time. After this the King asked Sri Sunthornvoharn whether he could find any grammatical error in his Pali speech. When the secretary replied in the negative the King told him to take down his last message to the Holy Brotherhood in Pali. . . . When it had been fully taken down, the King told Phraya Sri Sunthornvoharn to take it to Wat Raja-pradish temple and read it to the full congregation of the Holy Brothers there.

That evening at nine o'clock King Mongkut died.

This is the King's farewell testament of faith addressed to the Buddhist Brotherhood:

May My Lords of the Holy Brotherhood pay attention to the fact that while I was in Holy Order I was wont to say that, since I was born on the Day of Great Dedication, if I should be near-ing the time of my death and should my illness show signs of increasing graveness on the Day of Great Dedication, would some Holy Brothers and novices help to carry my person into the presence of the Assembly of the Holy Brothers, gathered for the Dedication Ceremony in the Uposatha Assembly Hall? With whatever strength that might be left in my body at the time, I would thrice dedicate myself to the Holy Order and then would meet my death in the presence of the Holy Brother-hood. Such action, were I in the position to carry it out, would be a good action. That action, if performed by me, would be appropriately performed. Such words did I oft say while I was a mendicant priest.

Now that I have become a layman, what can I do? For this reason have I sent tokens of veneration to the Vihara, to be humbly placed before the Holy Brothers in congregation for the Dedication Ceremony and before the Dharma. These tokens shall represent myself.

This Day of Great Dedication having fallen upon a Thursday, the same as on the day I was born, and my illness being ex-tremely grave, I fear that my time will at last come upon me to-day. I beg to take leave of My Lords of the Holy Brotherhood. I lift up my hands in veneration of the Illustrious One, Who has attained the Perfect Wisdom, even though He has long reached Nirvana. I lift up my heart in worship of the Law. I bow before the True Disciples of the Lord Buddha. I have reached my refuge in the Triple Gems.

For whatever offenses committed by me, who have erred, who have been ignorant and who have been unwise in various ways, I beg to admit their causes to the lack of diligence on my part. For the future composure of their minds, may the Holy Brothers accept my past offenses as a warning unto themselves.

At the present moment my mind is firmly resolved in the Five Precepts. I am attentive to the following Truth, that the five Constituent Elements of Being, the six Internal Means of Communication, the six External Means of Communication, the six forms of Consciousness, the six senses and the six sensations through the six channels are merely illusory. Hence no man can, without offense, hold as reality any worldly thing. I believe that all worldly manifestations are impermanent and that all worldly sensations and perceptions are not identifiable to self, being variable according to circumstances. That is to say, such things as we deem ours are not ours, and such beings as we deem us are not ourselves. The death of all beings is not to be wondered at, since death is natural to all things.

I beg of My Lords to dwell always in diligence. I beg to take leave of you. I salute you. As a favour unto me, I beg of My Lords to bear patience with me in my past offenses.

Even though my body is suffering, my mind is at rest.

Thus have I followed the Teaching of Buddha.[12]

APPENDIXES

I

Exchanges of Presents

THE exchange of gifts between heads of states is one of the oldest conventions of diplomacy—one that has largely disappeared in this egalitarian age.

Readers may be interested to know what gifts, a century ago, it was thought suitable that the President of the United States should present to the King of Siam, what King Mongkut forwarded to Washington in return, what presents Queen Victoria sent to the King, and what gifts King Mongkut had his embassy take to London to be offered to the royal ruler of Great Britain, the most powerful kingdom in the world.

Below is a list of the gifts presented on behalf of President Pierce to the Major King of Siam by Townsend Harris in 1856:

Two splendid mirrors very thick plates measuring 80 inches by 56 inches, with frames finely carved out of solid wood and richly gilt.

Two Superior Solar Chandeliers each 8 lights ormolu gildings, after the premium models of the World's exhibition in 1851. Thirty six cut Glass globes for the same   Thirty six plain glass chimneys   Seventy two dozen of Lampwicks.

One Compound Achromatic Microscope of the most approved form for the magnifying of minute objects, with 3 eyepieces of different powers   Four sets of achromatic object glasses of different focuses, double mirror moveable stage, diagonal eyepiece, Condensor, dissecting intruments, box of objects, and Camera Lucida, by which an accurate drawing of any object viewed in the Microscope may be taken.

One Solar Microscope, by which a magnified image of any object is represented on a white wall or screen, has 3 rack adjustments, 3 inch condensing lens, 3 object glasses of different magnifying powers and 3 objects finely prepared.

A small box containing twelve finely prepared objects for the Solar Microscope.

One Small Box containing twelve finely prepared objects for the compound achromatic Microscope   A book descriptive of the objects most interesting for the Microscope, with many plates.

One Sharps Patent primer rifle octagon Barrel, globe sight, number 32 guage and german Silver mounted.
Two lb of Sharp's primers.
One hundred cartridges.

One rich engraved, extrafine, finished, richly gilt ivory handled Colts   5 inch Pistol, in rich brass bound rosewood case, velvet lined with fine extra plated flasks, moulds, wrench key &c. best percussion caps, powder, balls, &c &c complete.

One Portrait life size of Gen[l] Washington.

One Portrait life size of Gen[l] Pierce.

One Republican Court or society in the days of Gen[l] Washington illustrated and splendidly bound, scarlet, turkey morocco, full gilt.

One American Scenery, or Principal Views in the United States, with full description, bound in antique morocco.

One illustrated description of the works of art, &c., exhibited at the New York Exhibition, bound Turkey morocco, gilt.—

One Iconographic Encyclopoedia, or The Arts and Sciences Fully Described and splendidly Illustrated, bound Turkey morocco, gilt.

One Webster's American Dictionary, unabridged, bound in Scarlet, Turkey, morocco, full gilt and lett[d] "Presented to his Majesty the King of Siam by Franklin Pierce, President of the United States of America."

1 Coloured view of the city of Washington
1   do   do   "   "   New Orleans
1 Coloured view of the city of New York from St. Pauls Church
1   do   do   do   do   do   from the Bay
1   do   do   do   do   Boston
1   "   "   "   "   Senate Chamber at Washington
1   "   "   "   "   Philadelphia
1   "   "   "   "   West Point
1   "   "   "   Crystal Palace New York
1 tinted   "   "   city of New Orleans,
1 view of an express railway train.

One map of the United States from Atlantic to Pacific Oceans, on rollers.[1]

The gifts to the Second King were very similar, but a little less in quantity. There was one oval mirror instead of two rectangular mirrors. There were no chandeliers. There were only six colored prints instead of eleven. Electrical apparatus was substituted for the microscopes. The other items were the same on both lists.[2]

These gifts for the Kings of Siam were shipped from the United States on the United States steam frigate "San Jacinto" which was to pick up Townsend Harris, the American envoy, at Penang (he went by way of Europe), take him to Bangkok and afterwards to Japan. The "San Jacinto" stopped first at Madeira and then Ascension. On leaving Ascension instead of steaming to the Cape of Good Hope, which would have taken about eighteen days, it was decided to sail, a procedure that took one month and ended with all hands on water allowance. Surgeon to the Fleet William Maxwell Wood in his delightful book *Fankwei, or The San Jacinto in the Seas of India, China and Japan* wrote of this period in the South Atlantic: "Here we lay upon its bosom in a calm—the winds lulled, the engines and the engineers rusting, the occupation of coal-heavers and firemen gone. We pity Mr. Marcy [the Secretary of State], if he wants that treaty with Siam made. We pity the King of Siam for the delay in receiving all these magnificent mirrors, these chandeliers, and other presents of our liberal minded Uncle. We pity Mr. Harris, who is delayed in making that treaty, and may be cut out by some swifter keeled nation. We mourn for Manifest Destiny, which is so long delayed in its diplomatic entrance to Siam. We mourn for those who are awaiting our relief in the China seas, but, most of all, we mourn for our pent up selves, and grieve that we are not rich enough to refund to the national treasury the cost of the coal which would take us to the Cape of Good Hope." [3]

What with more sailing and more pleasant stops—Simons Bay twenty-four miles from Capetown, Port Louis in Mauritius, Galle in Ceylon—149 days had elapsed from the time the "San Jacinto" left the United States until it dropped anchor at Penang. "Two ordinary merchant ships that left the United States after the *San Jacinto,*" wrote Harris, "both arrived out before her—one in 87 days, and the other 94 days. Our men-of-war never hurry." [4]

When the presents were unpacked at Bangkok, the only damage found was to "one book, which was injured by a nail which had been carelessly driven into the box." [5] Harris had been concerned for the mirrors; "I had feared," he noted in his diary, "that the concussion of the ship's guns firing salutes might have broken the plate (as is often the case), but all was safe. Indeed, I owe this probably to the kindness of Commodore Armstrong, who gave orders that no *shotted* guns should be fired for exercise while the mirrors were on board, although the standing orders of the Navy Department require that the men shall be exercised at target firing as often as (I think) once a month." [6]

After he left Siam Harris reported to the Secretary of State: "I was informed that both the kings had large quantities of ornamental but useless articles; and I was much gratified in hearing the praise bestowed on the presents by both Kings, not only for their intrinsic merits but from the fact that they were *not useless toys*. . . . I hoped to be able to select some articles from the great exhibition in Paris, but I found that the English had selected everything I should have selected for their presents to the Kings of Siam." [7]

Below are listed the gifts which King Mongkut in return forwarded, in 1856, for President Pierce. President Buchanan was in office when they reached Washington. For some years they were exhibited in the National Institute in

the old Patent Office, Washington; then they were transferred to the Smithsonian Institution, where a number of
them are still kept on public display. The words printed below in *italics* were filled in by the King in his own handwriting in the original list in English which accompanied
the presents.

1. A Royal portrait or likeness of His Majesty Somdetch Phra
   Paramendr Maha Mongkut the first King of Siamese
   Kingdom and His Majesty's queen consort Her Royal
   Highness the Princess Rambery Bhamarabhiramy made
   in daguerreotype.*
2. The sword or dagger (made of mixed steels of different
   color) with its case of Kuw wood mounted on silver
   richly gilt.
3. A finest Kris made of mixture of steels of different colours,
   with its case and handle made of Kuw wood ornamented
   with gold.
4. A Siamese spear in bamboo-cane ornamented with gold.
5. Two pairs of spears, one pair of which were mounted with
   gold, and the other with silver.
6. A Siamese hair-cutting scissors diversified and bottomed
   with gold.
7. The pipe of finest Rajwang bamboo headed and bottomed
   with enamelled gold together [with] a beautiful tobacco-
   box of solid gold finely enamelled.
8. A snuff box of solid gold, beautifully enamelled, contained
   a small little finger ring made in Siamese ornaments manner decked with *cat eyes* that were production of Siam.
9. An enamelled golden pocket Inkstand with the golden pen
   pointed with platina manufactured in Siam.
10. Five kinds of silver articles engraved and coloured with
    metallic black color and richly gilt diversifiedly manu-
    factured by Siamese Goldsmiths,—namely a water pot,

* Reproduced in this book.

a vessel with its standing vase, a cigar case, a cigar box, and their plate connected with stand.

11. A pair of Japanese vases, embroiled with cut or engraved mother of pearl shells, smoothly made by Siamese manufacturers.
12. A great Siamese drum or tom-tom peaked with silver peaks.
13. A set of a pair of long drums and flageolets.
14. Two pieces of *gilt silk* cloth.
15. Two pieces of Poom cloth of first quality, and two of second quality.[8]

Harry Smith Parkes (afterwards Sir Harry Smith Parkes, K.C.B., K.C.M.G., one of the most distinguished of British diplomats in China and Japan) served as Bowring's private assistant during the negotiation of the treaty of 1855. Following the signing of the treaty he was charged with taking it to London for ratification. While he was in England, one of the duties assigned to him by the Foreign Office was that of advising on the purchase of suitable royal presents to be sent by Queen Victoria to this unusual King of Siam.

One of the gifts selected brought forth a panegyric from *The Times* under the caption "Splendid Present for the King of Siam." "An inkstand," read the article, "probably the most brilliant and beautiful article of the kind ever made, has been manufactured by Mr. P. G. Dodd, jeweller, of Cornhill, intended as a present from Her Majesty to the King of Siam. It is of silver, electro gilt, and, although not of very great intrinsic value, yet deserves notice as a work of art. The figures, emblematical of science, and the ornamental portions generally are executed with great taste, and if good writing could be inspired by the beauty of the vessel from which the ink is drawn the King of Siam might become the most popular author of the day." [9]

Then Parkes was directed to take the Queen's gifts with him and deliver them to the King when he presented the royal reply to Mongkut's letter and exchanged ratifications of the treaty.

Despite the necessary transshipment in Egypt all went well as far as Singapore. It had been decided, in order to give appropriate dignity and importance to the occasion, that Parkes and his bride should arrive in Siam on a British man-of-war. Accordingly the "Auckland" put into Singapore to pick them up and take them on the last leg of their journey to Bangkok. On March 3, 1856, young Parkes, just turned twenty-eight years, nine weeks married, and on his first independent mission, wrote to his brother-in-law: "At this moment I have great cause for grief. This morning (Monday) I should have put to sea in the *Auckland,* and on Saturday I shipped off my traps, public ones first, consisting of the presents for the King of Siam sent by the Queen, and private ones later in the day. A gale sprang up as the former were going off, and the boat with difficulty obtained shelter under a hill, far from the point whence she started. News of this having reached us, carts, etc., were sent to bring off the packages up to town, but through perversity or misconception of orders the boat again ventured out, and this time *filled and sank!* Picture my distress, with all my presents gone! By dint of great exertion no less than thirty-six out of forty-five packages were recovered, but with the exception of three only, the contents were completely saturated and spoiled. My masters at the Foreign Office will be ill pleased to hear of the loss of about two thousand pounds' worth of property, and my misery on the occasion is very great." [10]

There was of course nothing to do but proceed to Bang-

kok, where the King was understanding and, at least out-
wardly, "did not appear concerned about the presents, as
he said 'it was the kind will of the Queen which he valued.' " [11] Parkes, the King wrote, "repaired several articles
of the Royal presents sent to us from Her Britannic Majesty
according to his ability, and the conveniences obtainable
here, and has delivered us certain portion thereof in due
times, at the last of which times he has a sealed written
document from us in their receipt, in which we have stated
he is harmless or blameless indeed." [12] A year later, Mongkut sent his "heartful thanks sincerely" when he learned
that Queen Victoria had "given her direction to prepare
some other articles to replace those parts of Her Majesty's
last presents designed for my acceptance." [13]

The receipt which Mongkut gave Parkes is dated May 7,
1856:

Whereas Mr. Harry S. Parkes the Bearer to Our Court of Her
Britannic Majesty's Ratification of the Treaty of Friendship and
Commerce lately concluded with Us and Our Royal brother the
Second King has reported to us on his arrival at Bangkok the
accident which had befallen the presents in his charge designed
for Us by Her Britannic Majesty whereby some had been injured and others entirely lost.

We have accordingly to acknowledge the receipt from Mr.
Parkes of the following articles as described and numbered in
the List of Presents subjoined to the letter addressed to Us by
Her Britannic Majesty.

1. A silver inkstand richly gilt with figures emblematical of
   science and art.
2. Two pairs of globes 36 inches in diameter.
3. Two coloured engravings representing the Coronation of
   Her Majesty Queen Victoria.

4. A best improved revolver pistol silver mounted in a case.
5. A gold enamelled double eye-glass with watch and gold cable neck chain.
6. A camera and complete photographic apparatus.
11. A collection of ornaments in glass, china &c.

The above articles have been received by Us in good condition; and of the injured articles Mr. Parkes has also delivered to us.

7. Digby Wyatt's industrial Arts 2 volumes highly illuminated.
12. A collection of coloured diagrams illustrative of physiology, machinery, natural history, etc.
13. A complete set of charts of the Indian and China Seas, all of which have been discoloured or greatly damaged by the action of salt water.

We are informed by Mr. Parkes that by far the larger portion of the collection of philosophical apparatus, illustrative of astronomy, electricity and optics, numbered 8 in the List of Her Majesty's presents are irretrievably damaged.

We have received from him in good order a model of a steamer, a model of a Locomotive Engine and carriages, an air pump and a solar gun.

Also a polar clock, gyroscope and stereoscope, but the three latter instruments are of no avail in their present injured state.

The arithmometer and dressing case numbered 9 and 10 in the List of Her Majesty's Presents have not been delivered to Us by Mr. Parkes in consequence, as he informs Us, of their having been completely destroyed.

We do not blame Mr. H. Parkes in any term for the portions of the presents designed for Us by Her Gracious Britannic Majesty some being entirely lost some very injurious in being of no use and losing of their fine appearance, for the stated unfortunate accident is believable and heard by Us from many others, and such the unforeseen accident is in difficulty of human

power to promptly prevent; merely we are thankful to Mr.
Parkes for his great endeavour to reobtain their portion for
Us. . . .[14]

The two pairs of globes and the model locomotive and
cars are included in the exhibits permanently on display in
the National Museum, Bangkok.

Several years later, in a letter to Victoria, King Mongkut referred to these presents: "Certain part is for service to
mystercit knowledge and promotion of science, as Asmouth
and optic instruments, sample of astronomical position &c.
In certain number of those instruments, ourselves and our
native servants can examinate and understand the design
and contrivance of the invention thereof throughout, till we
could fulfill their management to produce their good effects,
but in certain number of those we and our native servants
could not understand to work well." [15] He appealed to the
British consul for help, but the latter appears to have lacked
the requisite skills and suggested the King wait for foreign
visitors who might have "intelligeable knowledge thereof.
For instance . . . the photographic cammera was to postponed very long because Siamese have no facility to work.
Afterward however we have met with a Swesdent photog-
rapher being visitor here, and the other English gentleman,
who was a person of good understanding of photographic
work introduced to us by your Majesty's Consul Sir Robert
Schomburgk, who both have given some instruction and
assistance to our native worker who become now in some
facility in the photographic work. Wherefore we on this
occasion have liberty to let our native photographers take
the likeness of ourselves, when we adorned with the watch
decked with diamonds and the double edged sword, which
were honorary royal gracious gift from your Majesty, re-

ceived by us a few years ago, and seated ourselves by the tables containing the gift silver inkstand and desk together with the revolving pistol and rifle, wholly being gracious gift from your Majesty, in a framed piece of paper, have caused another photographic likeness of our royal affectionate Queen consort to be done in another framed paper, and let the painter paint both according to their ability, and got the said two photographic portraits . . . entrusted to the care of the present [1861] Siamese Embassy in accompany here with—designed to be offered to your Majesty."

The first Siamese embassy left Bangkok in the fall of 1857 and was carried by the British steam frigate "Encounter" to Suez together with the presents which King Mongkut was sending Queen Victoria. From Suez the ambassadors, their retinue, and the presents proceeded overland to Alexandria, where they were taken aboard Her Majesty's steam despatch yacht "Caradoc." They reached Malta on October 8. There

they were saluted by Her Majesty's ship Hibernia and afterwards by Fort St. Angelo. They were received at the palace by his Excellency the Governor, Sir William Reid, and Rear Admiral Sir Montagu Stopford, with their respective staffs. Their Excellencies took up their abode at the Imperial Hotel, much, it is said, to their dissatisfaction, as they expected they would have been the guests, according to the custom of their country, of the Governor. In the evening, attended by Commander Clavering, R.N. of the Caradoc they were presented in the Governor's box at the opera, where the richness and novelty of their costume attracted much attention, and on the following morning Lieutenant-General Sir John Pennefather had the troops out in review order on the Floriana parade ground, in honour of their arrival.[16]

The English began to be curious. On October 15 *The Times* had noted briefly that the "Caradoc" was due to leave Malta for England on October 10 with the Siamese ambassadors on board.[17] On the nineteenth appeared the story of their reception in Malta. Then on October 20 *The Times* carried the following article derived obviously from someone who had been aboard the "Caradoc":

The Siamese Ambassadors:—The Ambassadors about visiting England are said to be—first and second from the first King of Siam, and the third from the second King of Siam—there being two kings, the first sending two ambassadors, the second one. The second Ambassador is the adopted son of the King; the first is the brother of the Prime Minister. Another younger brother and son are in the suite, coming here to be educated. They are Buddhists, and consequently do not eat beef or mutton, or use milk, cheese, butter, or anything produced from bulls or cows. Hog's lard is the only fat allowed to be used in cooking. For the information, however, of those who may wish to invite them in England to parties we may state that they eat freely of game, poultry, pork, and curry of the hottest at every meal. They drink moderately of brandy, wine, champagne and pale ale. They are very fond of tea which they drink at every meal, and all day long, without milk. They eat no pastry or sweets. Eight of the principal members of the embassy dine together; the others, excepting servants, have a separate table, and pay great respect and homage whenever they address one of the superior eight. They are very cleanly, and all make a point of bathing every day. Their teeth are black from the use of the betel-nut. They have all sorts of European articles for ordinary purposes. They have splendid presents aboard for Her Majesty, among them two crowns and a state saddle, enriched with diamonds, rubies and other precious stones, spears with gold heads, &c. They have also 50,000 *l* in dollars on board, besides bars of gold; so they are tolerably well provided. Their dress is very splendid—a rich tunic with a belt of gold clasped in front with a buckle ornamented with diamond and rubies; loose trousers, and small richly-ornamented skull-cap, with a spire running from the top. Their faces are perfectly Chinese, and they look amazingly like the nodding figures in the large tea-shops in England. A number have changed their gay oriental dress for slop-made paletôts and Jim Crow hats. The change is not an improvement.[18]

It was not until the evening of October 27 that the "Caradoc" arrived at Spithead "from Alexandria with the Siamese Ambassadors on board. Heavy weather, and being compelled in consequence to lay to and bear up, has been the cause of their non-arrival at the time anticipated, several days since. Their Highnesses will remain on board the Caradoc to-night, and land in the morning under Royal honours. There are three Ambassadors and 25 in suite." [19]

The Times devoted the major part of a column to the landing of the Siamese embassy.

At 9:30 A.M., the Caradoc steamed into this harbour [Portsmouth] with the Siamese standards of the First and Second Kings flying from her main and fore masts, and which were saluted by the Governor's battery *en passant*. On coming to moorings in the harbour, abreast of the dockyard, Admiral Sir George Seymour, K.C.B., the Commander-in-Chief, went off in his barge to pay his respects and offer the hospitalities of the Admiralty-house to the long-delayed voyagers, who received him with every demonstration of high reverence as the representative of the Queen, of whom they have come so far to seek an audience. Meanwhile the dockyard wharves, the ships in docks adjacent, and the ground abutting on the reception jetty became thronged with the officers of the dockyard and their friends, a large number of ladies among them, to witness the disembarcation of the illustrious strangers.

At 11 o'clock the Caradoc ranged up alongside the jetty, her progress to which point was cheered by the enlivening strains of the band on board the Diadem. Rear-Admiral-Superintendent Martin had made the best preparations that could be managed on so sudden an occasion for the landing of their Highnesses, and General Scarlett, commanding the district, had posted a detachment of the third battalion of the Scots Fusileer Guards on the spot to keep the ground. The guard of honour was furnished by the 68th Regiment, and commanded by Major Grier. On the chief Ambassador landing on the jetty he cordially shook hands with Admiral Martin, General Scarlett, Colonel Wright, deputy-assistant quartermaster-general; Captain Gordon, aide-de-camp; and Town-Major Breton, which courtesy was followed by the other Ambassadors, and the flagship Blenheim fired the usual salute. The Port Admiral's carriage was in waiting, into which the chief personages were ushered by Admiral Martin and General Scarlett, and the other members of the Siamese Commission having entered other equipages the whole were escorted to the Admiralty-house, where a superb breakfast was in waiting, to which all the captains and commanders of the fleet at Portsmouth, Admiral Martin and staff, General Scarlett and staff, and Lieutenant Clavering, commanding the Caradoc, were invited.

After the *déjeûner* the "distinguisher foreigners" were conducted over the dockyard by Admiral Martin and staff, and shown every object of interest, with most of which they exhibited and expressed unfeigned surprise. This occupied until nearly 3 o'clock, when the entire *cortége* were driven, under the conduct of Flag-Lieutenant Malcolm and other officers, to the quarters prepared for them by Her Majesty's Government at the George Hotel, within the garrison of Portsmouth. Here their appearance was greeted by a large concourse of spectators of all classes, and certainly their Excellencies would not have felt in any way flattered could they have understood the remarks made by divers of the lower class of the auditory as they alighted from their equipages. Their State costume certainly borders closely upon the theatrical pantomimic, only that it is of a richer quality in material than the usual "property" of the supernumeraries in a stage burlesque of the Christmas and Easter family; but they appear to enjoy themselves and their position, and exhibit the utmost cordiality and affability to all who tender them the like courtesies.

This evening they will amuse themselves by visiting the Portsmouth Theatre Royal and witnessing the spectacle of *The Jewess,* which is as well put upon the stage by Mr. Rutley, the lessee, as it could be at any theatre of the like dimensions. The house will no doubt be crowded by anxious sightseekers, and it is questionable whether the objects before the curtain will not eclipse in attraction the efforts of those behind it.

To-morrow the embassy will move to London by special train. Mr. Fowell, an *attaché* from the Foreign-office, has been at Portsmouth for some days past awaiting the arrival of the Caradoc, and has the charge of the mission. The treasures brought by their Excellencies as presents from the Kings of Siam for Her Majesty have been landed carefully to-day, under the superintendence of Lieutenant H. W. Hall, director of dockyard police, and stowed away in safe custody. No foreigners have ever landed at Portsmouth who have created the interest and curiosity of the Siamese, and their hotel is attended by large assemblages of gazers who look at them as they sit smoking at the open windows with eyes and impudence such as only the lower members of John Bull's family indulge in.

The chief Ambassador acknowledges to the luxury of 58 wives, and it is related of him that on going round the dockyard to-day his eye lighted on a young lady whom he would have liked to make the 59th, at the purchase-money of 3000 *l.* This was related to us by a lady to whom the eastern Mormon confessed the weakness, with whose charms he also acknowledged himself smitten.

After their siesta the whole of the illustrious chiefs walked about the town, and visited the jewelry establishment of Messrs.

E. and E. Emanuel, of High-street, and were engaged in inspecting their numerous objects of vertu and value, with which they expressed themselves much pleased, and on retiring presented cigars to Mr. Emanuel and his friends in the establishment.[20]

The ambassadors were received by Queen Victoria at Windsor Castle on Thursday, November 19. In the words of the Court Circular:

Her Majesty the Queen held this day a Court for the reception of the Ambassadors from the Kings of Siam.

The Ambassadors arrived at Windsor Castle shortly before 1 o'clock, attended by Mr. Fowle and Captain Clavering, Royal Navy. . . .

Their Excellencies were passed up the Grand Staircase and into the Guard Chamber (which were lined by the Yeomen of the Guard under the command of Captain Morton Herbert, the Exon in Waiting), and were conducted into the Tapestry-room.

Soon after 1 o'clock the Queen was conducted by the Lord Steward and the other Officers of State to the Throne-room. Her Majesty was accompanied by His Royal Highness the Prince Consort and her Royal Highness the Princess Royal, and was attended by the Dutchess of Athol and Lady Caroline Barrington, Ladies in Waiting, and the Gentlemen in Waiting.

His Royal Highness Prince Frederick William of Prussia, attended by the gentlemen of his suite, was present at the reception in the Throne-room.

The Earl of Clarendon, K.G., the Queen's principal Secretary of State for Foreign Affairs, stood in attendance near her Majesty at the audience.

The Ambassadors were conducted by Major-General the Hon. Sir Edward Cust, K.C.H., Her Majesty's Master of the Ceremonies, and Mr. Norman Macdonald, Gentleman Usher, from the Tapestry-room, through St. George's-hall and the Grand Reception-room to the door of the Throne-room, where they were received by Lord Ernest Bruce, Vice-Chamberlain, Sir

William Martins, and Sir Frederick Smith, Gentlemen Ushers, by whom their Excellencies were conducted to the Queen on the Throne.

Phya Mantri Suriywanse, one of the representatives of the First or Major King of Siam, bore autograph letters from the Kings, written in gold. The presents from the two Kings of Siam to Her Majesty the Queen were arranged on either side of the room. They comprised an Eastern crown of gold and enamel, enriched with diamonds, emeralds and rubies; a gold collar, thickly studded with rubies; a large star; a massive ring, set with diamonds and a variety of precious stones; a golden belt, enriched with rubies; a chair of State or Throne; a rare and valuable white shell, having a number of jewels inserted; a cup and saucer of agate; a State palanquin; a State saddle and bridle; a number of umbrellas covered with gold embroidery; boxes and cups of solid gold; silver salvers with gilt embossed edges; a metal drum, and a variety of other articles of rarity and curious workmanship, together with a painting of the Court of the Kings of Siam.[21]

A formal address was delivered by the ambassadors in the course of which they said that they had been directed

to convey both their Majesties' Royal letters with the accompanying presents, and lay the same at your Royal Majesty's feet, as a mark of respectful and sincere homage of both their Majesties the two Kings of Siam to your most gracious Majesty, the all-powerful and enlightened Sovereign of the united kingdom of Great Britain and Ireland, and the vast British colonies in different parts of the world, on which the sun, we know, never sets.

When the address had been concluded,

The First Ambassador then presented the autograph letters from the Kings of Siam.

Her Majesty was pleased to return a most gracious answer.

At the termination of the audience their Excellencies returned to St. George's-hall, and were afterwards ushered into the Waterloo Gallery, where luncheon was served.

That the royal Siamese gifts commanded deep interest in England is clear. Three days later *The Times* carried a more detailed description taken from the *Court Journal:*

The crown brought by the Siamese Embassy is a high conical cap of gold filigree, with bands of gold and enamel running round it, and ornamented with a few jewels. In general appearance it is not unlike the triple crown of the Pope; and, as it is intended to be worn, it is made exceedingly light. The "umbrellas" are apt to suggest very undignified notions to our minds, as presents from one Sovereign to another; but they are very different affairs from our umbrellas. Our readers must imagine a golden stick, and on it a flat shade, or umbrella, of gold tissue; above it, on the same stick, and at some distance, a smaller shade, and then again a smaller, until they taper to a point; they are all of gold tissue, and are standards emblematical of regal dignity, being as such planted before the throne at Siam. The star is more like a very small, but boldly projecting, shield, studded with beautiful jewels. A conch shell of great beauty ornamented with precious stones is among the presents. The ring is a massive hoop, set with a variety of stones all of the same size; among them is a very fine cat's eye.[22]

A few months later the Queen sent all the Siamese presents to the South Kensington Museum for public exhibition, and Lord Palmerston added a Siamese sword that had been presented to him.[23]

The complete list of royal presents sent by King Mongkut in 1857 to Queen Victoria is as follows:

1. The Royal official customary letter slightly written in Siamese characters upon a solid golden plate and wrapped

in the Royal solid gold envelope and sealed with Royal peculiar seal and enclosed in a golden case richly enamelled.

The translation of this Royal letter in English annexed or appended therewith.

This is made according to the Siamese Royal custom for very respectful compliment to the Sovereign of superior Kingdom, not to the equal or inferior always—when the superior Sovereign does not allow to be omitted.

2. Two Royal Daguerreotype portraits, one of which is a likeness of His Majesty the First King of Siam dressed in full royal robes and decorations seated on his throne of state.

The other is the Daguerreotype of His Majesty with the Royal consort and two Royal children seated in Their Majesties knees.

3. A Royal Crown beautifully enamelled and set with diamonds and rubies.

4. A Royal Ribbon with circular gold brooches richly set with rubies locked together and fixed all round with blue satin.

5. A Royal golden Ring set with nine kinds of precious stones.

6. A Royal gold tissue cloth jacket with seven gold buttons set with diamonds.

7. A Royal gold tissue net work robe.

8. A Royal Girdle or band made of gold wire finely wrought with nine massive gold ornaments richly set with precious stones, and buckle of open gold work set with diamonds, rubies and emeralds.

9. A Royal gold tissue cloth scarf for the waist as worn by Siamese usage.

10. A Royal gold tissue of net worked sash worn over the former.

11. A pair of Royal Pantaloons of varied colors of tissue cloth richly ornamented with gold enamelled devices.

12. A gold tissue wove red silk sarong worn on state occasions.

13. A piece of Indian cloth stamped with gold tissue devices, worn on state occasions.
14. A red silk cloth figured worn daily.
15. A conch shell with golden stand richly enamelled. The shell being ornamented with gold and enamel and precious stones.
16. A golden water vessel with its golden stand,—both richly enamelled.
17. A tea-pot with golden handle and ornamented, and gold-enamelled stand,—also jasper cup with gold saucer and gold enamelled tray for whole.
18. Two tea cups with covers, one of gold richly enamelled with various devices, the other of silver gilt inlaid with black metal elaborately worked.
19. A golden cigar case beautifully enamelled.
20. Two pairs of hair-cutting scissors inlaid with gold, one set in diamonds, the other in rubies together with a pair of combs in gold and enamelled and ornamented with emeralds.
21. A gold knife, fork and spoon of rich pattern and set with diamonds.
22. Two large silver stands or dishes with gilt edges and gilt tissue covers.
23. A state sword of twisted steel with gold enamelled scabbard, richly mounted with precious stones, and having a small knife of twisted steel to fit in scabbard.
24. A state gold sword of twisted steel with rich gold scabbard.
25. and 26. A pair of different shaped state spears with silver gilt sheaths.
27. A pair of state spears with hair of Thibet goats streamers.
28. A Malay creese with gold handle and pinchbeck scabbard.
29. Different kinds of state paraphernalia consisting of one sun screen, one large state umbrella, four pairs of different shaped umbrellas all made of silk and figured.
30. A Royal Sedan Chair richly gilt and ornamented.

31. A Royal metal Drum and ivory fife which precede the Royal Chair.

32. A Royal Saddle and Bridle with their attendant trappings and ornaments of gold.

33. Three drawings of Budh's image within the Royal Temple of the Palace of the First King at Bangkok.

34. Four painted plates shewing different views of the Coronation of the First King of Siam which took place on 15th May 1851.

Sixty seven of the different articles of merchandize mentioned in the tariff annexed to the Treaty and eight other articles produced in Siam. His Majesty the King of Siam has ordered a sample to be collected by the proper officers and given them to His Lordship Chau Phaya Phraklang, Siamese Minister for Foreign Affairs to forward to Her Majesty's Government as specimens of the various kinds of merchandize produced in Siam. The names and particulars of all these will appear in the letter of His Lordship Chau Phaya Phraklang to the Right Honorable the Earl of Clarendon on the occasion of the Siamese Embassy.[24]

II

The Band of the "San Jacinto"

THE band of the "San Jacinto" gave rise to a small curiosity of history. A slush fund is, as described by Wood,

the product of the sale of the grease skimmed from the water in which the crew's rations are boiled, and during a cruise it amounts to several hundred dollars. Now where rests the proprietorship of this fund? With the crew, with the officers and ship generally, or with the United States government? . . . I believe the government, for the first time, became a claimant on the fund in the following circumstances. It seems to have asserted the arbiter's right to the oyster, leaving the shell to the litigants.

"Navy Department, September 29, 1855.
"SIR:—Your letter of the 28th instant, requesting authority to ship a band, and for the purchase of musical instruments for the 'San Jacinto' has been received.

The Commandant at New York has been directed to cause a band to be enlisted.

You will direct the purchase of the musical instruments, and the payment, for the present, out of 'Contingent,' to be replaced, in time, from the 'Slush Fund.'

I am respectfully,

Your obedient servant,

J. C. DOBBIN

"COMMANDER H. H. BELL,

Commanding U.S. Steam Frigate 'San Jacinto,' New York." [1]

Aboard the "San Jacinto" there was considerable disagreement about the propriety of this use of the slush fund. Many felt it should be spent for the benefit of the crew since it was derived from food intended for their consumption. "This party admitted that a band might be a legitimate claim upon the 'Slush Fund,' provided a band was not regularly allowed by the government, because the crew had the benefit of the music. But the band being regular government allowance to a 'flagship,' to tax the 'Slush Fund' with it, this party contended, was the rich man's infringement upon Naboth's vineyard."

During Townsend Harris' stay in Siam the band became an adjunct of diplomacy. It accompanied Harris and his suite from the "San Jacinto" to Bangkok. "Our band," wrote Surgeon to the Fleet Wood, "was the first one of western music ever heard upon the Menam, and as we passed along its waters our approach was made known to the natives by the notes of the bugles and drums, sounding, besides our national airs, German waltzes, the 'Old Dog Tray,' 'Old Folks at Home,' etc. etc." [2] Nostalgically, Dr. Bradley noted, "Mr. Harris and his suite came into town about sunset. . . . They had their band with them and they played charmingly as the boat was coming up to the landing before the barracks which was prepared especially for their accommodation. Having heard nothing like it for many a year it was powerfully impressive." [3]

In Bangkok the musicians of the band and the marines of the guard were housed by the Siamese authorities in "a separate and lower building, though still elevated from the ground," from that built for Mr. Harris and his suite. "A new light mattrass, made of white muslin, with red edges, filled with a light silk cotton; a mat, mosquito curtain, and pillow, were all ready for every man." [4]

Rounds of courtesy calls were begun. When Prince Wongsa, the King's brother, who was a physician and a member of the New York Academy of Medicine, paid a return call on Mr. Harris he asked to hear the band, but he "preferred to have it up in the room where we were. The crash of 'Hail Columbia,' 'The Star Spangled Banner,' and 'Yankee Doodle,' on a base drum, drum and fife, with horns in proportion, was tremendous." [5]

A day or so later Harris and some of his suite called on the Chief Councillor, the aged uncle of both the Prime Minister and the Foreign Minister. He too asked to hear the band. After the Americans had concluded, he reciprocated by having his own band play. Then, "the band crouching on the floor before us, having finished its performance, the Somdetch waved his hand towards the apartment behind us, and immediately a large band of female musicians, concealed by a light screen, struck up their tinkling notes. The music and the airs were very harmonious to my ear," wrote Wood, "the music resembling that of a piano combined with the tinkling of bells." [6] Even Harris thought the music "from a distance sounded rather sweet and contrasted favorably with the ear-deafening noise given us by his band of male musicians." [7]

But the climax for the band—musical as well as social—

took place on May 9, at the "festival called Rak-na, or festival of opening the agricultural labors of the year." "On the King's expressing a wish for our band being sent for," Harris wrote in his diary, "this was complied with, and our band and the King's orchestra, vocal and instrumental, played together different tunes at the same time, which created a most barbaric confusion, the singing women each armed with two long flat sticks, which they struck every time together, accompanying this with some lamenting cries just the same as poor girls in New York on a wintry night produce by crying 'Hot Corn.' " [8]

III

"An account of the most lamentable illness and death of Her young and amiable Majesty,

the Queen Somanass Waddhanawathy, the lawful royal consort of His most gracious Majesty Somdetch Phra Paramender Maha Mongkut, the reigning King of Siam" [1]

THIS princess was born on the 21st of December, 1834 and was the only daughter of his royal highness Prince Laks Nanugun, who died in the beginning of June, 1835, six months after the birth of this princess. Whereupon his late gracious majesty Somdetch Phra Nang Klau C.Y.H. took great compassion on the orphan princess and took her to the grand royal palace, adopting her as his own daughter. She was placed under the care of her aunt her royal highness the princess Welasee, who also died during her niece's infancy. After this event, the late king had exceedingly great compassion on his adopted child, and made a royal mandate endowing her with all the estate and retainers of her natural father, as also with those of her royal aunt. He also conferred upon her all the honors and privileges belonging to the highest rank of royal children, and gave her the title of Phra Ong Chau Somanass Waddhanawathy. At the ceremony of cutting off her hair, she being then twelve years of age, her adopted father made a royal procession suitable to princesses of the highest royal birth, who are entitled Chau-fa, or children of royalty by a princess of royal birth. The ceremonies of the hair's cutting of their present Majesties, the first and second Kings, were also celebrated in the same manner, they both being of the highest royal birth. This princess was, therefore, respected by a great many people, both native and foreign, and by all the adjacent tributary countries during the late reign.

On the demise of His Majesty Somdetch Phra Nang Klau C.Y.H., the late King of Siam, and accession to the throne of his successor, Somdetch Phra Paramender Maha Mongkut, the reigning King, the whole council of royalty and nobility, seeing that this princess was without a protector, had great compassion on her, and unanimously proposed that she should be united by marriage and coronation to his majesty the reigning king, as his royal consort. Not a single dissenting voice was heard at this proposition, as they knew that his majesty had just retired from the priesthood, (which he had avowed for twenty-seven years) and had no lawful consort by whom he might expect an heir to future royal authority.

The ceremony of the royal nuptial and coronation took place on the 2d of January, 1852, his majesty being then forty-eight [47] and the queen sixteen [17] years of age. Since she was married and crowned in full dignity as queen-consort, she was respected both in private and in public, and was treated with the highest honor by the whole Siamese nation, and often received respectful compliments and presents from the adjacent tributary communities, and even friendship presents from certain noble persons and gentlemen of foreign countries who were formerly correspondents of his majesty, the present king, so that she was well and happy for six months, in what time she became with child in due course of nature. But alas! it was the pleasure of Superagency (God, merits and demerits, demons, etc., according to different faiths) that it should be otherwise; an unfortunate event befel her, and she became ill of a fatal disease, which at first appeared curable by all the physicians both foreign and native, they professing it to be only a natural consequence of her condition.

On the 25th of June, 1852, the disease first showed itself by great pains in the umbilical region, accompanied by vomiting; at this time the physicians then observed that the disease was in the abdomen. After the eclipse of the moon on the 1st of July, she seemed to recover her health; but alas! after forty days her former painful suffering returned, until the 18th of August, when her disease became serious.

On the 21st of August (at 1 P.M.) her majesty was safely delivered of a male royal infant. Her royal son was alive, but very feeble, crying and giving the usual signs of infantile life. A great many persons of royalty and nobility were immediately assembled with the officers of the palace, and welcomed the royal heir's arrival by birth, with the highest order of music, and other demonstrations of joy. They made its bed in the golden seat, covered with white, and surrounded with valuable royal weapons, a book, pencil; and in accordance with the ancient royal custom. Alas, the weak royal infant only lived three hours after its birth! it died at 4 P.M., on the same day, its life being but a brief one. The officers then secretly carried away the body, letting her majesty believe that it was well, and in another room, as her former sickness was still on her.

That same night her Majesty became worse, and vomited so frequently that she almost died from the attack. The Siamese official physicians tried to revive her, but they could not succeed to stop the painful vomiting even for half an hour. His Royal Highness the Prince Krom Hluang Wongsa Dhiraj Sniddh administered some homeopathic medicines, from the effect of which her majesty's frequent vomiting was relieved, and she had the happiness to have a good sleep, at four or five o'clock, A.M.

Next day, the 23rd of August, his majesty the king, and his royal highness the Prince Krom Hluang Wongsa Dhiraj Sniddh, and a great many princes and princesses, with the servants of her majesty, consulted with several Siamese physicians, and took the counsel of all who were in her service, as to placing her under the care of Dr. Bradley, one of the American physicians now in Siam, who had been called to consult with them. Dr. Bradley treated her majesty's disease according to the homeopathic mode, which has but lately been introduced into Siam by himself. His system of applying medicines is not so much believed in by the Siamese as it ought to be.

It was thought necessary to indulge her majesty a little in her desire to follow the Siamese mode of being confined. She, accordingly, lay alongside of a fire (the universal practice of Siamese females after child-birth), although Dr. Bradley, and a few believers in his system of medicine, who were present, were of a contrary opinion; and her majesty was then placed under the homeopathic mode of treatment of Dr. Bradley. Under his care, her majesty was a little relieved from her frequent attacks of squeamishness, vomiting, and fever.

She had frequent attacks of this disease for seven or eight days, until the 28th August, being the seventh day after the death of her royal son, Prince Chau-fa (an honored appellation applied to children and persons born of the king by the queen, or of any high prince by a princess of the rank of Chau-fa, or, in other words, born of parents that are both Chau-fa), when her majesty having known of the death of her royal son. Their majesties (the king and queen) then prepared valuable presents, and offered them to an assembly of Buddhist priests, and scattered balls, containing coins, to the people, in every direction, from her majesty's residence. This money was prepared, as customary on such events, for offerings at the death of her majesty's son, Prince Chau-fa.

Since the 29th and 30th of August, however, her majesty, unfortunately, became worse, and discharged from her stomach large quantities of bile, of a dark and yellowish colour, and accompanied by fever. Dr. Bradley then begged of the princes and nobles that her majesty should withdraw from the fire, and entirely follow his mode of treatment. This was complied with, and, being entirely under the care of Dr. Bradley, at length her majesty seemed slowly to recover. The vomiting was less frequent, and the fever disappeared, but she continued gradually taking less food, and thereby became very feeble and thin.

In this state her majesty continued till the 11th of September, when her feet appeared to be swollen, and other bad symptoms appeared, which much alarmed her friends and relatives. They consulted together, and resolved to try a Siamese physician. In fact, her majesty had not much belief in Dr. Bradley's system of medicine, as he was a foreigner, and she would not credit the statements of Dr. Bradley, and others that believed in homeopathy, that a few drops of spirits in a spoonful of water would cure her disease. Her majesty, therefore, tried again a Siamese physician, who administered to her medicines after the Siamese mode. But she got no better under his treatment, and even grew worse, so much so that no Siamese physician would take her case in hand. Dr. Bradley was, therefore, sent for again, who treated her after his own mode. While under the treatment of the Siamese physicians, the vomiting of black and yellow matter continued, accompanied by painful affections in her breathing, etc. These attacks occurred seven or eight times a day.

Since the return of Dr. Bradley to attend her majesty, up to the 16th of September, her majesty seemed to be a little better, as the vomiting of the black and yellow substance, supposed to be bile, became less frequent, and other bad symptoms being less than when she was under the treatment of the Siamese physicians; but alas! her majesty's weakness and refusal of sustenance yet prevailed on account of her continued vomiting. There was not a single day passed without severe vomiting, which obstinately refused to yield to any remedies. After the lapse of a few days, Dr. Bradley had not succeeded in making her vomiting less frequent, the intervals between her attacks of vomiting now became less distant, and unfavorable symptoms appeared, and her face and body presented a yellow appearance. In consequence of this she was again put under the care of official Siamese physicians; but they refused to take her in hand.

Upon this a proclamation was issued, offering a reward of many peculs of money to anyone who could restore her majesty to her former health. Since the time her majesty became worse under the hands of Dr. Bradley, her pulse became very quick and violent, and on 27th September she became delirious. On the same day a royal proclamation was issued to the people of the city, offering a reward of two peculs of money [about U.S. $4,800 at that time] to any one who could make her better. An old Siamese official physician then came to examine her majesty, and wished to try his skill, and was therefore permitted to see her. On seeing her majesty he misunderstood her complaint, and attributed her disease to mismanagement during childbirth or time of confinement, because she did not lay near the fire. From his statements, it appeared that he would cure her majesty in a short time, and got the consent of her majesty's relatives and friends, and even that of his majesty, to try his skill. But alas, two or three hours after drinking three or four spoonfuls of his aromatic medicines her majesty became so delirious that she could not speak so correctly as before, and occasionally cried out with a loud noise, and became much agitated, and continually moving to and fro.

His majesty then immediately rejected the old ignorant and covetous physician, and again called Dr. Bradley, who attended her majesty till her death, of which she appeared to be soon a victim. The doctor restored her by homeopathic medicines, but his success was only partial, and, on the 1st day of October, her majesty's eyes became strangely fixed, and she remained silent, refusing medicines and nourishment. On this day it was observed that there was an abscess which must have occurred probably (early), and had been broken by the violent agitations of her body during her illness; pus and matter, mixed with blood, found an outlet at her umbilicus; it continued to discharge freely and by degrees for days. Her majesty, by means of some remedies and applications in various ways, was restored to consciousness, although she was manifestly failing in strength, until the 6th of October.

During this interval his majesty the king and her majesty's kindred brought many gifts of yellow cloths, etc., to her, and induced her to present them as her last offering to the priesthood, and to receive the sacred instructions for her last meditation from the high priests, according to Buddhistical tenets—in which her majesty placed her faith. Her majesty then offered these cloths, etc., to many hundreds of Buddhist priests, and received their instructions and benedictions, though labouring under painful attacks of vomiting, and which caused her daily to lose her strength.

Alas, on the 6th of October, there was indubitable evidence that the abscess was also discharging its contents (internally). After this for three days her majesty sunk rapidly, and breathed her last on the 10th of October, 1852, at six o'clock P.M., greatly lamented, and bewailed by all the royal household.

Her majesty's remains were bathed and adorned with golden ornaments used for the dead according to the royal custom, in the full style and dignity of a queen, and wrapped in many folds of white cloth. Her remains were then placed in the golden urn or vessel called Phra-Kate, with a queen's crown on her head, and then covered with the cover of the golden urn. On the same night her majesty's remains were removed from the queen's residence to the "Tusita Maha Prasad," a great and richly gilded hall of the grand palace, and placed in the same apartment in which the royal remains of his late majesty laid during thirteen months, from April, 1851, to May, 1852.

Her late majesty's remains now lie there in state, surrounded with all the insignia of rank, until the burning takes place in about four or five months more, and will be attended with considerable ceremonies suitable to her late majesty's exalted rank. This event will take place about March or April proximo.

Her most amiable and youthful majesty the late Somanass Queen Waddahanawathy was the beloved and adopted royal daughter of his majesty Somdetch Phra Nang Klau, C.Y.H., the late King of Siam, since her infancy. At the thirteenth year of her age she was dignified to the highest rank of royal daughter, called Chau-fa, and became the queen consort of his present majesty Somdetch Phra Paramender Maha Mongkut Phra Chau Klau Yu Hud on the commencement of this present year, and lived happily with her much-esteemed and lawful royal husband, the King of Siam, for only seven months, from January to July, and from the 10th of August to the 10th of October, being sixty-two days and nights, her majesty was ill, making nine months and a few days that she lived as queen consort.

Her majesty's death happening in her youth and amiableness, and after such great prosperity and happiness which she enjoyed but for a short time, was much lamented and bewailed by his majesty, by the people of the city, and by foreigners of tributary countries.

After her majesty's death all the Siamese, Chinese and American physicians concluded that there was great reason to believe that the foundation of the disease which destroyed the valuable life of her majesty must have been laid some time previous to her espousal to his majesty, the present king, from her majesty's being uncommonly stout for a person of her age, and having suddenly become thin and emaciated, and being attacked at the same time with a severe fit of coughing; but the symptoms of her late majesty's disease did not show themselves till the 25th of June, as has already been stated.

As her late majesty was an orphan, and became the adopted daughter of the late king, by whom she was made to inherit the whole estates and retinues of her late royal parents and aunt, and being the only daughter, she has no half or full brothers and sisters, and has consequently no heirs. The whole of her property and large amount of money, together with her annual income or private fortune, will be placed in the royal treasury till after the funeral ceremonies are concluded. His majesty, the present king, has concluded that a portion of her late majesty's great property and money will be expended to refit the sacred places and monasteries belonging to her late royal father and aunt, and another portion will be expended in the construction of a sacred building within the new wall of this city, and will be called Somonapwihari. The remainder will be employed in the royal treasure for the use of the public.

As there are many of her late majesty's acquaintances in almost every province of Siam and the adjacent countries, and among them are even some persons of foreign countries, of China, Batavia, Maulmain, etc., who were or are the intimate friends and agents of his majesty, and became her friends for his majesty's sake, his majesty therefore commanded that an account of the illness and death of her late majesty be prepared in Siamese, to be issued by proclamation throughout the Kingdom of Siam and adjacent countries; and also to prepare an account of the same in the English language, to be printed and sent to all her English friends, so that they may know accurately about her.

Printed in lithographic press at the royal printing office, 21st December, 1852, which is the second year of the reign of his Siamese majesty Somdetch Phra Paramender Maha Mongkut.

VI

Anna as Historian

ANNA Leonowens published her two books on Siam, *The English Governess at the Siamese Court* and *The Romance of the Harem,* either stating or implying that they were true; and they were accepted at face value by most western readers who had no opportunity to know otherwise. A serious historian like Professor D. G. E. Hall has questioned the accuracy of her characterization of King Mongkut, suggesting that she used much imagination in her descriptions of his domestic life,[1] but only recently has there been any examination of her books as works of history. In his article, "King Mongkut in Perspective," Alexander B. Griswold has made some comments on Anna as a historian which seem worth reprinting here in case a reader may still have memories of a sadistic Mongkut flinging annoying wives into a dungeon, burning an unchaste concubine and her priestly lover at the stake, or seizing and burying casual strangers beneath a palace gate—and having remembered these and similar tales still have doubts of the real Mongkut:

The method she used sparingly in the first book is carried so far in the second that it gives itself away. Glancing through some earlier writer on Siam, or even on neighboring countries, she would seize on a lurid story that appealed to her; she would remove it from its context and transpose it to Bangkok in the 1860's; and then, after a moment's reflection, she would rewrite it with a wealth of circumstantial detail, and with contemporary men and women as the protagonists. King Mongkut, being the principal target of her malice, became the posthumous victim of this reckless method; I shall cite specific instances later.

Anna's two books, after having quite a success, lay unnoticed for many years. More recently they have had a series of reincarnations.

Mrs. Landon reduced them to a single volume and more coherent form (*Anna and the King of Siam,* New York, 1943). Careful readers will exonerate her from any share in the blame for giving a false picture of the King. She stresses the constructive factors more than Anna did; but her stated purpose is not to describe him objectively, it is to exhibit him through Anna's eyes without correcting the faults of Anna's vision. She refuses to vouch for the accuracy of Anna's account; it is, she says, a romance with an historical setting, *not* a history; it is "probably seventy-five per cent fact and twenty-five per cent fiction based on fact."

In the musical comedy and the film the truth loses out altogether, and King Mongkut presents the astonishing appearance of Rousseau's Noble Savage with a bow to Gilbert and Sullivan. These trifles are intended more to entertain than to instruct, but it is disconcerting to find them advertised as if they were documentaries.

Even more disconcerting is a reissue of *The Romance of the Harem* (under the title *Siamese Harem Life*) in London in 1952, illustrated with drawings that are a fantasy of every seraglio from Turkey to China, and with an introduction by Miss Freya Stark containing the following description of Anna among the Court ladies: "Harassed and indomitable, she loved the women in their royal slavery and trained a new and happier generation of children to carry light into the future: and few people can have wielded a stronger influence in that corner of Asia."

It has become almost an article of faith among westerners that every virtue the Royal Family have displayed since Anna's time stems from her tactful inculcation of Christian ideals. Yet virtue was not unknown in Siam before her arrival, and a cool assessment suggests that Anna did not loom very large in the life of King Mongkut and his children.[2]

Turning later to specific stories related by Anna, Griswold refers first to the tale of the concubine, Tuptim, who

having run off with a monk, was publicly tortured and burned at the stake with the partner of her guilt. The Siamese have always had a horror of death by fire—whether for themselves or anyone else; and even in medieval times they seldom if ever inflicted this punishment. King Mongkut, more humane than his predecessors—and more humane than many contemporary governments in the west, for that matter—did everything within reason to reduce the severity of punishments. So far from being a sadist, he hated even to sign a death-warrant for a common murderer, and whenever he had to do so he would sit up all night in an agony of mind, repeating to himself passages from the Buddhist scriptures. The alleged burning of the lady and her lover, though described as a public affair seen by the whole of Bangkok, escaped the notice of all other writers, Siamese or European. Anna herself seems to have had some qualms: "To do the King justice," she writes, "I must add here that, having been educated a priest, he had been taught to regard the crime of which they were accused as the most deadly sin that could be committed." She quotes him as saying, "Our laws are severe for such a crime."

But were they? The law provided only that an unchaste monk was to be expelled from the Order, given a beating, and made to cut grass for the Royal elephants. In an Order that numbered scores of thousands, unchaste monks were not so rare that the elephants ever lacked grass; if the punishment had been as Anna says, the gruesome blazes would have been a common sight. Or are we to believe the crime was aggravated by the fact that one of the ladies of the harem was involved? Hardly; for in such a case even the ancient law, which was no longer enforced, provided death by drowning for the lady and by impalement for the man—a cruel enough punishment, but *not* death by fire. King Mongkut allowed his wives to resign at will; and it is a matter of record that when a boatman abducted one of them he was let off with a fine amounting to about six dollars.

The fact is that Anna must have made up the whole story after finishing her first book, for it appears only in her second. She may have gotten the idea from a silly piece of doggerel quoted in a book by an Englishman * who had spent several months in Siam many years before King Mongkut came to the throne. It purports to be a translation of an old song—"a lament supposed to be uttered by a guilty priest, previous to his suffering along with the partner of his guilt the dreadful punishment attached to his transgression." The last stanza is worth repeating:

> "Behold the faggots blaze up high,
> The smoke is black and dense;
>
> The sinews burst, and crack, and fly;
> Oh suffering intense!

* None other than Neale, whose assertions about the floating houses of Bangkok so annoyed Townsend Harris and fascinated the King (pp. 53–54, 57).

The roar of fire and shriek of pain,
And the blood that boils and splashes,

These all consume—the search were vain
For the lovers' mingled ashes."

Some of her fabrications are easier to spot—as when she
tells us that King Mongkut locked up disobedient wives in a
subterranean dungeon in the Palace. Anyone who has lived in
Bangkok knows it is impossible to build any sort of under-
ground room in that watery soil.

Another episode can be brought to justice by literary detec-
tive work. Referring to a new gate built in the palace wall in
1865, Anna says that King Mongkut had some innocent pass-
ersby butchered and their corpses buried under the gate-posts
so that their restless spirits might forever haunt the place and
drive intruders away. Now it is a fact that this brutal form of
insurance had been practised in much earlier days. But it was
the sort of thing that King Mongkut, who was both humane and
rational, was utterly opposed to; no other writer accuses him
of resorting to it. There is, however, a detailed account of just
such a sacrifice in a French missionary's report for 1831—
long before King Mongkut came to the throne. Anna gives the
same details, uses the same phraseology, and carelessly leaves
a proof of her transposed plagiarism: she translates the French
word *cordes* as "cords" rather than "ropes." Obviously she had
moved the incident thirty-four years forward and accused the
wrong man.*

* After quoting the passage in Anna's book describing the event,
and the French version contained in a letter of Bishop Bruguière,
published in 1831 in a French missionary publication, Griswold
continues: "Bruguière was in Siam a rather short time (1829–
1831), and perhaps got the story from some older source; Anna
was neither the first nor the last European writer on Siam to quote
without acknowledgment large sections of earlier books. The old
stories keep cropping up again and again, and are attributed to

This is the kind of thing that makes her books so exasperating to the sober historian. Though there is much good in them, it is useless, for not a single statement can be accepted without confirmation from elsewhere. Analysis sheds a rather cruel light on her methods.[3]

---

successive reigns from the 17th century to the 20th. Not many writers are as scrupulous as Sir John Bowring and Pallegoix. Bowring, who made a quick but intelligent study of Siam in 1855, says he could find no vestige of the practice described by Bruguière: " 'It has probably fallen into desuetude,' he says. (*The Kingdom and People of Siam,* I, 140) Pallegoix says: 'Quant à moi, je me rappelle avoir lu quelque chose de semblable dans les annales de Siam; mais je ne voudrais pas affirmer le fait tel qu'il raconte.' (*Description du royume Thai ou Siam,* II, 50) He then goes on to quote Bruguière's letter in full, and it was doubtless this quotation that came to Anna's attention." [4]

SOURCE NOTES, BIBLIOGRAPHY,

AND INDEX

Source Notes

Preface

1. "Anna and Mr. Griswold," editorial, *Evening Sun*, Baltimore, Aug. 24, 1957, p. 4.

2. John Thomson, *The Straits of Malacca, Indochina and China* (London, 1875), pp. 96–97.

Chapter 1. "High Prince of the Crown"

1. Letter to "the Gentleman G. W. Eddy &c &c &c," dated at "Wat Pawarnives, Northern King Street, Bangkok, Siam," July 14, 1848, in Seni and Kukrit Pramoj, "The King of Siam Speaks" (typewritten MS [Bangkok, 1948]), pp. 12–13; quotations p. 13. Cited hereafter as Pramoj MS.

2. Pramoj MS, pp. 1–2; quotation p. 2.

3. These comments and the following description of the tonsure rites are based on G. E. Gerini, *Chulakantamangala or the Tonsure Ceremony as Performed in Siam* (Bangkok, 1893), especially pp. 2–4, 93–137, 143–145.

4. O. Frankfurter, "King Mongkut," *Jour. Siam Society*, I (1905), 192.

5. R. Lingat, "La vie religieuse du Roi Mongkut," *Jour. Siam Society*, XX (1926), 132.

Chapter 2. In the Buddhist Priesthood

1. Pramoj MS, p. 3.

2. Léon Feer, "Le bouddhisme à Siam: une soirée chez le phraklang en 1863," *Memoires de la Societé Academique Indo-Chinoise de France*, I (1877–1878), 155.

3. Letter from King Mongkut to M. Stephan, 1868, in Jean Marie Edouard Stephen, *Rapport sur l'observation de l'éclipse de soleil du 18 août, 1868* (Paris, 1869), p. 15n.

4. "These notices were written by the King of Siam, and prepared for the press by Dr. Dean." They are reprinted from the *Chinese Repository* in John Bowring, *The Kingdom and People of Siam* (2 vols.; London, 1857), II, 341–367.

5. Frankfurter, "Mongkut," p. 194.

6. Pramoj MS, pp. 6–7.

7. Feer, p. 155.

8. R. Lingat, "History of Wat Pavaraniveça," *Jour. Siam Society*, XXVI (1932), 76–77.

9. *Ibid.*, pp. 80–81.

10. Alexander B. Griswold, "King Mongkut in Perspective," *Jour. Siam Society*, XLV (1957), 16–18.

11. *Ibid.*, pp. 18–19.

12. Lingat, "Wat Pavaraniveça," pp. 85, 87.

13. Pramoj MS, p. 10.

14. George Haws Feltus, ed., *Abstract of the Journal of Rev. Dan Beach Bradley, M.D., Medical Missionary in Siam, 1835–1873* (Cleveland, 1936), pp. 26–28, 30.

15. *Ibid.*, p. 64.

16. Mary Backus, ed., *Siam and Laos as Seen by Our American Missionaries* (Philadelphia, 1884), p. 364. Also Feltus, *Bradley*, pp. 170, 222, 225, 234, 239.

17. George Haws Feltus, *Samuel Reynolds House of Siam* (Chicago and New York, 1924), pp. 53–54. Cited hereafter as *House*.

18. Pramoj MS, p. 11.

19. J. Thomson, pp. 94–95.

20. Letter from King Mongkut to the Earl of Clarendon, July 24, 1857, in "English Correspondence of King Mongkut," *Jour. Siam Society,* XXI (1927), 1–33, 127–177, and XXII (1928), 1–18; letter printed XXI, 133–138. Letters appearing in Vol. XXI cited hereafter as "Corr.," I; letters appearing in Vol. XXII cited hereafter as "Corr.," II.

21. Jean Baptiste Pallegoix, *Description du Royaume Thai ou Siam* (2 vols.; Paris, 1854), II, 126.

Chapter 3. His Majesty's Gracious Advices

1. Letter to "Lieutenant Colonel W. J. Butterworth, C.B., the Governor of Prince of Wales Island [Penang]," April 21, 1851, "Corr.," I, 3–6; quotation pp. 3–4.

2. Translation of letter to Phraya Suriyawongse Vayavadhana, Siamese ambassador to Paris, March 4, 1867, in Pramoj MS, pp. 179–186; quotation p. 186.

3. O. Frankfurter, "The Mission of Sir James Brooke to Siam," *Jour. Siam Society,* VIII (1911), pt. III, 31.

4. R. S. le May, "The Coinage of Siam: The Coins of the Bangkok Dynasty 1782–1924," *Jour. Siam Society,* XVIII (1924), 185.

5. *Ibid.,* pp. 191, 182–183, 166, 193–194, 178–179, 196.

6. G. E. Mitton, ed., *Scott of the Shan Hills* (London, 1936), p. 14.

7. Feltus, *Bradley,* p. 92.

8. *Ibid.,* p. 186.

9. William Maxwell Wood, *Fankwei, or the* San Jacinto *in the Seas of India, China and Japan* (New York, 1859), p. 208.

10. Seni Pramoj, "King Mongkut as a Legislator," *Jour. Siam Society,* XXXVIII (1950), 40, 41, 42. For translation of complete text see Pramoj MS, pp. 55–58.

11. Pramoj, "Mongkut," pp. 55–58. The text is complete except for the date: "Given on Sunday, the 7th of the Waxing Moon of the Third Month in the Year of the Great Snake, being the 8th year in the Decade by the Stars" (Pramoj MS, p. 54).

12. Bowring, I, 172.

13. *Ibid.,* p. 444.

14. Pramoj, "Mongkut," pp. 52–53.

15. *Ibid.,* pp. 33–34.

16. *Ibid.,* p. 35.

17. *Ibid.,* pp. 38–39. An additional paragraph is included in Pramoj MS, p. 66.

18. Cornelius Beach Bradley, "The Oldest Known Writing in Siamese: The Inscription of Phra Ram Khamhaeng of Sukhothai 1293 A.D.," *Jour. Siam Society,* VI (1909), 26.

19. Malcolm Smith, *A Physician at the Court of Siam* (London, 1947), p. 32.

20. Pramoj MS, pp. 62–64; quotations pp. 62–63, 62.

21. Pramoj, "Mongkut," pp. 61, 62, 64–65. The article omits several paragraphs and the date: "Enacted on Monday the 1st of the Waxing Moon of the Second Month in the Year of the Cow, the 7th in the Decade, being the 5332nd day in the Present Reign" (Pramoj MS, pp. 73–80).

22. Pramoj, "Mongkut," pp. 53–55. The article omits names, which have been taken from the Pramoj MS, and the date: "Given on Saturday the 12th of the Waxing Moon of the Second Month in the Year of the Horse, the completing year of the Decade, being the 2857th day in the Present Reign" (Pramoj MS, pp. 35–36).

23. M. Smith, pp. 61, 62.

24. Translation of an extract from a memorandum sent by King Mongkut to the Council of Ministers, 1863, in Pramoj MS, pp. 204–205; quotation p. 205.

25. Pramoj MS, pp. 196–197.

Chapter 4. *Agreement with England*

1. Bowring, II, 211.

2. Letter to "Lieutt. Coll. W. J. Butterworth, C.B., The Governor of Prince of Wales Island, Malacca and Singapore," May 22, 1851, "Corr.," I, 7–10; quotation pp. 8–9.

3. Frankfurter, "Brooke," p. 31.

4. "Corr.," I, 13–15; quotation pp. 14–15.

5. Dec. 27, 1854, *ibid.,* pp. 16–17.

6. "Our recomendation and approval of the agreement which Mr. Harry Parkes has written in stipulation with our Royal Commissioners," May 14, 1856, "Corr.," I, 21–29; quotations pp. 24–25.

7. Treaty of Friendship, Art. 4, in Bowring, II, 217. Also, Parkes' Agreement, Art. 11, in *ibid.*, pp. 239–240.

8. Letter to "M^r & M^s Eddy of New York, unite States," "Dated a place of sea surface 13° 26′ N. latitude/and 101° 3′ E. longitude in Gulf of Siam/18th November Anno Christi 1849/In touring or voyage of the undersigned," in Pramoj MS, pp. 14–19; quotation pp. 17–18.

9. Letter to "M^r & M^s Eddy of Waterford, Sar[atoga] Co. State of New York," dated at Wat Parawaniwesa, Dec. 27, 1849, in Pramoj MS, pp. 20–22; quotation p. 21. "I have most faithful opportunity to send my letter. . . . Therefore I beg to write again as the duplicate of the foregoing" letter of Nov. 18, note 8, above.

10. Bowring, II, 257.

11. July 24, 1857, "Corr.," I, 133–138; quotation p. 136.

12. "Corr.," I, 143.

13. Samuel J. Smith, *The Siam Repository,* I (1869), 61.

14. Feltus, *Bradley,* p. 61.

15. Stephan, p. 15.

16. Letter to Prince Krom Mun Bavorn Vichaicharn, 1862, in Pramoj MS, pp. 167–175; see pp. 173–175.

17. Bowring, I, 446, 447.

18. Feltus, *Bradley,* p. 177.

19. Backus, p. 326.

20. Bowring, I, 441.

21. J. Thomson, p. 93.

22. Ludovic Beauvoir, *Java, Siam, Canton: Voyage autour du monde* (5th ed.; Paris, 1871), pp. 303, 306.

23. Feltus, *Bradley,* pp. 27–28. Smith, p. 43.

24. Anna Harriette Leonowens, *The English Governess at the Siamese Court* (Boston, 1870), p. 246.

25. Feltus, *Bradley,* p. 170.

26. *Ibid.,* pp. 263, 264, 265, 267.

27. Pramoj MS, p. 197.

28. Harris to Secretary of State, Despatch No. 6, Confidential, June 4, 1856, bound in volume entitled "Diplomatic Despatches, Japan, T. Harris, Mar 17, 1855–June 29, 1858, Department of State," National Archives, Washington, D.C. Cited hereafter as "Despatches."

29. Frederick Arthur Neale, *Narrative of a Residence at the*

Capital of the Kingdom of Siam, with a Description of the Man-
ners, Customs and Laws of the Modern Siamese (London, 1852),
pp. 30, 33.

30. Mario Emilio Cosenza, ed., *The Complete Journal of Town-*
send Harris, First American Consul General and Minister to Japan
(New York, 1930), pp. 128–129.

31. Feltus, *Bradley,* pp. 148–149.

32. Bowring, II, 303.

33. June 30, 1858, "Corr.," I, 158–163; quotation p. 160.

34. Translation of letter to Phraya Montri Suriyawongse, ambassador to London, and Chao Mun Sarapeth Bhakdi, vice ambassador,
1858, in Pramoj MS, pp. 222–227.

35. Letter to "Her Gracious Majesty Victoria the Queen of the
United Kingdom of Great Britain and Ireland, the powerful Sov-
ereign of British Colonies almost around the Globe of Human
World," March 21, 1861, "Corr.," I, 166–177; quotation p. 168.

36. *The Times,* London, Oct. 29, 1857, p. 12.

37. Cyril Pearl, *The Girl with the Swansdown Seat,* p. 174.
Copyright © 1955. Used by special permission of the publishers,
The Bobbs-Merrill Company, Inc., Indianapolis.

Chapter 5. The Americans

1. Harris to Secretary of State, Despatch No. 6, Confidential,
June 4, 1856, *supra,* "Despatches."

2. Official translation accompanying original Siamese letter to
President Franklin Pierce, June 10, 1856, bound in volume en-
titled "Ceremonial Letters, Roumania, Russia, Salvador, San
Marino, Serbia, Siam, Department of State," National Archives,
Washington, D.C. Cited hereafter as "Ceremonial Letters."

3. Despatch No. 6, Confidential, June 4, 1856, "Despatches."

4. Cosenza, *Harris,* pp. 27, 28n.

5. Wood, pp. 201–202.

6. Cosenza, *Harris,* pp. 130–131.

7. Stanley Lane-Poole and Frederick Victor Dickins, *The Life*
of Sir Harry Parkes, K.C.B., K.C.M.G. (2 vols.; London, 1894),
I, 206. Cited hereafter as *Parkes.*

8. *Ibid.,* I, 205.

9. Harris to Secretary of State, Despatch No. 7, June 5, 1856, "Despatches."

10. Wood, p. 202.

11. Cosenza, *Harris,* p. 132.

12. Wood, p. 203.

13. Cosenza, *Harris,* pp. 132–133.

14. Wood, pp. 203–204.

15. Cosenza, *Harris,* p. 123.

16. *Ibid.,* pp. 133–134.

17. *Ibid.,* p. 135.

18. Wood, pp. 205–206, 207.

19. Cosenza, *Harris,* p. 135.

20. *Ibid.,* p. 136.

21. Wood, p. 208.

22. Cosenza, *Harris,* p. vii.

23. Letter from Townsend Harris to President Pierce, Aug. 4, 1855, in *ibid.,* p. 9.

24. *Ibid.,* pp. 106, 139.

25. Harris to Secretary of State, Despatch No. 6, Confidential, June 4, 1856, *supra,* "Despatches."

26. Cosenza, *Harris,* p. 107.

27. *Ibid.,* p. 140.

28. Wood, pp. 153–154.

29. Despatch No. 6, Confidential, June 4, 1856, *supra,* "Despatches."

30. Cosenza, *Harris,* p. 146.

31. Wood, p. 175.

32. Cosenza, *Harris,* p. 151.

33. *Ibid.,* p. 151.

34. *Ibid.,* p. 153.

35. *Parkes,* I, 211.

36. Letter to Mr. W. Lockhart, June 28, 1856, *ibid.,* p. 215.

37. Cosenza, *Harris,* p. 153.

38. Harris to Secretary of State, Despatch No. 4, April 7, 1856, "Despatches."

39. Feltus, *Bradley,* p. 191.

40. Cosenza, *Harris,* pp. 154–155.

41. Letter from Phra Klang to Secretary of State, May 30,

1856, bound immediately after Harris Despatch No. 5, June 5, 1856, and its enclosures, "Despatches."

42. Cosenza, *Harris,* p. 155.

43. *Ibid.,* p. 156.

44. *Ibid.,* p. 157.

45. *Ibid.,* p. 158.

46. *Ibid.,* pp. 159–160, 161–162.

47. Wood, p. 159.

48. *Ibid.,* p. 151.

49. Cosenza, *Harris,* p. 83.

50. *Ibid.,* p. 162.

51. "The Siamese—The Franks of Asia," *Harper's Weekly,* I (July 18, 1857), 456.

52. Letter from President James Buchanan to King Mongkut, May 10, 1859; official copy transcribed in volume entitled "Communications to Foreign Sovereigns and States, 1854–1864," pp. 84–86; quotation pp. 84–85, National Archives, Washington, D.C. Cited hereafter as "Communications."

53. Official translation accompanying original Siamese letter to President Buchanan, Feb. 14, 1861, "Ceremonial Letters."

54. Exec. Doc. No. 62, U.S. Senate, 34th Cong., 3d sess. (Washington, 1857).

55. Official translation accompanying original Siamese letter to President Buchanan, Feb. 14, 1861, second letter of same date, "Ceremonial Letters."

56. "Message of the President of the United States transmitting a copy of two letters from his Majesty the Major King of Siam to the President of the United States, accompanied by certain presents, and of the President's answer thereto," Exec. Doc. No. 23, U.S. Senate, 37th Cong., 2d sess. (Washington, 1862).

57. Letter to King Mongkut, Feb. 3, 1862, "Communications," pp. 184–186; quotation pp. 185–186.

Chapter 6. The Whale and the Crocodile

1. March 21, 1861, *supra,* "Corr.," I, 166–177; quotations pp. 170, 172, 175.

2. Feltus, *Bradley,* p. 136.

3. *Ibid.,* p. 138.

4. J. Thomson, p. 100.

5. Henri Mouhot, *Travels in the Central Parts of Indochina (Siam), Cambodia and Laos* (2 vols.; London, 1864), I, 46–49.

6. Feltus, *Bradley,* p. 242.

7. *Ibid.,* p. 248.

8. *Ibid.,* p. 253.

9. *Ibid.,* pp. 191, 192.

10. D. G. E. Hall, *A History of South-East Asia* (New York, 1955), p. 579.

11. *Ibid.,* p. 558.

12. Letter to "Sir Robert Schomburgk, Her B. Majesty Consul for Siam &c &c," July 21, 1862, "Corr.," II, 10–11.

13. Letter to "Sir Robert Schomburgk, the Consul of Her Britannic Majesty for Siam &c. &c. &c.," July 23, 1862, "Corr.," II, 12–13.

14. Hall, pp. 451–452.

15. Translation of letter to Prince Krom Mun Bavorn Vichaicharn, 1862, *supra,* in Pramoj MS, pp. 167–175; quotations pp. 167–173, 175.

16. Translation of letter to H. R. H. Prince Mahamala, 1863, in Pramoj MS, pp. 176–178; quotation p. 177.

17. R. Stanley Thomson, "Siam and France 1863–1870," *Far Eastern Quarterly,* V (Nov., 1945), 35.

18. Feltus, *Bradley,* p. 254.

19. *Ibid.,* pp. 257, 258.

20. R. S. Thomson, pp. 36, 37.

21. Beauvoir, p. 343.

22. *Ibid.,* p. 340.

23. Lawrence Palmer Briggs, "Aubaret and the Treaty of July 15, 1867 between France and Siam," *Far Eastern Quarterly,* VI (Feb., 1947), 136.

24. Leonowens, pp. 277–278.

25. Translation of letter to Phraya Suriyawongse Vayavadhana, Siamese ambassador to Paris, March 4, 1867, *supra,* in Pramoj MS, pp. 179–186.

Chapter 7. White Elephants

1. Beauvoir, pp. 344–345.

2. Translation of letter to Nai Netr Khun Srisayamkich, vice consul for Siam in Singapore, written by the King's secretary at

the direction of King Mongkut, 1867, in Pramoj MS, pp. 231–233.

3. Feltus, *Bradley,* pp. 179–180.

4. Bowring, II, 229.

5. *Ibid.,* I, 476.

6. Leonowens, pp. 140–142, 143–144.

7. Backus, pp. 136–137.

8. Feltus, *Bradley,* p. 216.

9. *Ibid.,* p. 240.

10. Translation of letter to H. R. H. Prince Mahamala, 1863, *supra,* in Pramoj MS, pp. 176–178.

11. Translation of letter to H. R. H. Prince Mahamala, 1866, in Pramoj MS, pp. 202–203; quotation p. 202.

Chapter 8. The Inner Palace

1. Backus, p. 372.

2. Bowring, II, 312.

3. M. Smith, pp. 37–40.

4. Pramoj MS, p. 193.

5. *The Times,* London, May 26, 1868, p. 9.

6. Feltus, *Bradley,* p. 205.

7. *Ibid.,* p. 182.

8. Translation of letter to Chao Mun Sarapeth Bhakdi, vice ambassador to London, 1857, in Pramoj MS, pp. 219–221; quotation pp. 219–220.

9. *Ibid.,* p. 193.

10. *Ibid.,* pp. 194–195.

11. Quoted in Bowring, I, 435.

12. M. Smith, pp. 58–59.

13. Feltus, *Bradley,* p. 147.

14. *Ibid.,* p. 147.

15. *House,* p. 115.

16. *Ibid.,* pp. 115–116.

17. M. Smith, p. 59.

18. Leonowens, p. 247.

19. Translation of letter to Lady Phung, 1852, in Pramoj MS, p. 198.

20. Translation of letter to Lady Phung, 1854, in Pramoj MS, pp. 199–201.

21. Translation of letter to Phraya Montri Suriyawongse, ambassador to London, and Chao Mun Sarapeth Bhakdi, vice ambassador, 1857, in Pramoj MS, pp. 215–218; quotation pp. 215–217.

22. Pramoj, "Mongkut," pp. 47–49. For translation of complete text, see Pramoj MS, pp. 206–209. For clarity, the manuscript text has been substituted in one paragraph, an "and" substituted for a "wherefore," and an obvious error corrected.

23. Pramoj, "Mongkut," pp. 49–51. The article omits the date: "Given on Monday, the 1st of the Waxing Moon of the First Month in the Year of the Horse, the completing year of the Decade, being the 2742nd day in the Present Reign." It also omits the signature: "Lady Aab, Bearer of Royal Command" (Pramoj MS, pp. 210 - 212). The manuscript text has been substituted in one instance as being probably more accurate.

Chapter 9. *"However Differently Perceived and Worshipped"*

1. Bowring, I, 377.
2. *House*, p. 49.
3. *Ibid.*, pp. 54–55.
4. Griswold, p. 16.
5. *House*, p. 52.
6. Feltus, *Bradley*, p. 106.
7. *House*, p. 137.
8. Letter to Mr. and Mrs. Eddy, Nov. 18, 1849, *supra*, in Pramoj MS, pp. 14–19; quotation p. 15.
9. Feltus, *Bradley*, p. 248.
10. *Ibid.*, p. 253.
11. *Ibid.*, p. 253.
12. J. Thomson, p. 82.
13. Feltus, *Bradley*, p. 250.
14. *Ibid.*, p. 251.
15. *Ibid.*, p. 250.
16. *Ibid.*, p. 245.
17. Samuel J. Smith, *The Siam Repository*, I (1869), 65–66.
18. Backus, p. 376.
19. Feltus, *Bradley*, p. 169.
20. *Ibid.*, p. 173.

21. *Ibid.,* p. 179.

22. *Ibid.,* p. 240.

23. *Ibid.,* p. 143.

24. Translation of letter to Pope Pius IX, 1861, in Pramoj MS, pp. 187–191; quotations pp. 187–188.

25. *Ibid.,* p. 9.

26. Bowring, I, 106.

27. Pramoj, "Mongkut," p. 44. For translation of complete proclamation, see Pramoj MS, pp. 67–70.

28. Pramoj MS, p. 68. This paragraph is not included in Pramoj, "Mongkut."

29. Pramoj, "Mongkut," p. 46.

30. M. Smith, p. 23.

31. Pramoj, "Mongkut," pp. 45–46.

32. M. Smith, p. 41.

33. Feltus, *Bradley,* p. 141.

34. Backus, p. 372.

35. *Ibid.,* p. 325.

36. Feltus, *Bradley,* p. 188.

37. Backus, p. 333.

38. Feltus, *Bradley,* p. 188.

39. Letter to "Wm. Adamson Esquire the Manager of the Branch of Borneo Company Limited at Singapore &c &c," about 1862, in Pramoj MS, pp. 228–230.

Chapter 10. *"Thus Have I Followed the Teaching of Buddha"*

1. Bowring, I, 444.

2. *Ibid.,* II, 280.

3. Letter to Sir Robert Schomburgk, Dec. 7, 1859, "Corr.," I, 164–165; quotation p. 165.

4. Letter to M. Stephan, 1868, *supra,* in Stephan, p. 15n.

5. Pramoj MS, p. 234.

6. Feltus, *Bradley,* p. 276.

7. George Bladen Bacon, *Siam, the Land of the White Elephant* (New York, 1873), p. 149.

8. Feltus, *Bradley,* p. 278.

9. *Ibid.*, p. 278.

10. Translation of "Extracts from the Diaries of Chao Phraya Mahindr, describing the last days of King Mongkut," in Pramoj MS, pp. 235–247; quotations pp. 236–244, 247.

11. Griswold, p. 34.

12. Translation of "Last Letter of the King written in Pali on his deathbed, addressed to the Buddhist Brotherhood," in Pramoj MS, pp. 245–246.

Appendix I. Exchanges of Presents

1. Original receipt for presents signed by King Mongkut, May 31, 1856, Harris to Secretary of State, Despatch No. 5, Enclosure No. 5, June 2, 1856, "Despatches." This receipt does not list the three volumes: American Scenery, the New York Exhibition, and the Iconographic Encyclopoedia; but that was clearly an error by the Siamese scribe. They are included in Harris' numbered list of presents for the King (Cosenza, *Harris,* pp. 566–567), and the correct number of volumes was receipted for by the Phra Klang in his letter to the Secretary of State, May 30, 1856, *supra,* "Despatches."

2. Cosenza, *Harris,* pp. 568–570.

3. Wood, p. 57.

4. Cosenza, *Harris,* p. 75.

5. *Ibid.*, p. 124.

6. *Ibid.*, p. 126.

7. Harris to Secretary of State, Despatch No. 10, July 3, 1856, "Despatches."

8. Official translation accompanying original Siamese list of presents "designed for Franklin Pierce the President of the United States of America," [July, 1856], "Ceremonial Letters."

9. *The Times,* London, Dec. 27, 1855, p. 10.

10. *Parkes,* I, 199.

11. *Ibid.*, p. 205.

12. "Our recommendation and approval of the agreement which Mr. Harry Parkes has written in stipulation with our Royal Commissioners," May 14, 1856, *supra,* "Corr.," I, 21–29; quotation p. 27.

13. Letter to the Earl of Clarendon, July 24, 1857, *supra,*
"Corr.," I, 133–138; quotation p. 133.

14. Receipt for the presents from Queen Victoria actually delivered by Mr. Harry Parkes, May 6, 1856, "Corr.," I, 18–20;
quotation pp. 18–19.

15. March 21, 1861, *supra,* "Corr.," I, 167–177; quotations pp.
172–173, 173–174.

16. *The Times,* London, Oct. 19, 1857, p. 9.

17. *Ibid.,* Oct. 15, 1857, p. 5.

18. *Ibid.,* Oct. 20, 1857, p. 9.

19. *Ibid.,* Oct. 28, 1857, p. 6.

20. *Ibid.,* Oct. 29, 1857, p. 12, *supra.* The accents are as in the
original.

21. *Ibid.,* Nov. 20, 1857, p. 6.

22. *Ibid.,* Nov. 23, 1857, p. 10.

23. *Ibid.,* April 14, 1858, p. 9.

24. "The list of Royal presents alluded to in the accompanying
Royal Letter [July 22, 1857] and designed for the acceptance of
Her Most Gracious Majesty Victoria, . . . from Her Majesty's
distinguished friend and, by regal race, an humble and affectionate
Royal Brother," "Corr.," I, 139–142.

Appendix II. The Band of the "San Jacinto"

1. Wood, pp. 25–26.

2. *Ibid.,* p. 165.

3. Feltus, *Bradley,* p. 189.

4. Wood, p. 167.

5. *Ibid.,* p. 182.

6. *Ibid.,* p. 186.

7. Cosenza, *Harris,* p. 117.

8. *Ibid.,* pp. 137–138.

Appendix III. "An account of the most lamentable illness and death of Her young and amiable Majesty"

1. Wood, pp. 245–254. An incomplete version of this same
account (with some minor differences in the text) is available in
M. Smith, pp. 159–162. Mr. Smith's text was transcribed from a

pamphlet in the reference library of the London Missionary Society, from which some pages were missing.

Appendix IV. Anna as Historian

1. Hall, p. 579.
2. Griswold, pp. 5–6.
3. *Ibid.*, pp. 29–31.
4. *Ibid.*, pp. 40–41, n. 21.

Bibliography

(*Books and articles cited in the source notes*)

Backus, Mary, ed. *Siam and Laos as Seen by Our American Missionaries.* Philadelphia, 1884.

Bacon, George Bladen. *Siam, the Land of the White Elephant.* New York, 1873.

Beauvoir, Ludovic. *Java, Siam, Canton: Voyage autour du monde.* 5th ed. Paris, 1871.

Bowring, John. *The Kingdom and People of Siam.* 2 vols. London, 1857.

Bradley, Cornelius Beach. "The Oldest Known Writing in Siamese: The Inscription of Phra Ram Khamhaeng of Sukhothai, 1293 A.D.," *Jour. Siam Society,* VI (1909), 1–64.

Briggs, Lawrence Palmer. "Aubaret and the Treaty of July 15, 1867 between France and Siam," *Far Eastern Quarterly,* VI (Feb., 1947), 122–138.

Cosenza, Mario Emilio, ed. *The Complete Journal of Townsend Harris, First American Consul General and Minister to Japan.* New York, 1930. Rev. ed.; Rutland, Vt., 1959.

"English Correspondence of King Mongkut," *Jour. Siam Society,* XXI (1927), 1–33, 127–177; XXII (1928), 1–18.

Feer, Léon. "Le bouddhisme à Siam: une soirée chez le phraklang, en 1863," *Memoires de la Société Academique Indo-Chinoise de France,* I (1877–1878), 129–148.

Feltus, George Haws. *Samuel Reynolds House of Siam.* Chicago and New York, 1924.

———, ed. *Abstract of the Journal of Rev. Dan Beach Bradley, M.D., Medical Missionary in Siam, 1835–1873.* Cleveland, 1936.

Frankfurter, O. "King Mongkut," *Jour. Siam Society,* I (1905), 191–207.

———. "The Mission of Sir James Brooke to Siam," *Jour. Siam Society,* VIII (1911), pt. III, 19–33.

Gerini, G. E. *Chulakantamangala or the Tonsure Ceremony as Performed in Siam.* Bangkok, 1895.

Griswold, Alexander B. "King Mongkut in Perspective," *Jour. Siam Society,* XLV (1957), 1–41.

Hall, D. G. E. *A History of South-East Asia.* New York, 1955.

Lane-Poole, Stanley, and Frederick Victor Dickins. *The Life of Sir Harry Parkes, K.C.B., G.C.M.G.* 2 vols. London, 1894.

le May, R. S. "The Coinage of Siam: The Coins of the Bangkok Dynasty 1782–1924," *Jour. Siam Society,* XVIII (1924), 153–220.

Leonowens, Anna Harriette. *The English Governess at the Siamese Court.* Boston, 1870.

Lingat, R. "History of Wat Pavaraniveça," *Jour. Siam Society,* XXVI (1932), 73–102.

———. "La vie religieuse du Roi Mongkut," *Jour. Siam Society,* XX (1926), 129–148.

Low, Charles Porter. *Some Recollections.* Boston, 1905.

Mitton, G. E. ed. *Scott of the Shan Hills.* London, 1936.

Mouhot, Henri. *Travels in the Central Parts of Indochina (Siam), Cambodia, and Laos.* 2 vols. London, 1864.

Neale, Frederick Arthur. *Narrative of a Residence at the Capital of the Kingdom of Siam, with a Description of the Manners, Customs and Laws of the Modern Siamese.* London, 1852.

Pallegoix, Jean Baptiste. *Description du Royaume Thai ou Siam.* 2 vols. Paris, 1854.

Pearl, Cyril. *The Girl with the Swansdown Seat.* Indianapolis, 1955.

Pramoj, Seni. "King Mongkut as a Legislator," *Jour. Siam Society,* XXXVIII (1950), 32–66.

Pramoj, Seni and Kukrit. "The King of Siam Speaks." Type-written MS [Bangkok, 1948].

"The Siamese—The Franks of Asia," *Harper's Weekly,* I (July 18, 1857), 456–457.

Smith, Malcolm. *A Physician at the Court of Siam.* London, 1947.

Smith, Samuel J. *The Siam Repository,* I (Jan., 1869).

Stephan, Jean Marie Edouard. *Rapport sur l'observation de l'éclipse de soleil du 18 août, 1868.* Paris, 1869.

Thomson, John. *The Straits of Malacca, Indochina and China.* London, 1875.

Thomson, R. Stanley. "Siam and France 1863–1870," *Far Eastern Quarterly,* V (Nov., 1945), 28–46.

United States Senate, 34th Cong., 3d sess. Exec. Doc. No. 62. Washington, 1857.

United States Senate, 37th Cong., 2d sess. Exec. Doc. No. 23. Washington, 1862.

Wood, William Maxwell. *Fankwei, or the* San Jacinto *in the Seas of India, China and Japan.* New York, 1859.

Index